TAKING
THE
CONSTITUTION
SERIOUSLY

WALTER BERNS

TAKING
THE
CONSTITUTION
SERIOUSLY

WALTER BERNS

MADISON BOOKS
Lanham • New York • London

Taking the Constitution Seriously *was originally published in hardcover in 1987 by Simon and Schuster and has been reprinted in paperback by Madison Books 1992.*

Published by Madison Books
4720 Boston Way
Lanham, Maryland 20706

3 Henrietta Street
London WC2E 8LU England

Distributed by National Book Network

The paper used in this publication meets the minimum requirements of American National Standard for Information Sciences—Permanence of Paper for Printed Library Materials, ANSI Z39.48–1984. ∞™
Manufactured in the United States of America.

Library of Congress Cataloging-in-Publication Data

Taking the constitution seriously / Walter Berns.
p. cm.
Reprint. Originally published: New York :
Simon and Schuster, © 1987.
Includes bibliographical references and index.
1. United States—Constitutional law.
2. United States—Constitutional history.
I. Title.
[KF4550.B39 1991]
342.73'029—dc20 [347.30229] 90–21730 CIP

ISBN 0–8191–7970–1 (paper : alk. paper)

British Cataloging in Publication Information Available

FOR ABIGAIL RUTH FRADKIN,
THE FIRST OF HER GENERATION.

Contents

Preface

This book was written to appear in 1987, the Constitution's bicentennial year. It is not a history of the founding of the United States, although the first two chapters are largely historical in character; nor, although I have a lot to say on the subject, is it a theoretical study of constitutionalism. It is, instead, an explanation of sorts, an explanation of the Constitution by reference to the Declaration of Independence, the first of our founding documents. The Declaration holds it to be self-evidently true that human beings are equally endowed with "certain unalienable rights," and that governments are instituted in order "to secure these rights." The problem the Framers* faced (and, I would insist, solved) was to devise a government that would best do

---

* I prefer the term "Framers" to "Founding Fathers" in part because, as I once heard William Safire say, the latter term was first coined by President Warren G. Harding.

11

this. How best to secure those rights? That was the simple question, and the Constitution was (and is) the rather more complex answer, but both—question and answer alike—are in need of an explanation.

Publius (Alexander Hamilton, in this case) begins his defense of the Constitution by emphasizing that "it seems to have been reserved to the people of this country, by their conduct and example, to decide the important question, whether societies of men are really capable or not of establishing good government from reflection and choice, or whether they are forever destined to depend for their political constitutions on accident and force." Now, 200 years later, we are in a position to say that, under some conditions, some "societies of men" are so capable, but most are not.

This fact was impressed on me—although not for the first time—in September 1983, when, at the Supreme Court of the United States, the American Enterprise Institute convened a meeting of some twenty-odd countries on the subject of constitution writing. With the exception of the American representatives, the persons present had themselves played a major role in the writing of their countries' constitutions—most of them written in the 1970s—and, again excepting the American, the oldest of these was the French constitution of 1958, the fifth of the republican constitutions adopted by France during the period in which we have had one. And since that September meeting, the Nigerian constitution, so ably discussed and defended on that occasion by one of its authors, has been cast aside, much as the previous four French republican constitutions were. It seems that societies of men are capable of establishing good government from reflection and choice, but only rarely or exceptionally. Why we Americans should be an exception to this dismal rule is an interesting question. Luck had a little to do with it, but, as I hope to make clear, only a little; of greater consequence were the Americans who gathered in Philadelphia during the summer of 1787 and the Constitution they managed to write *and* then to have ratified.

That Constitution is unique not only because of its longevity but because of the place it occupies in the hearts of ordinary Americans. Their attitude toward the Constitution has recently been described as a "curious blend of reverence and ignorance," but there is really nothing curious about it. They may indeed be ignorant of its particular provisions, but they are not unaware of its role in securing for them and, they hope, for their posterity too the blessings of liberty. Respecting the Constitution, they respect constitutionality—which is to say, the distinction between what is politically desired and constitutionally permitted—and that cannot be said of some of our judges and constitutional lawyers. If, as seems likely, we will not much longer have reason to celebrate these constitutional anniversaries, it will not be because of any failing on the part of ordinary Americans.

Unlike Tennessee Williams's Blanche Dubois, I have not depended on the kindness of strangers; in preparing this book I have depended instead on the labors, wisdom, and kindness of friends: Philip Kurland and Ralph Lerner, of the University of Chicago, who made available to me in manuscript form their magnificent collection—some 8,000 pages in all—of documents on the founding of the United States; Harvey C. Mansfield, Jr., of Harvard University, whose various writings on the theory and practice of constitutional government I have studied with care and also, I hope, with profit; and Herbert J. Storing, of the University of Chicago and then of Virginia, whose untimely death in 1977 deprived this country of the person best qualified to write on the subject of the Founding. For their support over the years, I want also to express my gratitude to the various officials of the John M. Olin Foundation, and especially to its president, William E. Simon. This book probably could not have been written—it certainly could not have been completed—without that support.

Washington, D.C.
September 1986

Introduction

We Americans might be excused for believing that the outcome of the Civil War would have set to rest all doubt concerning the date of this nation's founding and the principles on the basis of which it was founded. Chief Justice
Roger B. Taney's depreciation of the Declaration of Independence in his opinion for the Supreme Court in the infa-
mous case of *Dred Scott* v. *Sandford* was answered not
only on the battlefield of Gettysburg but, a few months
later, by Abraham Lincoln's address on the site of that battle. Lincoln insisted there, in November 1863, as he had in
many other places and on many other occasions, that the
nation was born at Philadelphia in 1776, four score and
seven years earlier. Taney, and the South in general, had
denied this, or had come to deny it—the time came when
John C. Calhoun and Alexander H. Stephens said the assertion that all men are created equal is a self-evident lie and
went so far as to denounce Thomas Jefferson for making

it. But what the South, that old South, lost in battle it seems now to be winning back in the groves of academe and the pages of contemporary journalism.

It has become common to hear scholars dismiss the Declaration as mere propaganda, or a clever lawyer's brief with a dash of natural law added for spice, a convenient weapon to wield against the British, and no more. But this is belied by the evident care with which the Declaration is written. To say nothing for the time being of its famous philosophical second paragraph, what propagandist, what lawyer wanting no more than a ceremonial weapon to brandish, would bother to compose—or would be capable of composing—Jefferson's indictment of George III? In its organization alone, that indictment is a kind of disquisition on political morality. It begins with the mildest of strictures— George had exercised poor judgment by refusing his assent to wholesome and necessary laws—and proceeds, crescendo-like, through a series of ever more serious offenses, culminating in the most serious charge Jefferson could level against anyone: by "captivating and carrying" a distant people into slavery, George had "waged cruel war against human nature itself." The Declaration was intended to be read as it was written, carefully, and not as a piece of ephemera to be discarded, like a newspaper, after it had served its immediate purpose.

But what was its immediate purpose? Not to declare independence; that had been done on July 2, when the Continental Congress formally adopted a motion to that effect. Besides, as Lincoln pointed out, the assertion that all men are created equal "was of no practical use in effecting our separation from Great Britain; and it was placed in the Declaration, not for that, but for future use." Lincoln said,

Its authors meant it to be, thank God, it is now proving itself, a stumbling block to those who in after times might seek to turn a free people back into the hateful paths of despotism. They knew the proneness of prosperity to breed tyrants, and they meant when such should re-appear in this fair land and commence their vocation they should find for them at least one hard nut to crack.

There are historians who assure us that Jefferson and his colleagues—primarily John Adams and Benjamin Franklin, his colleagues on the committee that drafted the Declaration—never intended their appeal to the laws of nature and of nature's God to be taken seriously; they never intended, we are told, that the laws of nature be used as a measure of "the rights and wrongs of colonial life." And for this knowledge we are supposed to be grateful and by it comforted: it is supposed to prove that the Founders were just like us, happy moral relativists who, as one law school dean puts it, rightly reject the "notion of a discoverable and objectively valid set of moral principles." Put in the language of the Declaration itself, we are supposed to find happiness in the opinion that we have no right to pursue it. Incapable of serious thought themselves, these writers are unwilling to believe the serious declarations of others.

There are still other historians who would deny the Declaration its rightful place precisely because they take it seriously; they know, with the Bible, that "in the beginning was the word," and they do not want America's word to be the word spoken in the Declaration.* They know that it matters when this nation was founded; it mattered in Lin-

* No one in our time has worked harder to dislodge the Declaration from its rightful place in the country's foundation than Garry Wills. For a critique of his argument, see the Appendix, pp. 242–51.

coln's time and it matters still; it matters because important issues turn on the answer.

It is probably true that all countries are affected in one way or another by the manner of their beginnings. To take an example close at hand, Canada came into being in 1759 on the battlefield outside the city of Quebec when the English, under General Wolfe, defeated the French, under General Montcalm, and much of its subsequent history derives from the enmity born that day between English and French Canadians. What is true of Canada—or of Mexico, France, Britain, and the others—is even truer of America. More than being affected by its beginning, this country is characterized by it. This, as I indicated above, was Lincoln's view:

> All this is not the result of accident. It has a philosophical cause. Without the *Constitution* and the *Union*, we could not have attained the result; but even these, are not the primary cause of our great prosperity. There is something back of these, entwining itself more closely about the human heart. That something, is the principle of "Liberty to all"—the principle that clears the *path* for all—gives *hope* to all—and, by consequence, *enterprize* [sic], and *industry* to all.
>
> The *expression* of that principle, in our Declaration of Independence, was most happy, and fortunate. *Without* this, as well as *with* it, we could have declared our independence of Great Brittain [sic]; but *without* it, we could not, I think, have secured our free government and consequent prosperity. No oppressed people will *fight*, and *endure*, as our fathers did, without the promise of something better, than a mere change of masters.
>
> The assertion of that *principle*, at *that time*, was *the* word, "*fitly spoken*" which has proved an "apple of gold"

18

to us. The *Union*, and the *Constitution*, are the *picture* of *silver*, subsequently framed around it. The picture was made, not to *conceal*, or *destroy* the apple; but to *adorn*, and *preserve* it. The *picture* was made *for* the apple—*not* the apple for the picture.

These reflections, found among Lincoln's papers after his death, were obviously inspired by Proverbs 25:11: "A word fitly spoken is like apples of gold in a setting of silver." I quote them to make the point that, as understood by the greatest of our presidents, we were first constituted by the Declaration of Independence, and the Declaration must figure prominently in a proper study of American constitutionalism.

Having adopted the Declaration, and as if to mark the occasion, the Continental Congress immediately constituted a new committee, consisting again of Jefferson, Adams, and Franklin, and charged it with the task of preparing "a device for a seal of the United States of America." The committee submitted its design to the Congress on August 10, 1776, but only two of its features are preserved in the Great Seal as we know it. (It is reproduced, both obverse and reverse, on every dollar bill.) Missing is the motto, attributed to Franklin, "Rebellion to Tyrants is Obedience to God." Missing also is a depiction of "Pharaoh sitting in an open chariot, a crown on his head and a sword in his hand passing through the divided waters of the Red Sea in pursuit of the Israelites," which, in the sketch accompanying this description, proved to bear an uncanny resemblance to the subsequently familiar picture of Washington crossing the Delaware. What is preserved is the Eye of Providence peering out of the triangle atop the unfinished pyramid, above which the final designer inscribed the words, *Annuit Coeptis,* thereby indicating that it was Providence that "favored our undertakings." Also preserved in the final design is the more familiar motto, *E pluribus unum.* On the whole, however, the committee's design did not meet with a favorable reception.* Yet the design finally approved by Congress in 1782 is one that Jefferson, Adams, and Franklin could well have favored. Prominently displayed on it is the motto, *Novus ordo seclorum,* or, in English, a new order of the ages, and they, as well as the other Founders, were very conscious of the fact that the nation they were building represented not only an experiment but something altogether new. To adopt a phrase of our own time, America was the first new nation, the first nation to embody the principles of the new or improved science of politics, and the first to be built on the foundation of the rights of man.

---

* The final design of the Great Seal was the work of an otherwise unheralded resident of Philadelphia, William Barton, who is said to have "improved" upon a design submitted by the secretary of Congress, Charles Thomson. Cut in brass, the seal was first used on a commission, dated September 16, 1782, granting General George Washington full powers to arrange a prisoner exchange with Britain.

CHAPTER I

Constituting
the People
of the United States

| | |

Our habit of speaking of "Americanism" grates on the ears of other peoples, in part because, as the late Martin Diamond used to point out, no other country has an expression similar to it.[1] There is no such expression—because there is no such thing—as Frenchism, for example, or Englishism. Shakespeare's John of Gaunt (in *Richard II*) presumed to define England as

> This happy breed of men, this little world,
> This precious stone set in the silver sea,
> Which serves it in the office of a wall
> Or as a moat defensive to a house,
> Against the envy of less happier lands,
> This blessèd plot, this earth, this realm,
>   this England. . . .

But America is something in addition to a plot, an earth, a realm; something more than a place with a past; something, indeed, that was deliberately brought into being at a particular moment of time and for a specific purpose. At Gettysburg, our poet Abraham Lincoln defined it as a nation conceived in liberty and dedicated to a certain philosophical proposition, a nation brought into being by "our fathers," as Lincoln called them, who are related to us not necessarily or even essentially by blood but by a mutual dedication to that proposition. In principle, anyone can be Americanized, another term that has no analogue elsewhere; all that is required is a pledge of allegiance to the "ism," so to speak, to the flag of the United States, and, as Diamond emphasized, "to the republic for which it stands."

Not everyone, of course, has been willing to give that pledge. At the very beginning, and on grounds of political principle, the people we call Tories chose to remain loyal to George III rather than become part of the republican people of the United States. What is more, not everyone present at the beginning was permitted to give that pledge, because not everyone was thought to be suited for membership in the American political community; among the putatively unsuitable at the beginning were the Indians, the blacks, and, in the opinion of what proved to be an insignificant minority, the "Jews, Turks, Papists, and Infidels."

This chapter is an account of how, governed by political theory as well as by practical considerations, the American colonists and one-time British subjects constituted themselves a people. Before there could be a government of the United States there had to be a people of the United States, and like the government that people had to be constituted. To constitute is, in one sense, to make one out of many, and our familiar motto—*E pluribus unum*—can be said to refer

22

to the making of one people out of many persons, as well as to the making of one country out of many colonies.

In the various official compilations of American laws— *The Public Statutes at Large of the United States of America* (1854), *Revised Statutes of the United States* (1878), *The Federal and State Constitutions, Colonial Charters, and Other Organic Laws of the United States* (1877), and even the *United States Code*—the Declaration of Independence enjoys what might be seen as pride of place, ahead of the Articles of Confederation, the Northwest Ordinance, and the Constitution and its amendments.[2] What is noteworthy here, however, is not the Declaration's place in that list— after all, the Declaration is the earliest of the documents listed chronologically—but, rather, its presence in that list, a list of legal documents. Like the Northwest Ordinance and the Constitution, the Declaration is understood to be a law of the United States and, more precisely, an organic law. Indeed, in more than one of these compilations—for example, in the 1970 edition of the United States Code—it is classified as one of the "Organic Laws of the United States."

An organic law is an organizing or constituting law, and the Declaration is the first such American law because, according to the political theory informing it, before there can be legitimate government, there must be a people, a people to institute it, and before there can be a people there must be a compact among persons who, by nature, are free and independent—which is to say, independent of each other. That this was clearly understood by the Founders of the United States is, I think, manifest in this statement by James Madison, the Constitution's principal author. Writing to a

23

correspondent toward the end of his long life, Madison explained the nature of the two compacts upon which the entire structure of American government rests:

> Altho' the old idea of a compact between the Govt & the people be justly exploded, the idea of a compact among those who are parties to a Govt is a fundamental principle of free Govt.
>
> The original compact is the one implied or presumed, but nowhere reduced to writing, by which a people agree to form one society. The next is a compact, here for the first time reduced to writing, by which the people in their social state agree to a Govt over them.[3]

This is the political theory of our beginning, and its importance should not be minimized. Admittedly, Americans had not been living in a Lockean state of nature—and, therefore, had not been "free and independent" in the Lockean sense—prior to their association in 1776. And there can be little doubt that our subsequent political prosperity owes something to the fact that Americans had so much in common from the very beginning. John Jay was not writing nonsense in the second *Federalist* when he said,

> Providence has been pleased to give this one connected country to one united people—a people descended from the same ancestors, speaking the same language, professing the same religion, attached to the same principles of government, very similar in their manners and customs, and who, by their joint counsels, arms, and efforts, fighting side by side throughout a long and bloody war, have nobly established their general liberty and independence.

A connected territory; common ancestors, language, religion; similar manners and customs; common memories of

24

what Lincoln was later to call the "scenes of the revolution." No one can rightly gainsay the political importance of these factors. Yet, except for the last, each of them was shared by the Tories who fled (or were driven out) to Canada and England, and most of them were shared by George III and his ministers: they, too, spoke English, worshiped God in a Christian fashion, and followed similar customs. What separated George Washington from Thomas Hutchinson, the erstwhile governor of Massachusetts Bay, and Frederick, Lord North, the British prime minister, and, at the same time, united him with Thomas Jefferson, John Adams, Benjamin Franklin, and the officers and men of his army, was the Declaration of Independence and the compact that made it possible.* By that compact, they agreed—in Madison's words—"to form one society."

Compacts of one sort or another were a familiar feature of the American colonial experience, particularly in New England. Every Congregational church was founded on or arose out of a compact, a solemn covenant freely entered into by its members in the presence of God. "Where Congregationalism went"—and it went to many places in America—"there went also the theory and the fact of compact and covenant." So said one authority. Then there were plantation covenants, so called to distinguish them from the church covenants; in the most famous of these the Mayflower pilgrims did "covenant and combine [themselves] togeather in a civill body politick." Then, as time passed, there was a tendency on the part of the colonists to regard the colonial charters as if they were compacts between

---

* Washington's general orders of July 9, 1776, called for the parading of the "several brigades" of troops and, in "an audible voice," the reading of the newly adopted Declaration of Independence.

themselves and the king. These various covenants and charters were solemn, formal, and written; and they were also a real and familiar experience in the lives of many, and perhaps even most, Americans.

Unlike these covenants and charters, the compact to form one political society was unwritten—"nowhere reduced to writing," as Madison puts it—but it was and is nonetheless real, and not only real but necessary. Its necessity derives from its premise, which is the self-evident truth that, by nature, all men are equally endowed with certain unalienable rights. More specifically, men are equally endowed with the fundamental right of self-preservation, which entitles them to do whatever they think necessary to preserve their own lives. In Locke's terms, in the state of nature they are free "to order their actions and dispose of their possessions and persons as they think fit."

Unfortunately, but precisely because everyone is, in practice, entitled to do anything, the state of nature comes to be indistinguishable from the state of war, where, in Hobbes's familiar phrase, life is solitary, poor, nasty, brutish, and short; even in Locke's more benign version, and for the same reason, life in the state of nature is characterized by many unendurable "inconveniences." And why not? There may be a law of nature which prescribes that if at all possible—and one's "own preservation comes not in competition"—no one ought to harm another, but, as Locke immediately makes clear, the enforcement or execution of that law of nature is, in the state of nature, "put into every man's hands." Which means that everyone is entitled to punish offenders—after having himself determined who are offenders—and even to kill them.[4] No wonder life in the state of nature becomes unendurable, and no wonder the rights of nature prove to be insecure in the state of nature. To secure these rights, as the Declaration of Independence says, "governments [have to be] instituted among men," and instituted by men. Government does not exist naturally; it is an artifact, something made by man rather than provided by God.

What are its preconditions? It surely cannot be instituted—or, at least, free government cannot be instituted—if men insist on retaining their natural right to govern themselves; that right has to be surrendered. Each man must consent to be governed, which, as Hobbes puts it, he does when he lays down his natural right to govern himself. In Locke's version, civil society is formed when everyone "has quitted his natural power [to punish offenders], resigned it up into the hands of the community."[5] Paradoxically, security for rights requires the surrender of certain rights; they are surrendered into the hands of civil society.

Like government, civil society does not exist by nature (or in the state of nature). By nature, to repeat, every person is sovereign with respect to himself, free to do whatever in his judgment is necessary to preserve his own life. Civil society comes into existence when this person, acting in concert with others, surrenders his natural rights or sovereign power; upon this agreement, or social contract, civil society becomes sovereign over those who consent to this surrender. Civil society is the product of that first and usually unwritten compact to which Madison referred in that letter. By virtue of this compact, freely entered into by everyone with everyone, the naturally free and independent individuals are transformed into or *constituted* a social entity, a people, or a society, and it is this society that institutes and empowers government. So it was that "we [became] the People of the United States" in 1776, with the first compact, and, in the second and written compact of 1787, ratified in 1788, we ordained and established, in the words of its preamble, "this CONSTITUTION for the United States of America."[6]

This, as I said above, is the political theory (and, in one important respect, the true history) of our beginning; the account may appear unnecessarily pedantic, but the theory is by no means irrelevant, even today. Much of what we regard as politically valuable derives from it and depends on its validity. Unlike the ancients who spoke of virtue and judged political regimes in its light, we speak of rights and measure political things on a yardstick calibrated in rights. "By means of the idea of rights," said Alexis de Tocqueville in his celebrated study of American democracy, "[modern] men have defined the nature of license and of tyranny."[7] But it is only by recognizing that rights exist prior to and independent of government that they can serve effectively to measure or evaluate governments. Hence, it was the rights of man and not of Englishmen that the Declaration relied on when making the case against the king and for independence; after all, the king (or king-in-parliament) had the authority to define the rights of Englishmen and could be expected to know better than Jefferson, Adams, and Franklin what they were. And it is only by recognizing that these rights are grounded in human nature, possessed by everybody irrespective of nationality, color, faith, gender, or ethnic affiliation, that they can serve to measure foreign governments. For example, in the State Department's annual *Country Reports on Human Rights Practices,* Iran is criticized severely for its treatment of religious minorities, particularly members of the Baha'i sect, who are per-

28

secuted, imprisoned, and, for refusing to recant, not infrequently executed.[8] But Iran can be blamed for this only if freedom of conscience is truly a human right, belonging to man as man, and not merely an American or peculiarly Western idea of a human right, not even the United Nations' idea of a human right. Although some political good might be accomplished by having nations subscribe to the various U.N. human rights declarations—conventions, covenants, and protocols—such pronouncements cannot provide these rights with a firm grounding. A human right cannot be created by the U.N.'s secretary general or voted into existence by a majority in the General Assembly.

A human right properly and originally understood derives from or reflects an aspect of human nature, an aspect that distinguishes human from all other classes of beings and makes it possible for them alone to have rights. Man is not unique in having desires; for example, man and all other animals have planted in them "a strong desire of self-preservation." But only in man's case does this desire for preservation become transformed into a right or, as Locke himself puts it, does it serve as "the foundation of a right," a right to take and use what is "necessary or useful to his being."[9] Insofar as they have desires but not rights, animals are said by Locke to be "inferior" to man; they are directed "by their sense and instinct," whereas man is directed by "his senses and reason." In saying this—and this is all he says directly—Locke suggests that it is man's rationality that distinguishes him from other animals and allows him to be endowed with rights. To say that animals do not have rights is not to say we may treat them cruelly. On the contrary, it is human to know what pain is, human to know that we can inflict it and that animals can feel it, and, therefore, human (or humane) to seek to avoid inflicting it on them. When, contrary to the facts, someone issues a declaration to the effect that animals as well as men have rights, his purpose is not to protect animals from other animals but to protect them from other men; no one in his right mind expects the animals themselves to be influenced one way or another by such declarations. These animals can manifest desires, but only man, alone in his rationality, can speak—or has any reason to speak—the language of rights. Only a rational creature can claim a right for himself or recognize a right in another and—and this is the point—by so doing, curb, check, restrict, or himself delay the satisfaction of, his own desires. Only a rational creature can understand the need to do this, and how it is in his own interest to do this, and how, in practice, it can best be done. All of which is to say that it is human beings who have rights and, because they have rights not instincts, are in need of government and capable of instituting it.

Now the striking fact about this political theory of our beginning is that there is nothing peculiarly American about it. It was indeed the "people of the United States" who (in the second and written compact) ordained and established the Constitution, but by nature no person was ineligible for membership in that body. It was formed by the original compact—the one that is "nowhere reduced to writing"—and no one was foreclosed from being a party to that compact. At least not in principle. A person had only to be willing to give up his natural freedom—or his natural right to govern himself—and to assume the obligations attendant upon his new condition as a member of the "social state" formed by the compact. Any rational person could do that

30

and could appreciate the advantages of doing that: only in this way could his rights be secured in fact.

As I said above, the Americans of 1776 asserted their rights as men, not as Englishmen; they appealed not to the laws of the realm but to the laws of nature and of nature's God. In this important respect, the Declaration of Independence differs from, say, the celebrated Magna Carta. The barons who on June 15, 1215, met with King John in the meadow at Runneymede demanded and got what they said they were entitled to as English barons: "all the liberties [traditionally enjoyed by] the free men of [John's] kingdom." So, too, does the Declaration differ from the Bill of Rights of 1689. There the British Parliament appealed to and managed to restore "the Protestant Religion and the Lawes and Liberties of [that] Kingdome [which] the late King James the Second [had] endeavour[ed] to subvert and extirpate." As Hannah Arendt correctly pointed out, when, the year before, the Stuarts were expelled and the royal power was placed in the hands of William and Mary—an event known today as the Glorious Revolution—it was not thought of as a revolution at all, "but as a restoration of monarchical power to its former righteousness and glory."[10] But the American appeal was to nature, not to tradition or the customary law, and it was, therefore, both more radical and less parochial. The consequences of this have been profound: on this foundation we built not only a nation of immigrants, but a nation of immigrants from every part of the globe. In the words of the old Book of Common Prayer, we became and remain a haven for "all sorts and conditions of men."

This is not to deny that our laws have sometimes been

31

biased or our citizens prejudiced; it is merely to say, what is surely true, that in no other place is a prejudice against foreigners so inappropriate, so foreign, so difficult to justify. Xenophobia is, to use another term for which there is no analogue elsewhere, un-American. Precisely because America is something other than a place and a tradition, because words constitute the principal bond between us, anyone (in principle) may become an American. He has only to be Americanized, and, as I say, all sorts and conditions of men have been able and willing to do that.

THE TORIES

While true, however, that statement has to be qualified. The Tories or loyalists were not willing to become Americanized, and they constituted a significant proportion of the white population, about 20 percent—or approximately 500,000 persons—according to the best estimates. Some of them were Tories because—as officeholders, soldiers, or Anglican clergy—they had a vested interest in the imperial establishment in America. A second group was composed of cultural or religious minorities, such as the Quakers, who refused to fight in the war for independence. The third, and politically most interesting, were what might be called the "throne and altar" Tories, dedicated monarchists loyal to the king as head of church and head of state.

More than sentiment was involved in their loyalty; more than an attachment to the forms of monarchy; more even than an aversion to the likes of Tom Paine. They had their reasons and could state them coherently. Men are not born in a Lockean state of nature, said Charles Inglis; they are born in society and from the moment of their birth have social obligations. (An Anglican clergyman, Inglis departed for England in 1783, and died in Halifax, where he served as the first bishop of Nova Scotia.) Nor are men born equal. God intended that they be social creatures, wrote Jonathan Boucher, and He therefore prescribed that there be "some relative inferiority and superiority among them." A musical instrument composed of equal and identical "chords, keys, or pipes," could not, he concluded, produce anything resembling harmony. (He returned to and died in England.) There is no such thing as an inherent right to change a form of government or a "race of kings," wrote Daniel Leonard; contrary to Locke, Paine, Jefferson, and the rest, government is part of God's providence. Besides, by admitting that such a right might be exercised in a single province or "in a number of provinces"—which is to say, in the American colonies—"we unhinge all government." (Leonard fled first to Nova Scotia and then to England, where he, too, ended his days.)[11] Put simply, what Jefferson, Adams, Franklin, and their colleagues held to be self-evidently true, these Tories held to be palpably, foolishly, even dangerously false.

Holding such views, and especially after the British defeat at Yorktown, they had no choice but to become exiles; some 35,000–40,000 of them went to Nova Scotia alone. In 1784 they persuaded the British government to partition this "New Scotland" and to establish for them another colony which, in the course of time, was to become (along with Nova Scotia) one of the ten Canadian provinces. Appropriately enough, it was named New Brunswick.* And

* The so-called Hanoverian kings of England came from Brunswick-Lüneburg in what is now part of the West German state of Lower Saxony. Thus, George I of England was George Louis of Brunswick-Lüneburg, son of Ernest Augustus, elector of Hanover.

there they lived out their days. Their descendants, there and elsewhere in Canada, congregate under the banner of United Empire Loyalists.

THE INDIANS

The Tories can be said to have rejected an implicit invitation to join in the constituting of the people of the United States. No such invitation was extended to the American Indians. A century or more had to pass before many of them were given the opportunity to become citizens, and the day has not yet come when many of them are, like other Americans, simply citizens. Their situation was complicated formally by their tribal affiliations and informally by their inability to persuade Congress—to say nothing of the Indian agents, soldiers, traders, and state officials with whom they came into frequent contact—that they had adopted, or were capable of ever adopting, the habits of civilized life. As members of tribes, they were "Indians not taxed" and, under Article I, section 2 of the Constitution, not counted for the purpose of apportioning representatives and direct taxes among the states. Their tribes were regarded as alien nations, which would have made them simply aliens except for the fact that the tribes were not simply, or not exactly, foreign nations. In the leading case on the subject (decided in 1831), Chief Justice John Marshall said that the tribes might—"perhaps"—be denominated "domestic dependent nations," nations in a state of "pupilage." Thus, an Indian "alien" was not in the same position as, say, a French alien; his relation to the United States, Marshall said, "resembles that of a ward to a guardian." And while, under Article I, section 8 of the Constitution, Congress might regulate the commerce with "the Indian tribes," and like other foreign nations the tribes might enter into treaties with the United States, they were held not to be "foreign States" in the sense in which that term is used in Article III, section 2. That is, they were not so foreign that they might (like France, Peru, Monaco, and the others) file suit in the federal courts.[12]

Unlike that of the emancipated slaves, the legal status of Indians was not even immediately affected by the Fourteenth Amendment. Adopted in 1868, that amendment provides that "all persons born or naturalized in the United States, and subject to the jurisdiction thereof, are citizens of the United States and of the State wherein they reside." Except for the occasional person born to a foreign visitor, by this provision alone every black person—and, for that matter, every Oriental—born in the United States was made a citizen, a member of that body known as the people of the United States. Not so the Indians. They may have been born within the geographical limits of the United States, but they were not born in the United States and subject to its jurisdiction; they owed their allegiance to their tribes, tribes recognized by the United States as "alien though dependent" powers. Even an Indian who had severed all connections with his tribe and was living in the wider community was held not to be a citizen of the United States. Not being a citizen by birth—because he was born in a tribe—he could become a citizen only by being naturalized, and no one, the Supreme Court said, can be naturalized or become a citizen of the nation without the consent of the nation.[18] That consent had to be given (and on occasion had been given) in treaties or statutes permitting certain tribes, or certain categories of Indians, to be naturalized. In addition to taking an oath of allegiance and, like other applicants, satisfying the federal district courts of their good character, Indians were typically required to show that they had "adopted the habits of civilized life." Not until 1924 did Congress finally enact a general statute declaring all Indians "born within the territorial limits of the United States . . . to be citizens of the United States"; and even then it continued to recognize tribal associations: "*Provided*," the statute continues, "that the granting of such citizenship shall not in any manner impair or otherwise affect the right of any Indian to tribal or other property."[14]

The special character of Indian citizenship, or of the relation of Indians to the United States, is reflected in the cases (as well as in the number of cases) that continue to reach the Supreme Court every year. These are cases involving, for example, the right of the Crow Indians to regulate non-Indian fishing in Montana's Big Horn River, or the right of the Jicarillo Apaches to impose a severance tax on oil and gas production, or, for one more example, the right of a female member of the Santa Clara Pueblo to bring an action in federal court to protest a tribal ordinance denying membership to the children of female members who marry outside the tribe but not to the children of men who marry outside the tribe.[15] In this last case, the Court acknowledged that the purpose of the Indian Civil Rights Act of 1968 was to ensure Indians "the broad constitutional rights secured to other Americans," including, presumably, the right to equal protection of the laws, but held nevertheless that Mrs. Martinez, the Indian involved, could not bring this action against her tribe in a federal court; the tribe was held to enjoy a sovereign immunity from suit. The groups, corporate entities, and other associations to which other citizens belong are not so insulated or immune from suit, but, the Court implied, Indians are different and Congress may treat them differently.

Congress has always treated them differently. Even in 1775, almost exactly one year before they adopted the Declaration of Independence, the Continental Congress had cause to compose a letter of greater length, on a related subject, but written in an entirely different mode or style. The Declaration was written in a manner designed to pay a "decent respect to the opinions of mankind." As historian Carl Becker said, "The purpose of the Declaration is set forth in the first paragraph—a striking sentence, in which simplicity of statement is somehow combined with an urbane solemnity of manner in such a way as to give that felicitous, haunting cadence which is the peculiar quality of Jefferson's best writing."[16] The congressional letter, however, was written not to mankind but to particular Indian tribes—the Mohawks, Oneidas, Onodagas, Tuscaroras, Cayugas, and Senekas—to persuade them not to "take up the hatchet" against the colonists in their war with "the king's troops." Congress's opinion of Indians can, probably, be glimpsed in the unsophisticated, indeed, naive style of this letter. "Brothers, Sachems, and Warriors," it begins, "When our fathers crossed the great water . . . the king of England gave them a talk [a promise?]: assuring them that they and their children should be his children." It proceeds by complaining of the king's "proud and wicked" counsellors who persuaded him "not to send us any more good talks." It then complains of being taxed without being represented, but expresses that complaint as follows: "They [the wicked counsellors] now tell us they will slip their hand into our pocket without asking." Here and there it directs the bearers of the letter to offer a present of *"a small belt,"* or *"three strings, or a small belt,"* or *"the large belt of intelligence and declaration."* And it concludes by saying that the Congress intends "to kindle up a small council fire at Albany, where we may hear each other's voice," and where, presumably, these gifts were to be proffered.

Such a letter—a longer sample is printed in the footnote[17]—would probably be regarded as an insult today; but no offense was taken in 1775, and none was intended. It apparently never occurred to the men of that Congress— Patrick Henry, Benjamin Franklin, James Wilson, and Thomas Jefferson, among others—that Indians were fit to be citizens of the American republic. Certainly Jefferson did not think so; he said they were barbarians. This judgment may have been severe but it was not made out of ignorance; on the contrary, Jefferson was an avid student of Indians, especially of their languages, just as he was an avid student of natural philosophy in general. Asked by a "foreigner of Distinction" (François Barbé-Marbois) to give an account of the natural and political environment of America, Jefferson responded in a book entitled *Notes on the State of Virginia.* In it, he treated the subject of Indians in a chapter devoted to natural resources: the mines, trees, plants, fruits, wild animals, and the "aborigines." He took some satisfaction in reporting that, contrary to the opinions held by some Europeans, not only were the wild animals of North America as large as those of Europe, but the "aborigines" were as well formed in mind and body as *"Homo sapiens Europaens."* But they had no experience of law or government, being ruled only by their manners and "that moral sense of right and wrong, which, like the

38

sense of tasting and feeling in every man, makes a part of [their] nature." For them, as for every other "barbarous people," force is law, which explained why their women, the weaker sex, were subjected to "unjust drudgery." Only in a civilized place are women allowed to enjoy their "natural equality," and only in a civilized condition are men and women alike taught to subdue their selfish passions and "to respect those rights in others which we value in ourselves."[18] Once again taking his cue from Locke, Jefferson seemed to be suggesting that only as men develop those faculties that distinguish them from the inferior animals can they devise the means of securing their rights.

In saying all this, Jefferson reminds us that while the rights of man—being the gift of nature's God—are the same everywhere, the other attributes of men vary with men as well as with time and place. Of greatest significance is the fact—and Jefferson understood it to be a fact—that men and peoples are not equally civilized, a consideration to be weighed when deciding with whom to contract when constituting a civil society. As Jefferson's fellow Virginian, St. George Tucker, asked rhetorically in 1796, "Have not men when they enter a state of society, a right to admit, or exclude any description of persons, as they think proper?"[19] Not only inequalities but simple differences may properly be weighed when making this decision. After all, they are contracting "to form one society," as Madison put it, to live together, and living together—freely and peacefully— requires more than a legal or quasi-legal agreement; it requires mutual trust and some sense of fellow feeling. In short, a civil society must have elements of a community. As the French say, not only *liberté* and *égalité*, but *fraternité*, and it appears to have been Jefferson's judgment that the former British colonists and the Indians (although addressed by Congress as "Brothers," as well as "Sachems, and Warriors") were not, and in the foreseeable future were not likely to be, brothers. Nor in the foreseeable future did it seem likely that the Indians would want to be brothers to the colonists; they wanted to be left alone in their tribes. (Unfortunately, while they were left in their tribes, they were not left alone.)

THE BLACKS

Thus, the Indians, unlike the Tories, were effectively denied the choice of becoming part of the people of the United States; but given the choice they, in this case like the Tories, had a right to refuse it. So, too, the persons who became the people of the United States had a right to refuse to contract with the Indians and the Tories, the former because they were uncivilized and the latter because they were antirepublican. They also had a right, which they exercised, to refuse to contract with the blacks who were slaves but who, by right, should have been free. For, to quote Herbert J. Storing, "there is nothing contradictory in arguing that while the Negroes have a human right to be free, they do not have a human right to be citizens of the United States."[20] Some well-known historians of our own time would contest this. Winthrop D. Jordan, for one, quotes a New Hampshire abolitionist who (in 1795) called for emancipation of the slaves and their resettlement in a separate Negro state. "What was striking in this proposal was that fervent equalitarianism led directly to Negro removal," Jordan writes. "Evidently the right to live in the

40

white man's country was not one of 'the rights belonging to human nature,' since Negroes did not seem to share in it."[21] But there is no inconsistency here. Just as the Negroes constituting that separate Negro state would have had a right to exclude the whites, the white and erstwhile British colonists, when constituting the people of the United States, had a right to refuse to contract with the blacks.

What they did not have a right to do, however, was to exclude the blacks from their society—along with the Indians and the Tories—while continuing to govern them. This was a violation of natural right, and, what is more, they knew it. Indeed, they acknowledged it. "Is it not amazing," wrote Patrick Henry,

> that at a time, when the Rights of Humanity are defined & understood with precision, in a Country above all others fond of Liberty, that in such an Age, & such a Country we find Men . . . adopting a Principle as repugnant to humanity. . . . Would any one believe that I am Master of Slaves of my own purchase! I am drawn along by the general inconvenience of living without them, I will not, I cannot justify it.[22]

And because he failed publicly to acknowledge his transgression, a group styling themselves "The Yeomanry of Massachusetts" dared to denounce even George Washington himself. "We cannot think the noble general has the same ideas with ourselves, with regard to the rules of right and wrong," they wrote. "He wielded the sword in defence of American liberty, yet at the same time was, and is to this day, living upon the labours of several hundreds of miserable Africans, as free born as himself; and some of whom very likely descended from parents who, in point of property

41

and dignity in their own country, might cope with any man in America."[23] At his death in 1799, Washington owned some 317 slaves and, like Henry, made no effort to justify himself, except occasionally to wonder whether, if freed, the slaves could support themselves. Nevertheless, in his last will and testament he provided for their emancipation—but only after "the decease of [his] wife."

Slaveowners some of them were, but a better index of the Framers' attitude toward slavery can be found in the Constitution they wrote. That Constitution has three provisions relating to slavery, but nowhere in it is there to be found the word "slave" in any of its forms. The term employed in its stead is person or persons, as in "three fifths of all other Persons" (Article I, section 2, #3), "the Migration or Importation of Such Persons as any of the States now existing shall think proper to admit" (Article I, section 9, #1), and, finally, "No person held to Service or Labour in one State, under the Laws thereof, escaping into another, shall, in Consequence of any Law or Regulation therein, be discharged from such Service or Labour, but shall be delivered up on Claim of the Party to whom such Service or Labour may be due" (Article IV, section 2, #3). Everyone knew the persons referred to meant, in the main, slaves, but, so far as we can learn from the records of the Convention, the majority of the delegates insisted on the euphemisms, and no one objected to them.

The development or tranformation of the last-mentioned provision is instructive on this point. First introduced on August 28, 1787, by the South Carolinians Pierce Butler and Charles Pinckney, it spoke frankly and brutally of requiring "fugitive slaves and servants to be delivered up like criminals." After some discussion, this was withdrawn and, the next day, replaced by the following version: "If any person bound to service or labor in any of the U——— states shall escape into another state, he or she . . . shall be delivered up to the person justly claiming their service or labor." Upon objection to the implication that a person may "justly" claim the services of a slave, this was changed by the Committee of Style to read, "shall be delivered up on claim of the party to whom such service or labour may be due." But this committee's version began with the words, "No person legally held to service or labour in one state," and on September 15, on the floor of the Convention again, an unidentified delegate objected that the term "legally" might be understood to favor "the idea that slavery was legal in a moral view." The Convention responded by striking the word "legally" and substituting the words "under the laws thereof."[24]

There was no doubt as to why these changes were made or why, in general, the euphemisms were employed. As Luther Martin explained in his account of the Convention delivered to the legislature of his state of Maryland, the delegates "anxiously sought to avoid the admission of expressions which might be odious in the ears of Americans"—although, he added, "they were willing to admit into their system those *things* which the *expressions* signified."[25] That is an accurate statement of what happened. With the exception of an occasional Southerner—for example, Rawlins Lowndes, who, during the ratification debates, told the South Carolina legislature that the Northern delegates "don't like our slaves, because they have none themselves"[26]—the Founders looked upon slavery as "inconsistent with the principles of the revolution," as Martin put it. It was also an evil but, they said, an evil they had to tolerate.

43

Lincoln, for one, was willing to concede this point to the Founders. As they marked it, he said at the Cooper Institute in February 1860, so let it be again marked, *"as an evil not to be extended, but to be tolerated and protected only because of and so far as its actual presence among us makes that toleration and protection a necessity."* Our contemporary historians are unwilling to be so generous. The common view today is that, for some reason, the Founders thought it necessary to denounce slavery but found it convenient, even easy, to tolerate it. Jefferson especially has been harshly treated of late. Playwright (and sometime Princeton professor) Martin B. Duberman had only to have a character "recite selected passages from [Jefferson's] *Notes on Virginia,* often in a supercilious tone, to transform the father of democracy into the father of American racism." So writes David Brion Davis in his definitive study of the slavery issue during the revolutionary period. Davis then adds that Winthrop D. Jordan, "in a brilliant dissection of Jefferson's attitudes toward race," is somewhat more charitable when he says Jefferson "never realized how deep-seated his anti-Negro feelings were." Somewhat more charitable still, but still a long way from Lincoln, Davis himself speaks of Jefferson's "uncertain commitment" to the antislavery cause and, giving it as his opinion that his views changed—and changed for the worse—over time, suggests that Jefferson's reputation would be better had he died earlier.[27]

Much of this criticism is unfair, and the more extreme—for example, Duberman's—is an abuse of Jefferson's writings. Nevertheless, what someone said of Nietzsche can also be said of Jefferson: his writings on slavery are singularly easy to abuse. In the *Notes on the State of Virginia,*

where he cast himself in his favorite role of the dispassionate natural philosopher, he examined the physical differences between whites and blacks—wondering, for example,
whether the "black of the negro resides in the reticular
membrane between the skin and the scarf-skin, or in the
scarf-skin itself," noting that whites secrete more by the
kidneys and blacks "more by the glands of the skin,"
which, he said, "gives them a very strong and disagreeable
odour" but also renders them "more tolerant of heat, and
less so of cold, than the Whites," and concluding that the
whites were superior in beauty—and not only the physical
differences between whites and blacks but what he saw as
the mental and moral differences. His judgment—one he
"hazarded with great diffidence"—was that the blacks were
the equal of the whites in memory but "in reason much
inferior . . . and in imagination . . . dull, tasteless, and
anomalous." If challenged for these and similar judgments,
he might have said they were based on observation and,
of course, were subject to amendment when the facts war-
ranted it. Indeed, a decade later, having received an astro-
nomical almanac from its author, a black mathematician,
he wrote, "No body wishes more than I do to see such
proofs as you exhibit, that nature has given to our black
brethren, talents equal to those of the other colors of men,
and that the appearance of a want of them is owing merely
to the degraded condition of their existence, both in Africa
& America." But he would have had a hard time convincing
anyone that he was merely acting as the detached observer
when, in the *Notes on Virginia,* he said that blacks themselves acknowledged their inferiority by preferring the
whites, and proceeded to liken this to the "Oranootan's"
preference of black women "over those of his own species."[28]

At best he might have said—what was true—he had not originally intended the *Notes* to be read by a public audience.

At his worst, however, Jefferson was no match for Chief Justice Taney and his majority colleagues in the *Dred Scott* case. Unlike them, he never denied the humanity of blacks and, therefore, the fact of their endowment with natural rights. As he wrote to the Abbé Grégoire in 1809, "Whatever be their degree of talent it is no measure of their rights." What he denied was their capacity to exercise these rights in company with white Americans. Why not incorporate the blacks into the state? he asked. "Deep rooted prejudices entertained by the whites; ten thousand recollections, by the blacks, of the injuries they have sustained; new provocations; the real distinctions which nature has made; and many other circumstances, will divide us into parties, and produce convulsions which will probably never end but in the extermination of the one or the other race." This dismal prospect, he thought, had become more likely by 1820 and the Missouri crisis when, he said, justice for the blacks was incompatible with the preservation of the whites. But his definitive statement of the issue was reserved for his autobiography: "Nothing is more certainly written in the book of fate," he wrote, "than that these people are to be free; nor is it less certain that the two races, equally free, cannot live in the same government."[29]

This may not have been the unanimous judgment of the Founders, but so far as we can learn from the record they left—from what they said as well as from what they left unsaid—it was the common judgment. As an instance of the former, Madison, in a memorandum written (apparently) on October 20, 1789, said manumission would

be justified if the freed slaves could be completely incorporated in the "Society," but this, he said, was "ren-
dered impossible by the prejudices of the whites, prejudices
which proceeding principally from the difference of colour
must be considered as permanent and insuperable." As an
instance of the latter—of what was left unsaid—consider
the behavior of the Continental Congress. In a letter of
October 26, 1774, the Congress invited the Inhabitants of
Quebec to unite with the American colonists "in one social compact, formed on the generous principles of equal
liberty and cemented by such an exchange of beneficial
and endearing offices as to render it perpetual [and] to
complete this highly desirable union . . . to chuse delegates to represent your province in the continental Congress to be held at Philadelphia on the tenth day of May,
1775."[30] In extending this invitation, the Congress was apparently willing to overlook the fact that Quebec was an
overwhelmingly French-speaking, and not only French-
speaking but Roman Catholic, province, and that, only two
weeks earlier, Congress had formally denounced the British government's Quebec Act as an intolerable attempt to
extend the boundaries of the province—and with them "the
evils of popery"—down to the Ohio River. But in a time of
danger, at least, Congress was willing to overlook the language and religious differences and issue this appeal for
union.

What the Congress could not, or, at any rate, did not
do was issue a similar appeal to any of the British West
Indian colonies, Jamaica, for example. Jamaica was Protestant, English-speaking, and populous, having twice the
number of people of Quebec; in fact, its population of
some 210,000 exceeded that of nine of the original thir-

teen states and dwarfed that of Georgia. But 94 percent of Jamaicans were black and 98 percent of the blacks were slaves.[31] Not only were Jamaica, Barbados, and the rest not invited to cast their lot with the Americans, but, so far as we know, the idea of asking them never crossed the mind of an American, North or South, Pennsylvanian or Virginian.[32]

As one might expect, the Northerners even then were much more openly antislavery than their friends and associates from the South. Not only Benjamin Franklin and Benjamin Rush in Pennsylvania but John Jay and Alexander Hamilton in New York were members of manumission societies and took active part in the effort to abolish slavery in their states. Prior to 1776, the Society of Friends—the Quakers—was the only organization to advocate emancipation, and by 1787 it could boast that none of its members owned so much as a single slave,[33] but with the Revolution and the Declaration came a marked increase in the number of slavery's opponents. As one Connecticut patriot said as he left for war, "I will not fight for liberty and leave a slave at home," whereupon he manumitted his one slave. Within a year of the conclusion of the Revolutionary War, not only Pennsylvania but all the New England states had enacted laws providing for the abolition of slavery. Somewhat later, but only after protracted struggles, New York and New Jersey joined the movement with laws providing—and once again we should remark the significance of the date—that all Negro children born in the states after July 4, 1799 (New York), and July 4, 1804 (New Jersey), would be free.

But two things must be said about abolition in the Northern states. First, there were not many slaves to begin with in these states and relatively few slaveholders, which made abolition easier. Winthrop Jordan concludes his discussion of this matter by saying that "in a region where every twentieth rather than every third person was a Negro, it was easier for principles to override [the unpalatable prospect of a mixture of blood]."[34] Second, even though the number of free Negroes in the North was limited—27,000 in 1790 and 122,000 in 1830—which ought to have facilitated the process, the Northern states were not successful in incorporating them in the larger society. Indeed, it would be more accurate to say these states made no effort to incorporate them. Negroes, nominally free, remained "members of a despised race, subject to countless indignities, denied the equal rights promised by the Declaration of Independence, and restricted to the most menial occupations."[35] As late as 1842, New Jersey refused to grant the franchise to (free) Negroes.

Like Jefferson and Madison in Virginia, the Northern opponents of slavery—even some of the Quakers—were inclined to favor abolition only when combined with colonization or, at a minimum, separation. During the early years of the republic especially, colonization was not a proslavery policy; Winthrop Jordan points out that in fact it was then supported "only by men of genuine antislavery feeling."[36] To this end, Benjamin Rush actually offered to donate a 5,200-acre tract of land in western Pennsylvania for resettlement of free Negroes who were to be trained as farmers, and the most famous of the Quaker abolitionists, Anthony Benezet, advocated colonization in "that large extent of country, from the west side of the Allegheny Mountains to the Mississippi, on a breadth of four or five hundred miles."[37] Another noted Quaker, Thomas Branagan, called for the establishment of a black state to be carved out of the Louisiana Territory "upwards of two thousand miles from the white population." White prejudice made it impossible, he said, to incorporate them into the body politic.[38] Everyone seems to have agreed about the prejudice, but not everyone agreed with Madison, for example, that the prejudice derived from the difference in color and was "permanent and insuperable." Occasionally someone even put forward a plan to overcome it. Here is James Sullivan, a Boston lawyer, writing in 1795 to Jeremy Belknap:

> The children of the slaves must, at the public expence, be educated in the same manner as the children of their masters; being at the same schools, etc., with the rising generation, that prejudice, which has been so long and inveterate against them on account of their situation and colour, will be lessened within thirty or forty years. There is an objection to this, which embraces all my feelings; that is, that it will tend to a mixture of blood, which I now abhor; but yet, as I feel, I fear that I am not a pure Republican, delighting in the equal rights of all the human race. This mode of education will fit the rising progeny of the black people either to participate with the whites in a free government, or to colonize, and have one of their own.[39]

Yet as that last sentence indicates, even he wondered whether, finally, that prejudice could be overcome.

Perhaps the most instructive episode—and surely one of the most disgraceful—was the manner in which Congress chose to dispose of what can only be called "contraband" slaves. In December 1806, Congress began debate on a bill (enacted on March 2, 1807) prohibiting the "importation of slaves into any part or place within the jurisdiction of the United States, from and after the first day of January [1808]," which, under Article I, section 9 of the Constitution, was the first day such prohibition was permissible. The bill passed the House of Representatives by a vote of 113 to 5, which is some indication of the extent to which members North and South agreed that the African slave trade ought to be ended. On that point there was agreement; what they debated at length were the secondary issues, for example, the severity of the punishment to be imposed on the captured slavers and, most of all, the disposition of the captured cargo, which is to say, the slaves. John Smilie of Pennsylvania proposed that they be sent back to Africa, Josiah Quincy of Massachusetts that they be disposed of at the discretion of the secretary of the treasury, various members that they be indentured for life or for a term of years, and James Sloan of New Jersey that they be freed. But Sloan was deceiving either himself or the House when, in support of his motion, he suggested that the "northern states would receive the freed Negroes willingly rather than have them enslaved."[40] This the states showed no willingness to do. Like the Framers, the Northern politicians regarded slavery as contrary to natural right and, moreover, as a curse. They wanted to abolish it, and did abolish it, but they also wanted to get rid of the freed slaves—and this they did not know how to do.

The question during these slave trade debates—What should be done with these particular slaves?—was merely an especially dramatic version of the general question to which the Framers and the succeeding generations of politicians were unable to provide an answer. "We have the wolf by the ears," as Jefferson put it in his letter to John Holmes during the Missouri crisis in 1820, "and we can neither hold him, nor safely let him go." In the event, Congress disgraced itself by providing that the illegally imported slaves be disposed of according to the laws of the states to which the captured vessel and its cargo were taken; in practice, this meant they were sold into slavery. In a case that reached the Supreme Court in 1825 on an ancillary question, we learn that in Louisiana the law provided that they be sold by the sheriff of New Orleans Parish and that the proceeds of the sale go half to the officer commanding the vessel responsible for the capture and—as a way of salving consciences—half to the New Orleans Charity Hospital.[41]

In their moments of despair (which were frequent during the Missouri crisis in 1820), both Jefferson and Madison were driven to propose even an expansion of slavery, this as a means, they argued, of facilitating the emancipation of slaves. An absurd idea, diffusion or dispersion would nevertheless appear to have been seriously advanced by both men. Shortly after Congress had allowed Missouri to come into the Union as a slave state, Jefferson wrote in that letter to John Holmes that the "diffusion" of slaves over a greater surface "would make them individually happier, and proportionally facilitate the accomplishment of their emancipation, by dividing the burthen on a greater number of coadjutors." (By "burthen," or burden, he probably meant the expense of colonizing the emancipated slaves.) At about the same time, Madison was writing the antislavery journalist Robert Walsh and, as was his custom, being much more specific about the alleged benefits of diffusion, benefits that would presumably accrue to black and white alike. In summary, so the argument went, holding the number of slaves constant and spreading them over a larger

52

territory would have the effect of reducing the ratio of blacks to whites everywhere. This would be likely to reduce the number of slaves owned by a single master, and, he said, this "lessening" of the number of slaves would improve their "moral & physical condition." Secondly, the smaller the proportion of blacks in a particular location, the greater the number of manumissions; and finally, and directly connected to the second benefit, the fewer the blacks, the smaller the risk of insurrections.[42] His conclusion was that Congress was mistaken—foolish and short-sighted—to exclude slavery from that portion of the Louisiana Territory north of 36°30'. Indeed, serving as a kind of harbinger of what the Court was to do in *Dred Scott* v. *Sandford*, he questioned whether Congress had the constitutional authority to exclude slavery from any federal territory.

But in this case it was Madison who was mistaken, not Congress. Diffusing slavery was calculated to strengthen it, not weaken it. Congress would have had to do in 1820 what Lincoln denounced it for doing with the Kansas-Nebraska Act in 1854, namely, acquiesce in the spread of slavery and, as a condition of this acquiescence, renounce the principle according to which slavery was wrong. The program would have required the newly created states to fashion a full range of slave institutions, which could only have increased the flow of slaveholding immigrants to them and thereby hastened their election of rigid proslavery governments. Such governments would have been likely to join South Carolina and Georgia, for example, and demand the repeal of the anti-importation law. In short, dispersing slaves over a wider territory would have been likely to have perpetuated slavery, in fact, to have nationalized it, which is why Lincoln was willing to lead the country into the bloodiest of its wars rather than countenance even the principle of slavery dispersion.

There were, undeniably, a few free blacks who were and who were understood to be citizens of the United States prior to the Fourteenth Amendment; that much was demonstrated by Justice Benjamin Curtis in his justly celebrated dissenting opinion in the *Dred Scott* case. And it is equally undeniable that there were public officials who, when the subject was openly and directly debated, championed the cause of black citizenship and their eligibility for naturalization. "The gentleman from Virginia says he must not be told that the term, we the people, in the preamble to the Constitution means, or includes, Indians, free negroes, mulattoes," complained Representative William Eustis of Massachusetts during the Missouri debates of 1820. But, he went on, the convention that drafted the Constitution did not consider the "complexion" of the persons included in the compact. "No, sir; they necessarily considered all those as citizens who were acknowledged as such by the constitutions of the states."[43] And among the states that acknowledged Negro eligibility for citizenship was, he proudly pointed out, his state of Massachusetts. The fact that by law a black man was forbidden to marry a white woman meant nothing at all, he insisted; the same law forbade a white man to marry a black woman.

The precise issue being debated by the House at this time was the effect on Missouri (and its proposed proslavery constitution) of the provision (Article IV, section 2, #1) in the national Constitution that the "Citizens of each State shall be entitled to all Privileges and Immunities of Citizens in the several States." Read literally, this would have permitted citizens of Massachusetts, for example, including black citizens of Massachusetts, to enter and move freely about the state of Missouri, engaging in business, entering into contracts, suing and being sued, and, generally, doing what Missouri citizens were permitted to do. That prospect was, of course, unacceptable to the defenders of slavery. Thus, no one was surprised when Charles Pinckney of South Carolina, who had been a prominent member of the 1787 Convention, replied to Eustis that he, Pinckney, was the author of that constitutional language and that, "at the time [he] drew that constitution, [he] perfectly knew that there did not then exist such a thing in the Union as a black or colored citizen, nor could [he] then have conceived it possible such a thing could have existed in it; nor [did he] now believe one does exist in it."[44]

At about the same time, with respect to a matter having nothing to do with the Missouri issue, the U.S. attorney general, William Wirt, issued a formal opinion to the effect that the term "citizens of the United States" as used in the Constitution referred only to those "who enjoyed the full and equal privileges of white citizens in the State of their residence," which excluded from national citizenship "free persons of color in Virginia" or any other state.[45]

William Eustis notwithstanding, this seems to have been the prevailing view on the subject of whether blacks were, or could be, part of the people of the United States. In 1779, for example, Jefferson could draft a "Bill Declaring Who Shall be Deemed Citizens of this [Virginia] Commonwealth" and simply and (so far as we know) indifferently confine those eligible to "all white persons born within the territory of this commonwealth." The idea that black persons—free black persons—might join in constituting the people of Virginia or of the United States was never seriously considered or, so far as we know, considered at all. The same thing can be said of Congress when, beginning in 1790 and continuing in 1794 and beyond, it debated and adopted legislation prescribing the rules of naturalization; to state the matter simply, eligibility in the 1790 law was limited to "free white persons"[46] and remained so limited in the subsequent amended versions. The conclusion is clear: the typical American was opposed to slavery but equally opposed to including black persons as part of the people of the United States.

Yet, when, during the ratification debates of 1787–88, "Agrippa" (probably James Winthrop) of Massachusetts complained of that clause in Article I, section 8, giving Congress the power to "establish a uniform Rule of Naturalization" and spoke of the need "to keep their blood pure," he meant pure of even European mixtures. Pennsylvania, he pointed out, "had chosen to receive all that would come there" and had succeeded in populating a great extent of territory—but only "at the expense of religion and good morals." The eastern states—"the small state of Rhode Island only excepted"—had preserved their religion and morals by "keeping separate from foreign mixtures."[47] It was during these naturalization debates especially that the men of the Founding generation paid some attention to the moral qualifications of republican citizenship.

When, for example, debate began in February 1790 on the first of the naturalization bills, objection was taken to the first clause not because it limited eligibility to "free white persons," but because it permitted naturalization after a residence of only "one whole year." This was said by some members of the House of Representatives to be far too brief a period; to acquire a "taste for this [republican] government" and come to appreciate "the truth of [its] principles," a term of residence of four or even seven years ought to be required. Madison did not at first commit himself to a specific term of years but spoke eloquently of the necessity of attracting only "the worthy part of mankind to come and settle amongst us." James Jackson of Georgia argued specifically that before a person "is admitted to enjoy the high and inestimable privilege of a citizen of America . . . he ought to pass some time in a state of probation, and at the end of the term, be able to bring testimonials of a proper and decent behavior."[48] In 1790, Congress settled on a term of two years of residence, which left many members dissatisfied, and four years later the subject was reopened and extensively redebated. The bill enacted January 8, 1795, called for a five-year minimum residency, and it was during this second debate that Theodore Sedgwick of Massachusetts delivered what was probably the most elaborate and eloquent statement on the moral prerequisites of republican citizenship. It deserves to be quoted at some length:

America, he said, if her political institutions should on experience be found to be wisely adjusted, and she shall improve her natural advantages, had opened to her view a more rich and glorious prospect than ever was presented to man. She had chosen for herself a Government which left to the citizen as great a portion of freedom as was consistent with a social compact. All believed the preservation of this Government, in its purity, indispensable to the continuance of our happiness. The foundation on which it rested was general intelligence and public virtue; in other words, wisdom to discern, and patriotism to pursue the

general good. He had pride, and he gloried in it, in believing his countrymen more wise and virtuous than any
other people on earth; hence he believed them better
qualified to administer and support a Republican Government. This character of Americans was the result of early
education, aided indeed by the discipline of the Revolution. In that part of the country with which he was best
acquainted, the education, manners, habits, and institutions, religious and civil, were Republican. The community was divided into corporations, in many respects resembling independent republics, of which almost every
man, the qualifications were so small, was a member. They
had many important and interesting concerns to transact.
They appointed their executive officers, enacted bye laws,
raised money for many purposes of use and ornament.
Here, then, the citizens early acquired the habits of temperate discussion, patient reasoning, and a capacity of enduring contradiction. Here the means of education and
instruction are instituted and maintained; public libraries
are purchased and read; these are (said he) the proper
schools for the education of Republican citizens; thus are
to be planted the seeds of Republicanism. If you will cul-
tivate the plants which are to be reared from these seeds,
you will gather an abundant harvest of long continued
prosperity.[49]

And it was in the course of discoursing on the moral requi-
sites of citizenship that some members of Congress spoke
openly of excluding persons on religious grounds.

"JEWS, TURKS, AND INFIDELS"

One might have thought that by adopting—and adopting unanimously—the Article VI proscription of any "religious test . . . as a qualification to any office or public trust under the United States," the Constitutional Convention would have made it clear to the subsequent congresses that the Constitution forbids as well any religious qualification for citizenship. Indeed—and this subject will be discussed at some length in Chapter 4—it could be argued that the inalienable right to pursue happiness as one himself defines it would forbid laws limiting citizenship to persons of a particular religious persuasion. In these early naturalization debates, however, some representatives chose to distinguish between qualifications for officeholding and qualifications for citizenship, arguing that the latter ought to be more stringent and, furthermore, that the constitutional office-holding proscription could be attributed to the convention's inability to agree on the precise terms of a national religious test. To support this latter contention they could and did point to the variety of religious tests and restrictions enforced—with the exception of Virginia—within each of the original states. Jews, for example, labored under one or another legal disability in every state except Virginia and New York, and New York balanced this apparent liberality by disqualifying Roman Catholics. Nor was this prejudice confined to New York. Thus, when one member of the 1795 Congress spoke of the desirability of excluding from citizenship members of the former European nobility, Samuel Dexter of Massachusetts responded by ridiculing "certain tenets in the Roman Catholic religion, and [saying] that the priestcraft had done more mischief than aristocracy."[50] This, in turn, led Madison immediately to indicate his displeasure at hearing such sentiments expressed on the floor of the House. There was nothing inconsistent, he said, between Roman Catholicism and "the purest Republicanism."

In the event, of course, religious tests or tenets were made no part of the qualifications for national citizenship; Madison and his constitutional colleagues were sufficiently influential to see to that. But they could not themselves put an end to religious bigotry or, at a minimum, intolerance. As late as 1826, James Kent could still refer to New York's anti-Catholicism as a public problem. It was of long standing, he pointed out, and so strong that Jesuits and "popish priests" were excluded from the colony by law, a law which, according to the historian of the colony, should be made perpetual.[51] That was written in 1756, and it was not until 1806 that the law in question was modified so as to permit a particular Roman Catholic to take a seat in the New York Assembly. And in the North Carolina ratifying convention of 1788, William Lancaster could complain of the Article VI proscription of religious tests because it admitted the possibility and legitimacy of a "Papist" or "Mahometan" becoming president of the United States.[52] When, in 1786, the Virginia legislature rejected the amendment "to insert the words 'Jesus Christ' after the words 'our lord' in the preamble" to the Virginia Act for Religious Freedom, Jefferson saw this as proof that Virginia, at least, "meant to comprehend, within the mantle of its protection, the Jew and Gentile, the Christian and Mahametan, the Hindoo, and infidel of every denomination."[53]

Yet the formal and organized effort to have this declared to be a Christian nation continued well into the nineteenth century; even in the midst of the Civil War both Congress and President Lincoln were importuned by the National Reform Association to support a constitutional amendment to effect this. (Congress tabled the association's memorial, and Lincoln, after listening courteously to its delegation, managed to ignore the request.) It was only in 1945 that the association dissolved, and even then its cause "to put Christ in the Constitution" was taken up by the National Association of Evangelicals.[54]

CONCLUSION

In his recent biography of Winston Churchill, the American William Manchester speaks of the privileges and amenities enjoyed by the not-yet-impoverished English nobility and its immediate descendants. Churchill himself, for instance, a mere grandson of a duke, was always dressed and undressed by someone else, and—whether schoolboy, soldier, public minister, or private citizen—never once in his long life had to draw his own bath. His cousin, the ninth Duke of Marlborough, was accustomed to even closer attendance. On only one occasion, apparently, was he required to travel without his valet and make do without the services the valet customarily provided; he didn't do well. An overnight visitor at the home of friends, he emerged in the morning holding his toothbrush and complaining that it didn't "froth properly." Manchester reports that "he had to be told gently that toothpaste had to be applied to the brush before it would foam."

61

This story suggests that in certain respects England had apparently not changed all that much in the century since the 1830s when Tocqueville, who knew it well, could refer to it as the country where both "enjoyment" and "power" were monopolized by the rich. Now, even in the twentieth century, there was still an aristocracy that expected to be served and, much to the despair of socialists like R. H. Tawney, still a class of Englishmen willing not only to serve them but, with a tip of the cap or a tug of the forelock, ready to defer to them.

Things were different in America and always had been. Our few aristocrats were dispatched in the years following the Revolution, and the "Tories" who remained here were soon absorbed by or, better, assimilated into our democratic population. Unlike England or Tocqueville's France, this country has never experienced or had reason to fear an attempt to restore the monarchy; there have been no American Bourbons or, more to the point, American Jacobites or "Georgians" secretly toasting "The King over the Water." In this respect, we were lucky; we were, as Tocqueville said, "born equal instead of becoming so."

In saying this, Tocqueville was—knowingly, of course—ignoring the treatment of Indians and slaves.[55] This country suffered no constitutional damage by excluding or quietly converting the Tories, and it has benefited enormously from the early decision not to exclude anyone on religious grounds; but it has required the Indians to pay a heavy price for their nominal independence, and it has paid a terrible price for its initial decision to exclude blacks from the people of the United States. ("What Country have I?" asked the young Frederick Douglass in 1847, when most of his people were slaves; and Malcolm X had reason to repeat the question a century and more later when all of his people were legally free.) The price reckoned in human suffering is the subject of a thousand and one books; the damage done to constitutional government is a subject treated below.

CHAPTER II

Constituting the Government: The Convention

|||

The real wonder is that so many difficulties should have been surmounted [by the Convention], and surmounted with a unanimity almost as unprecedented as it must have been unexpected. It is impossible for any man of candor to reflect on this circumstance without partaking of the astonishment. It is impossible for the man of pious reflection not to perceive in it a finger of that Almighty hand which has been so frequently and signally extended to our relief in the critical stages of the revolution.

—Federalist 37

The frequency with which the process has been repeated should not be allowed to conceal the fact that in 1787 the writing and formal adoption of a constitution of government was a novelty. This was well understood by Americans when they were asked "to deliberate on a new constitution for the United States of America,"[1] and even better understood by the fifty-five men who assembled in Philadelphia to write it.

The constitution they wrote and were instrumental in having adopted was not, however, the first to be written or adopted by Americans. In the period immediately preceding 1787, each of the states comprising the United States (with the qualified exceptions of Connecticut and Rhode Island) had adopted, and was governing itself under, a written constitution.[2] Some of the men assembled at Philadelphia had played an active part in this process at the state level.

The Constitution of 1787 was not even the first national constitution. At the very time the convention was deliberating and debating in Philadelphia, there was a Congress of the United States meeting and debating national policy in New York, a congress that derived its authority from an agreement—the Articles of Confederation and Perpetual Union—entered into by delegates of the thirteen states in November 1777, and declared formally ratified by the states in March 1781. It was, in fact, at the call of this Congress on February 21, 1787, that the convention met in Philadelphia.

Thus, the Constitution of 1787 was neither the first to be written nor the first under which the American nation was governed; nevertheless, as its Framers knew very well indeed, they were engaged in what was still a novel enterprise, an experiment, and one for which history provided little guidance. They also understood its significance. As one of them wrote, "The subject speaks its own importance," and not only for Americans. He and many of his colleagues thought they were setting an example for the whole of mankind.

> It has been frequently remarked that it seems to have been reserved to the people of this country, by their conduct and example, to decide the important question, whether societies of men are really capable or not of establishing good government from reflection and choice, or whether they are forever destined to depend for their political constitutions on accident and force.[3]

One other feature of this constitution deserves mention here: although written by delegates representing the particular states, it claimed to derive its authority from "the people of the United States," an assertion that gave rise to a good deal of controversy. "What right had they to say, *We, the people*," demanded Patrick Henry, one of the heroes of the American Revolution. "Who authorized them to speak the language of *We, the People*, instead of *We, the States*?"[4] Henry was not merely being querulous; he and the scores of others who made similar objections had legitimate cause to complain. The country was governing itself under a constitution—the Articles of Confederation and Perpetual Union—which, by its own terms, could be altered or amended only with the consent of "the legislatures of every state." The amending provision was wholly compatible with the governing principle of the Articles, namely, the quasi-sovereignty of the individual states, and that sovereignty was not recognized in the new constitution. Furthermore, Congress had called the convention "for the sole and express purpose of revising the Articles of Confederation and reporting to the Congress and the several [state] legislatures such alterations and provisions therein as shall when agreed to in Congress and confirmed by the states render the federal constitution adequate to the exigencies of Government and the preservation of the Union."[5] But everyone acknowledged that the constitution that came out of the convention was much more than a revision of the Articles of Confederation; it was wholly new, in its principle as well as its provisions. It recognized the sovereignty not of each individual state but, rather, of the people of the United States, and, Patrick Henry notwithstanding, its Framers could and did argue that they were fully justified in having it do so.

To understand the making of the Constitution of the United States, it is necessary to appreciate the extent to which the process (as well as the document that emerged from it) was informed and influenced by these two not necessarily compatible principles, popular sovereignty and state sovereignty. They were part of the political theory and the history that went into it.

POPULAR SOVEREIGNTY

Madison was expounding the political theory when, in the letter referred to in Chapter 1, he explained the nature of the two compacts upon which our government rests.[6] In the first of these, the erstwhile subjects of George III constituted themselves the people of the United States and, as such, declared their independence and their right to "assume among the powers of the earth, the separate and equal station to which the laws of Nature and of Nature's God entitle[d] them." The first compact points to, and of necessity must be followed by, a second, a compact, as Madison put it, "by which the people in their social state agree to a Govt. over them."

The formal renunciation of allegiance to one political authority (the British Crown) did not, and in principle could not, by itself institute a new political authority, or a new government. That much is suggested in Madison's letter and is clear on the face of the Declaration of Independence itself. There it is said to be self-evidently true that all men are created equal insofar as they all possess the natural rights to life, liberty, and the pursuit of happiness, and that "to secure these rights, Governments are instituted among Men, deriving their just powers from the consent of the governed." And there it is also said that, whenever any government becomes destructive of these ends, it is the right of the people "to alter or abolish it, and to institute new Government, laying its foundation on such principles and organizing its powers in such form, as to them shall seem most likely to effect their Safety and Happiness." This is followed by an indictment of George III listing his "usurpations" of power and the "repeated injuries" he had inflicted on the people of the United States, all, it was alleged, with the purpose of establishing "an absolute Tyranny over these States." The Declaration then concludes with a renunciation of "all Allegiance to the British Crown." In short, by declaring independence, the people of the United States exercised their right to "alter or abolish" a government that had become destructive of the proper ends of all government, but they did not exercise their right to "institute new Government." The Declaration speaks of the necessity of consent, of the withdrawal of consent and the reasons for that withdrawal, but it does not pretend to be a compact in which the people give their consent to a new government.

A necessary condition of legitimate government, consent must be given formally; as Madison put it, it takes the form of a compact that is "reduced to writing." The reasons for this may not be self-evident; after all, Americans had never formally consented to the government of George III, but, by declaring their independence when, in their judgment, his government had become tyrannical, they implied that they had consented to it, if only tacitly. Besides, if the first compact—that by which individuals agree to form one society—can be unwritten, there would seem to be no necessity for the second to be written. Written, but, as John Locke himself acknowledged, it might also be "tacit," and no less valid for that.[7] Nevertheless, for reasons that can be traced back to Locke, Madison was correct in suggesting that the constitution of government should take the form of a written compact. This was something new.

Our texts sometimes credit Aristotle with having "collected" well over a hundred constitutions, most of them the constitutions of Greek city-states, and go on to point out that, unfortunately, only one of these, his *Constitution of Athens*, has come down to us in print. Anyone opening the work bearing that title and expecting to find a document similar to the Constitution of the United States will surely be surprised by its contents. He will find no preamble beginning, "We the people of Athens," and no article declaring that all legislative powers therein granted shall be vested in some Athenian equivalent of the American Congress. Instead, what he will find at the beginning (or what has survived as the beginning) is this sentence: "With Myron acting as an accuser, a court, selected from the nobility and sworn in upon the sacrifices, passed a verdict to the effect that a sacrilege had been committed." Aristotle's *Constitution of Athens* is a sort of history, or a treatise on Athenian constitutional history, not a document bearing any resemblance to the Constitution of the United States or, for that matter, to any other modern constitution.

There were no written constitutions in classical antiquity. Moreover, although the term "constitution" is certainly not new and famous scholars have written learned texts on constitutionalism ancient and modern, the idea of a written constitution is altogether modern. So much so, that at the time of our founding most Americans would have agreed with Tom Paine that "an unwritten constitution is not a constitution at all." Why this is so, or how this came to be understood as the common sense of the matter, deserves an explanation.

If, as Locke wrote[8] and the Declaration of Independence repeated, all men are by nature free and equal, then no man has a natural right to rule another. As colonists, Americans had been governed by kings or queens who claimed such a right, a right to rule by the grace of God—*Dei gratia, rex* (or *Dei gratia, regina*); in abbreviated form this motto still appears on British and even Canadian coins. But on July 4, 1776, they declared this claim to be contrary to the self-evident truth that all men are created equal. Not equal in all respects, or even in most respects, but equal in the one respect that matters here, their natural rights. A superiority of birth, or strength, or intelligence, or beauty, or whatever, does not entitle anyone to rule. In Jefferson's words, the mass of mankind was not born "with saddles on their back, nor a favored few booted and spurred, ready to ride them legitimately, by the grace of God." On the contrary, because men are by nature free and equal, no man is entitled to rule another except with his consent. It is consent alone that makes an individual a member of a particular civil society, and only by or with its consent that that society may justly be governed. The power to govern society comes from the people constituting that society—as free and equal individuals each yields his right, or power, to govern himself, yields it to the government they collectively institute—and it is exercised at their pleasure. This is what is properly known as popular sovereignty.

It was not only Jefferson and his congressional colleagues who held these views, not only Madison or Hamilton (the author of the Letters from Phocion); these views were held by the common people of Pittsfield, Massachusetts, for example, a town even farther from sophisticated Boston then than now. In May 1776, they solemnly declared that "the people are the fountain of power"; that the dissolution of Britain's power would cause the colonies to fall "into a state of Nature"; that "the first step to be taken by a people in such a state for the Enjoyment or Restoration of Civil Government amongst them, is the formation of a fundamental Constitution as the Basis and ground work of Legislation"; and that "the Approbation of the Majority of the people of this fundamental Constitution is absolutely necessary to give Life and being to it."[9] Whether or not they were aware of it, in saying this they were merely repeating Locke.

On the occasion when government is instituted, that sovereignty will indeed be exercised by a majority; as Locke makes clear, on that occasion the majority rules.[10] Given the improbability if not the impossibility of unanimity on

71

the great issues to be determined, this is as it must be; with everyone casting an equally weighted vote, authority goes with the greater number. Acting, therefore, on behalf of the whole society, the majority is charged with the heavy responsibility of determining the form of government that will best secure the rights of all.

It should be understood that men might be in complete agreement on the right of the people to institute government and the ends to be served by the government instituted and yet have sharply divergent views on the best form of government. (That was surely the situation in the United States in 1787.) It is in this situation that the majority is authorized to act for all, and it is no derogation from the principle of popular sovereignty if it decides to institute a nonmajoritarian form of government. Popular sovereignty does not necessarily lead to popular or democratic government; it may even lead to monarchical government.[11] This is clear from the Declaration of Independence, which speaks of "governments"—governments in general—deriving their just powers from the consent of the governed, and not only of a particular form of government. Then, too, it speaks of "any form of government" becoming destructive of the ends of government, which suggests not only that a democratic as well as a monarchic government might misgovern, or even become tyrannical,[12] but also that a nondemocratic government is capable of governing properly. In short, the principles associated with popular sovereignty cover the authorization, the ends, but not the forms of government. Aware of this and of society's inability to agree as to the best form, and aware as well of the propensity of those who govern to misgovern under whatever form, those charged with the responsibility

72

of instituting government will act with great circumspec-
tion, leaving as little as possible to chance. Entering into a
compact according to which each of them gives up his natural right to govern himself in favor of a government whose
purpose is to secure the rights of all, they will see the necessity of reducing that compact to writing.

Modern constitutionalism is historically connected with
these rights and cannot be separated from them. They belong to men *in* nature (because they are an aspect of human nature) but cannot be enjoyed in nature, or in the
"state of nature," because they are not secured there. To
secure them, and thereby to make it possible to enjoy them,
government has to be instituted, but not just any kind of
government; for example, not "absolute, arbitrary" government, as John Locke put it. He said it passed belief that a
rational man should agree to leave the state of nature, where
at least he was his own boss, so to speak, and choose to live
under laws to be enacted by someone, or some body, that
"should still retain all the liberty of the state of nature, [but
now] increased with power and made licentious by impunity." In short, Locke was confident that most men were
not so foolish as to put themselves in a position where they
were likely "to be devoured by lions" merely to avoid the
mischief done them in the state of nature by "polecats or
foxes."[13]

But avoiding those lions is no simple matter. After all, if,
by natural right, every person may do whatever he has to
do in order to preserve himself, with the consequence that
the state of nature is or inevitably becomes a state of war,
and if, in order to secure peace and the opportunity to exercise rights in peace, each person contracts with everyone
else and agrees to surrender this natural right to govern

himself (Thomas Hobbes) or this natural liberty (Locke) into the hands of a sovereign brought into being by that contract, then the powers of that sovereign over the newly created society will be the sum of the powers each person had over himself in the state of nature. That is to say, since each person *was* free to do whatever he thought necessary to preserve himself—he was, as I said, his own boss—the new sovereign *is* free to do whatever he (or it) thinks necessary to preserve the society. By surrendering their liberty to a sovereign (even one of their own creation), men may indeed have created a lion capable of devouring them. And that, more or less and to say nothing more, is where Hobbes left the problem.

Locke is recognized as one of the founders of modern constitutionalism because he delineated the elements of a governmental structure that, in practice if not in principle, solved the problem Hobbes left unsolved and believed to be unsolvable: that of the devouring lion or, to drop the metaphor, of an absolute and probably tyrannical sovereign authority. In the words of a recent writer, Locke discovered the connection between absolutism and limited government.[14] Or, better yet, he discovered a way of avoiding in practice the absolutism to which his analysis (to say nothing of Hobbes's) pointed. Men leave the state of nature by contracting to form civil society, and that civil society, acting through its majority, must, Locke writes, "appoint the form of government, which is by constituting the legislative and appointing in whose hands it shall be." It is by means of this constituting act that the people delegate their powers, and it is from this constituting act that the government derives its powers. But precisely because men are not so foolish as to risk being devoured by lions, they will not delegate, and the government therefore will not receive, an "absolute arbitrary power." The people will want to put bounds or limits to the powers they hand over. Constitutionalism for Locke is government that respects "the bounds which the trust that is put in them by the society . . . have set to the legislative power of every commonwealth, in all forms of government."[15] As I mentioned above, Locke did not specify that the constituting act be "reduced to writing," but he made it very easy for subsequent political theorists to draw the conclusion that it should be reduced to writing. He accomplished this much merely by differentiating the powers of government—the legislative, executive, and so-called federative powers—which allowed his successors to devise the institutional techniques of keeping them separate, and limited. Safety would be found in the structure of government, and the elements of that structure ought to be precisely defined.

Within a few years of Locke's death in 1704, the Englishmen John Trenchard and Thomas Gordon, whose *Cato's Letters* were widely circulated and frequently quoted in America, did indeed draw the conclusion that constitutions had to be written. "No man in his senses was ever so wild as to give an unlimited Power to another to take away his Life, or the means of Living, according to the Caprice, Passion, and unreasonable Pleasure of that other," we read in Letter 60, and the argument proceeds step by step until in Letter 62 we arrive at the obvious conclusion:

> So that Civil Government is only a partial Restraint put by the Laws of Agreement and Society upon natural and absolute Liberty, which might otherwise grow licentious: And Tyranny is an unlimited Restraint put upon natural Liberty, by the Will of one or a few. Magistracy, amongst

75

a free People, is the Exercise of Power for the Sake of the People; and Tyrants abuse the People, for the Sake of Power. Free Government is the protecting the People in their Liberties by stated Rules.[16]

Here is the prescription for constitutional government: state the rules; state the terms according to which you agree to be governed; set them down in "some solemn and authoritative act," as Alexander Hamilton put it. Rational human beings will see the necessity of this.

They are not, after all, creating a sovereign with the unrestricted authority "to make laws for the Peace, Order, and Good Government" of the country;[17] the people themselves retain the sovereign authority.[18] The government they are instituting will have the limited purpose of securing their rights—including emphatically their right to pursue a happiness each of them defines for himself—and otherwise leaving them alone. They will, therefore, specify the powers granted and the powers withheld, and, in order to guard against the misuse of the powers granted, they will organize them in a certain way. It is conceivable (but not likely) that they themselves might tacitly agree to all the detailed provisions of the compact each is making with all the others, but, because that compact is binding on their posterity as well as on themselves, there is an additional reason to embody it in a written document. Besides, even the immediate parties to a compact sometimes forget their obligations under it, especially when it is to their advantage to do so. As Madison also said, "The legitimate meaning of the Instrument [of government] must be derived from the text itself,"[19] and that meaning can be confidently ascertained only when the text can be read and not merely recalled.

For all these reasons, popular sovereignty requires or leads to a written constitution.

Americans were divided on the issue of whether the Constitution deserved to be ratified—divided into groups known as Federalists and Anti-Federalists—but they were not divided on the questions of whether there had to be a constitution and whether constitutions had to be written. Not only Federalists like the Virginian James Madison but anonymous Anti-Federalists like the Virginian "Impartial Examiner" understood that government was instituted to secure rights and that, when designing it, every "precaution" must be taken, the powers withheld *"expressly stipulated."*[20] Unwritten constitutions, to refer once more to Tom Paine, were not constitutions at all. Asked to produce evidence of the existence of his constitution, an Englishman would be likely to point to the "numerous decrees and proclamations" issued over the years by the Parliament with a view not to limiting power but to enhancing its power by seizing powers formerly exercised by the monarch.[21] Unwritten constitutions go hand in hand with claims of parliamentary sovereignty, supremacy, and even omnipotence. In saying this, Paine discloses a fact of some importance: popular sovereignty, which gives rise to written constitutions, is incompatible with the principle of the supremacy of parliament, even a popularly elected parliament. Better than anyone else at the time, Paine makes it clear that producing a written constitution is an important and even necessary step in the assertion of the sovereignty of the people.

State Sovereignty

Even the motto of the United States—*E pluribus unum*—lends some plausibility to the state sovereignty argument. In the beginning there were indeed "many," and much of the early history of the United States was dominated by a dispute over the effort to make from, or of, or out of the many, one. No one disagreed that in the very beginning there were many colonies. The issue disputed was whether those colonies became states before there was a United States, and that was not resolved until 1865, when the self-styled Confederate States of America were defeated on the battlefield.

In the name of state sovereignty, the eleven states of the confederacy had "seceded" from the Union and fought what they were pleased to call the War Between the States. As sovereign powers (or so they claimed), they had been parties to a contract in 1787–88 which, as sovereign powers (or so they claimed), each of them was entitled to revoke, thereby ending its association with the others. Here, for example, is South Carolina's Ordinance of Secession of December 20, 1860:

> We, the people of the State of South Carolina, in Convention assembled, do declare and ordain, and it is hereby declared and ordained, that the ordinance adopted by us in Convention, on the 23rd day of May, in the year of our Lord 1788, whereby the Constitution of the United States was ratified, and also all Acts and parts of Acts of the General Assembly of this State ratifying the amendments of the said Constitution, are hereby repealed, and that the union now subsisting between South Carolina and other

78

States under the name of the United States of America is hereby dissolved.[22]

Four days later, in language strikingly similar to that used in the Declaration of Independence,* the state announced that with the Ordinance it had resumed its "separate and equal place among nations." Here, in a phrase, is embodied the essence of the state sovereignty argument: it was not as "one people" but as thirteen discrete peoples that independence was declared in 1776.

Historically, as I said, the persons who became the people of the United States had been separated into thirteen distinct colonies and, for some time, tended to refer to themselves as Pennsylvanians, New Yorkers, or Virginians. And it is true that in the last paragraph of the Declaration of Independence the "United Colonies" are declared to be not a free and independent state but "FREE AND INDE-PENDENT STATES." This permitted President James Monroe in 1822 to say that the sovereign power wrested from the Crown in 1776 passed directly "to the people of each colony and not to the people of all the colonies in the aggregate."[23] But it is also true that, prior to 1776, the colonies were joined by their association with the British empire, and the individual colonists were joined to each other by a common allegiance to the British Crown: Pennsylvanians, New Yorkers, and Virginians alike were British subjects. Were these ties, personal as well as collective, broken when allegiance to George III was renounced? North and South Carolina, for example, were no longer connected by virtue of their common status as royal colonies. Were they,

---

* ". . . and to assume among the powers of the earth, the separate and equal station to which the Laws of Nature and of Nature's God entitle them."

then, wholly separate and equal political entities? Had nothing replaced that allegiance to the British Crown? Evidently not; not, at least, as state sovereignty reads our history.

This argument has, of course, been a feature in that history. It was relied on in 1788 by some of those who opposed ratification of the Constitution, in 1828 by John C. Calhoun and the other South Carolina "nullifiers," in 1860 by the seceding Confederates, and, implicitly at least, in our own time by anyone who insists that the Union was created by the states. It also carries an interesting implication. If, after the Declaration of Independence but before the Articles of Confederation, the states were as free and independent of each other as they were of Great Britain, then they were legally—under the laws of nature—entitled to do to each other what they proposed to do to Great Britain: make war. That is to say, their delegates to the Continental Congress must have understood their states to be in this position. But, of course, the delegates neither said nor implied any such thing. They—John Hancock, Thomas Jefferson, John and Sam Adams, Benjamin Franklin, and the rest—claimed a right to engage in a course of action that they knew would necessarily involve the killing of British soldiers, but to each other they pledged their lives, their fortunes, "and [their] sacred Honor." It was not until later that some of their descendants claimed the right to make war on each other.

More than anyone else, Abraham Lincoln was responsible for the defeat of this Confederate project. It was he who challenged its pretensions—ultimately, the right of its people to enslave black people and carry them into the territories of the United States; he who forged a political coalition that captured control of the national government from its representatives in Washington; he who refused the compromise that might have precluded the war; he who · sustained the cause of freedom throughout the four terrible years of that war; and, as president, he who was charged with the responsibility of countering its argument of sovereign right.[24]

His argument was that the Union was older than any of the states and had created them as states. Before that, they had been "dependent colonies," and in this capacity they had created the Union that "threw off their dependence for them." Not one of them had ever been a state "*out* of the Union." What the Declaration of Independence declares to be "free and independent states," he pointed out, are described as the "United Colonies"; and the plain object of the men who issued it "was not to declare their independence of *one another*, or of the *Union*, but directly the contrary, as their mutual pledge, and their mutual action, before, at the time, and afterwards, abundantly show."[25]

In response to this, the Confederates of 1860 could point to the Articles of Confederation. Although written in 1777 by the "Delegates of the United States in Congress assembled"—a point for Lincoln—they were agreed to in 1778 by the "undersigned Delegates of the States," and, of course, during the subsequent three years, ratified by the legislatures of the states. Furthermore, the Articles flatly declare that "each state retains its sovereignty, freedom and independence"—a point for the Confederates. Beyond that, in the Congress, after as well as before the Articles, voting was done by states. (A plan prepared by Benjamin Franklin and providing for voting by individuals was rejected by the Congress.[26]) And finally, the Articles could be amended only with the consent of the "legislatures of every state."

On the basis of such textual evidence, the Confederates of 1860 concluded that the states existed before the United States, that it was the states that first constituted the United States when they ratified the Articles of Confederation and Perpetual Union, and that any state was free at any time to withdraw from the Union. On the basis of the same evidence, the "confederates" of 1787–88 opposed the new constitution. They did not, of course, succeed in preventing its adoption, but they did succeed in putting their mark on it.[27]

Try as they might, the advocates of popular sovereignty and consolidated government—the nationalists—learned that they could not ignore the states and the political authority they had accumulated. This fact was driven home to them by William Paterson, one of the New Jersey delegates to the 1787 Constitutional Convention. On the floor were two constitutional plans, one providing for a strong national government and the other, introduced by Paterson himself, providing for a system under which the states would have retained much of their power. In this context he issued the following, almost defiant challenge to the nationalists:

> If we argue the matter on the supposition that no Confederacy at present exists, it cannot be denied that all the States stand on the footing of equal sovereignty. All therefore must concur before any can be bound. . . . If we argue on the fact that a federal compact actually exists, and consult the articles of it we still find an equal Sovereignty to be the basis of it.[28]

This, as Herbert Storing once wrote, was the dilemma the proponents of the states challenged the nationalists to resolve. Within the Articles or outside, the states stood on a footing of sovereign equality. "The equality could be relinquished only with the consent of the states concerned, a consent which the states were under absolutely no obligation of any kind to give, and which the small states did not propose to give." Their position was strengthened by the fact that in the convention, as in the Congress, voting was done by states.

In their opposition to a strong national government there was, undeniably, an element of parochialism and perhaps a lack of vision. (Some historians have accused them of being "men of little faith.") But there was more to their opposition than a selfish desire to hold on to their local offices or a fear of being overwhelmed by men of greater talent. And they certainly could not be justly accused of a hostility to republican government. On the contrary, with the support of some of the greatest names in political philosophy—Aristotle, for example, Montesquieu, and Rousseau—they could argue that republican government could not be exercised over a territory so large as that comprehended by the thirteen states. As one of them wrote, so extensive and various a territory "cannot be governed in freedom" except in a confederation of states. Within each state, "opinion founded on the knowledge of those who govern, procures obedience without force. But remove the opinion, which must fall with a knowledge of characters in so widely extended a country, and force then becomes necessary to secure the purposes of civil government."[29] Their view of the American situation and what might safely be done about it is reflected in the letter by which the Continental Congress transmitted the proposed Articles of Confederation to the various state legislatures:

This business . . . has . . . been attended with uncommon embarrassment and delay, which the most anxious solicitude and persevering diligence could not prevent. To form a permanent union, accommodated to the opinion and wishes of the delegates of so many states, differing in habits, produce, commerce, and internal police, was found to be a work which nothing but time and reflection, conspiring with a disposition to conciliate, could mature and accomplish.[30]

If the size and diversity of the country made it difficult to unite under the Articles of Confederation, where Congress was charged mainly with providing the means of defense against possible foreign enemies, how much more difficult—and, indeed, hazardous—it was to unite for purposes of domestic governance.

In laying such stress on the diversity of the various peoples and economies, as well as on the great distances involved, these early proponents of state sovereignty—who, to do them justice, are better described as proponents of small republics—may have exaggerated the difficulties of union. After all, and leaving aside the African slaves, Americans were all, or nearly all, of British origin and spoke a common tongue, nearly all Christians (and the vast majority of them Protestants), and, as Tocqueville would later point out, had all "arrived at the same state of civilization."

I do not know of any European nation, however small, that does not present less uniformity in its different provinces than the American people, which occupy a territory as extensive as one half of Europe. The distance from Maine to Georgia is about one thousand miles; but the difference between the civilization of Maine and that of Georgia is slighter than the difference between the habits

84

of Normandy and those of Brittany. Maine and Georgia, which are placed at the opposite extremities of a great empire, have therefore more real inducements to form a confederation than Normandy and Brittany, which are separated only by a brook.[31]

He was, of course, writing of an America that had been living under the Constitution for almost fifty years, but it is doubtful that, in these cultural respects, it had changed all that much during that time. In the important respects, the Americans were one people living in thirteen states. They were united in their opinion that government was instituted in order to secure the rights with which all men are equally endowed and, in 1787, divided only on the question of the form of government that would best secure these rights. What would divide them later on, and would threaten to divide them permanently, was the slavery issue. The Framers of the Constitution had reason to believe, or at least, as we saw in the previous chapter, they chose to believe, that that problem would be resolved with the passage of time.

A More Perfect Union

The Americans of 1787 may not have agreed on the character of the Union or on when it was constituted, but they agreed that the Articles under which it was being governed were in need of revision. Even the state sovereignty men—soon to be given the name "Anti-Federalists"—were willing to concede that under the Articles the powers of Congress were inadequate to the "exigencies of the Union."

With the concurrence of at least nine of the thirteen

states represented, Congress had the authority to borrow money and "emit bills on the credit of the united states," but it had no sure source of revenue out of which to repay the loans or redeem the bills. For revenue, it had to rely on the willingness of the individual states to pay the assessments levied on them; it had no way to enforce payment. It was empowered by the Articles to discharge the debts incurred during the War of Independence, but, in the event, it lacked the funds out of which to pay the soldiers who had fought it. It could—again with the concurrence of nine states—enter into treaties with foreign nations, but it was unable to compel the British to honor certain provisions under the Treaty of Paris ending the War of Independence. It could regret what Madison called the "trespasses of the states on the rights of each other," but do nothing to prevent them. It could do little by way of promoting commerce among the states or protecting the means by which it was carried on with other nations. It could do nothing to compel, or even to induce, the attendance of delegates and, as a result, frequently lacked the quorum that would enable it to carry on its business. Thus, for example, aware of the powers it lacked, it might compose amendments to the Articles with a view to increasing its authority, only to be frustrated by the absence of the quorum required to bring them to a vote. With such evident displays of its impotence, it risked becoming an object of open contempt, not only to Europeans but, more pernicious in its consequences, to Americans of "weight and understanding," state sovereignty men and nationalists alike.

The former, while acknowledging the need of alterations to the Articles, were ever fearful of embarking on the course that would produce them. Richard Henry Lee, for example, agreed that Congress ought to be able to assure state compliance with its fiscal requisitions, but he was reluctant to concede the means by which it might be done. The difficulty, he wrote to George Mason, is "how to give the power in such manner as that it may only be used for good, and not abused to bad, purposes. Whoever shall solve this difficulty will receive the thanks of this and future generations."[32] Meanwhile, especially to a government not under the immediate and close control of the people, it was better to withhold than to grant powers. "I think Sir," Lee wrote to Samuel Adams, "that the first maxim of a man who loves liberty should be, never to grant to rulers an atom of power that is not most clearly and indispensably necessary for the safety and well being of Society."[33] Beyond this, he was of the opinion that mere structural changes would not solve the problem. "I fear it is more in vicious manners, than mistakes in form that we must seek for the causes of the present discontent."[34] And the cure for vicious manners could be prescribed only in the small republic in which the people would (in Rousseau's sense) be forced to be free and forced to be virtuous. As one New Yorker put it, government should rest on "a substantial yeomanry" because they are "more temperate, of better morals, and less ambitious, than the great."[35] Anyone harboring such sentiments was certain to distrust a government empowered to promote foreign commerce and become an active force in the world of nations.

The nationalists were united in the judgment that political salvation was not to be had in the small agrarian republic depending on the "substantial yeomanry" (whose existence in substantial number they tended anyway to doubt). It followed that, for them, the remedy lay not in amendments conceding a few additional powers to the Congress but, rather, in the replacement of the Articles with a wholly new constitution of government. As early as 1778, Alexander Hamilton was calling for radical measures; in due course, he was joined by Robert Morris, Rufus King, John Jay, James Madison (who, characteristically, prepared a careful draft of the "Vices of the Political System of the United States"), and others, including, most significantly, George Washington.

By the summer of 1786, Washington was describing the reluctance to admit the need of national powers for national purposes as "popular absurdity and madness"; the country was faced with a "crisis," and means had to be found to meet it.[36] He was especially impatient with anyone who hesitated to recognize the country's dependence on foreign commerce and to yield the powers required to promote and control it.

It has long been a speculative question among Philosophers and wise men, whether foreign Commerce is of real advantage to any country; that is, whether the luxury, effeminacy, and corruptions which are introduced along with it; are counterbalanced by the convenience and wealth which it brings with it; but the decision of this question is of very little importance to us: we have abundant reason to be convinced, that the spirit for Trade which pervades these States is not to be restrained; it behooves us then to establish just principles; and this, any more than other matters of national concern, cannot be done by thirteen heads differently constructed and organized. The necessity, therefore, of a controuling power is obvious; and why it should be withheld is beyond my comprehension.[37]

Still, the state sovereignty people hesitated. They could point to some solid advancements made by the country under the Articles (and the greatest of Congress's achievements—the Northwest Ordinance—was to be made in 1787 even as the convention was meeting), and it was only natural that they should be apprehensive of a general convention charged with proposing constitutional amendments. (Have we not heard our own contemporaries express fears that a constitutional convention called on the application of two-thirds of the states would be a "runaway convention"?) And perhaps the most difficult task faced by the nationalists was convincing their opponents that free republican government could be established in a country the size of the United States.

Conventional wisdom had it that that was impossible. Thus, while there was a general agreement on the need for changes to render the Congress "adequate to the exigencies of the Union," the contending parties disagreed on the sort of Union they wanted to build.

The attempts at union building began in 1754, when, at the instigation of Benjamin Franklin, commissioners representing eleven of the thirteen colonies drew up the Albany (New York) Plan of Union. Designed to promote a common and more effective defense against the French and Indians, as well as to foster further colonization under British auspices, the plan would have provided a measure of popular self-government combined with royal government in the person of a president general appointed by the Crown.[38] The extent of the disunity then existing among the colonies is reflected in the decision to submit the plan to Westminster, asking it to be established by act of Parliament. As Franklin explained, the jealousy and distrust then prevailing among the colonies persuaded the commissioners that nothing would induce the colonies to agree to a common plan of action, let alone a common government.[39] In the event, in Franklin's words, "the Crown disapproved it, as having plac'd too much Weight in the democratic Part of the Constitution; and every [colonial] Assembly as having allow'd too much to [royal] Prerogative. So it was totally rejected."[40]

A somewhat similar proposal was drawn up by loyalist Joseph Galloway in September 1774, after the outbreak of hostilities. Taking the form of a petition by the Continental Congress, it asked the king-in-parliament to establish a political union, "not only among [the colonies], but with the Mother State."[41] But by a vote of six to five, the Continental Congress (voting by colonies) rejected the plan, and by that rejection, the die was cast for war and the formal declaring of independence. The time had passed when a union could be forged—peaceably, at least—under the auspices of the Crown.

It was by no means certain, however, that a union "more perfect" than the one achieved under the Articles of Confederation could be forged even under the auspices of dire necessity. Somehow—British military ineptitude and the assistance of France had a lot to do with it—the war with Britain was won; but within less than a year after the last engagement of that war, Washington (still commander-in-chief) was warning the states of the impending crisis. Unless they could agree to forgo their jealousies and institute a proper national government, the Union, he predicted, could not be of long duration. "For, according to the system of Policy the states shall adopt at this moment, they will stand or fall, and by their confirmation or lapse, it is yet to be decided, whether the Revolution must ultimately be considered as a blessing or a curse: a blessing or a curse, not to the present age alone, for with our fate will the destiny of unborn Millions be involved."[42]

Although Washington's word carried a weight greater than that of any other American, not everyone was persuaded by it. Some remained irresolute. Others, including men who were later to become enthusiastic supporters of the new Constitution, had well-founded doubts as to the feasibility of a more perfect union of continental proportions and wondered whether the solution for the country's problems did not consist in regional confederations. "Some of our enlightened men," wrote Benjamin Rush in the fall of 1786, "who begin to despair of a more complete union of the states in Congress have secretly proposed an Eastern, Middle, and Southern Confederacy to be united by an alliance offensive and defensive."

> These confederacies they say will be united by nature, by interest, and by manners, and consequently they will be safe, agreeable and durable. The first will include the four New England states and New York. The second will include New Jersey, Pennsylvania, Delaware, and Maryland; and the last Virginia, North and South Carolina, and Georgia. The foreign and domestic debt of the United States they say shall be divided justly between each of the new confederations. This plan of a new continental government is at present a mere speculation. Perhaps necessity, or rather divine providence, may drive us to it.[43]

This theme was to be sounded again during the 1787 convention, as well as during the ratification debates, when Hamilton suggested that a man would have to be "far gone in Utopian speculations" to doubt that these "partial confederacies" would not have "frequent and violent contests with each other."[44]

Washington's efforts began to be rewarded in 1786, when nine states accepted Virginia's invitation to convene at Annapolis, Maryland, ostensibly to consider interstate commercial problems. Only five states (New York, New Jersey, Delaware, Pennsylvania, and Virginia), represented by the small total of twelve "commissioners," were actually present when the convention met in September; but among those twelve were Hamilton and Madison. Working together, and undeterred by the apparent lack of interest on the part of the states, or the real lack of legal authority from the Congress, they contrived to have the commissioners adopt a report (written by Hamilton) that called upon the legislatures of the five attending states (and by implication all the states) to appoint delegates to meet "at Philadelphia on the second Monday in May next, to take into consideration the situation of the United States, to devise such further provisions as shall appear to them necessary to render the constitution of the Foederal Government adequate to the exigencies of the Union." The report ended with an acknowledgment that the "Commissioners could not with propriety address these observations and sentiments to any but the states they [had] the honor to Represent," but they concluded nevertheless that it would not be improper to transmit "Copies" of the report, not only to the executives of the other states, but to the Congress.[45]

This démarche produced the desired result. In February 1787, on a motion by Massachusetts, Congress resolved that it was "expedient" that there should be a convention of the states "for the sole and express purpose of revising the Articles of Confederation and reporting to Congress and the several state legislatures such alterations and provisions therein as shall . . . render the federal constitution adequate to the exigencies of Government & the preservation of the union."[46] The convention would exceed the authority given it—by the Congress as well as by the twelve states (all except Rhode Island) that appointed delegates—but there could be no denying that it was authorized to meet and to do *something* on behalf of union. This was to have happy consequences.

THE PHILADELPHIA CONVENTION

There was no dispute concerning the principle governing the selection of delegates to the convention. Except in South Carolina, where the legislature authorized the governor to make the appointments, they were chosen by the state legislatures, which, in almost every instance, specified the number required to constitute a quorum of the state's delegation at the convention and, thereby, to cast its vote.[47] The delegates represented their particular states; their number was determined by the states—the smallest being New Hampshire's (two) and the largest Pennsylvania's (eight); they voted as states; and their expenses, when paid at all, were paid by the states, not the Congress.[48] Yet, with all that, many of them came to Philadelphia determined to diminish the political force of the states.

Some were unknown (and remained so), but most of them came not as strangers to each other. The more distinguished among them especially had worked together in the Congress or army and, even when that was not the case, knew each other by reputation. They were a remarkably learned and talented group of men. Even Richard Henry Lee, who did his best to prevent the ratification of the Constitution, acknowledged that "America probably never will see an assembly of men of like number more respectable." Their average age was forty-three, but Franklin at eighty-one and two members of the Connecticut delegation, Roger Sherman at sixty-six and William Johnson at sixty, were largely responsible for making it that high. Four of them were not yet thirty, and fully a third of them (including four of the most distinguished among them, James Madison, Alexander Hamilton, Gouverneur Morris, and Edmund Randolph) were in their thirties.

All being of British stock and native speakers of English, they had no need of simultaneous translation of speeches or materials. Their discourse was further facilitated by the fact that they had read the same books, lived under and, in many cases, practiced the same law, and shared in a common political tradition. Without exception, they respected the rules or forms of doing business, which was altogether to be expected because they were assembled to write a constitution. By secret ballot (but, as it turned out, unanimously), they elected George Washington to be the presiding officer (or president) of the convention, and, it being a custom or formality with which they were all familiar, two of them—Robert Morris of Pennsylvania and John Rutledge of South Carolina—"conducted" him to the chair. They elected a secretary, who would keep the official journal, and "appointed" a messenger and doorkeeper. On formal motion, they ordered that a committee be appointed to draw up the rules of order and then, by ballot, named Hamilton of New York, George Wythe of Virginia, and Charles Pinckney of South Carolina to that committee. Drawn up over the weekend and, following debate and amendment, adopted on Monday and Tuesday, the rules governed both the forms of behavior and of doing business.

In the first category were rules such as these: members wishing to speak shall rise and address the president (and, when another is speaking, they shall not hold discourse with each other "or read a book, pamphlet, or paper, printed or manuscript"); and "when the House shall adjourn every Member shall stand in his place until the President pass him." With such rules, the delegates demonstrated a respect not for each other as individuals or for George Washington the man (although they did mostly respect each other and unanimously and greatly respected Washington), but for the dignity and importance of the enterprise in which they were engaged. As they saw it, they were engaged in demonstrating the truth of what was then only an untested proposition, namely, that it was possible for men to govern themselves, or to be governed, by rules of their own devising. Formal rules serve as restraints on behavior, and because it depends on such restraints, constitutional government is government according to formal rules.[49] The men gathered in Philadelphia to write a constitution acted formally because they had an important example to set.

In the second category were rules of procedure designed in part to promote deliberation (but with an eye on the need for decision) and in part to permit compromise. Prominent among these were rules guaranteeing the privacy and, indeed, the secrecy of their deliberations. Separated from their constituents by the exclusion of the public and the press (to say nothing of the television cameras), the delegates were free to speak frankly and, if appropriate, tentatively rather than definitively—with no galleries to play to, delegates had little reason to score debating points against other speakers—and to listen carefully. It was understood that they might change their minds, and the rules made it easy to do so.[50] It was also understood that it might be desirable to reconsider matters, even those decided by majority vote, and the rules permitted that as well.

These rules were adopted on May 29, after little debate and remarkably little disagreement,[51] and they were to serve the convention well throughout the almost four months of its meetings. They helped to ensure deliberations that were serious—the record is free of any evidence of persiflage—and what is more important, efficacious: the convention produced a constitutional document to which Washington and thirty-eight delegates (at least one from each of the twelve states present) affixed their signatures.

Although the rules required secrecy—even the official journal was not printed until 1818—they did not forbid the members to take notes of the deliberations. It is to these, and especially to Madison's, that we owe our knowledge of what was said and done in the convention. Because he was impressed by the significance of their enterprise, Madison, working at night from notes compiled during the course of each working day, accomplished the herculean task of transcribing the debates, accurately and fully. In an unfinished paper written many years later, he explained what led him to do this:

The curiosity I had felt during my researches into the History of the most distinguished Confederacies, particularly those of antiquity, and the deficiency I found in the means of satisfying it more especially in what related to the process, the principles—the reasons, & the anticipations, which prevailed in the formation of them, determined me to preserve as far as I could an exact account of what might pass in the Convention whilst executing its trust, with the magnitude of which I was duly impressed, as I was the gratification promised to future curiosity by an authentic exhibition of the objects, the opinions & the reasonings from which the new System of Govt. was to receive its peculiar structure & organization. Nor was I unaware of the value of such a contribution to the fund of materials for the History of a Constitution on which would be staked the happiness of a young people great even in its infancy, and possibly the cause of Liberty through[ou]t the world.[52]

Madison did not explain why, in his judgment, future writers of constitutions could find instruction in an account of the *proceedings* of the 1787 convention, but Herbert Storing suggests that it could be found in the members' awareness of the need for decision. It was this that made compromise possible, and clearly, compromise was required if there was to be a constitution. The contending principles—popular and state sovereignty—were each represented in the convention, but, as Storing writes, an unyielding pursuit of either principle would, almost certainly, have resulted in its irretrievable loss.

The two sides found the grounds of compromise in their common desire to "form a more perfect union," though

their ideas of a perfect union differed. The debates leading to the Great Compromise yield insight into a great
question of principle lying at the heart of the American
political order. They also yield an example of how such
questions are properly approached in political life.[53]

It is to the debates culminating in that Great Compromise
that we must now devote our attention.

The rules adopted, the delegates turned immediately to
the substantive business of the convention. On behalf of
the Virginia delegation, Edmund Randolph (the state's
governor as well as a member of its delegation), after out-
lining what he described as the defects of the Confederation, formally proposed a set of fifteen resolutions that,
together, amounted to a comprehensive plan of government. Prepared mainly by the indefatigable Madison, the
so-called Virginia Plan called for the establishment of a
strong national government to replace the Congress of
states, a government with a national executive, a national
and independent judiciary, and a national bicameral legislature with the power to legislate "in all cases to which the
separate States are incompetent" and, most significantly,
the power "to negative all laws passed by the several States,
contravening . . . the articles of Union."[54] Its first branch
was to be elected directly by the people of the several
states—in itself a significant departure from the principle
of the Articles of Confederation—and the members of the
second branch were to be elected by the members of
the first, "out of a proper number of persons nominated
by the individual [state] legislatures." In each branch,
the number of representatives to which a state would be
entitled would depend on its quota of "contribution" or
the number of its free inhabitants. It was this provision that

98

gave rise to the dispute that occupied the convention for an entire month.

For the first two weeks after its introduction on May 29, however, the Virginia Plan dominated the debates and, by June 13, had been substantially adopted by the convention, thus illustrating the importance of being first in the field with a plan of action. Even the provision respecting the proportioning of representatives was "generally relished," and would have been adopted as early as May 30, had not George Read of Delaware moved that consideration of it be postponed. Reminding the convention that "the deputies from Delaware were restrained by their commission" from assenting to any such rule of representation—an instruction for which he was himself partly responsible—Read explained that, were the rule adopted, he and his Delaware colleagues might have "to retire from the Convention."[55] This threat marked one of the low points of the convention. By the time (June 9) debate on this rule was renewed, the number of delegates of Read's persuasion had grown to the point where they were able to offer effective resistance to what, up to then, had been a strong nationalist tide. Their state sovereignty motion—according to which states would be equally represented in the second branch of the legislature—failed by a single vote. By the same margin (six to five), the nationalists' motion calling for proportional representation in the second (as well as in the first) branch was adopted.[56] But so wide a disagreement could not be settled by a majority so narrow, not on so fundamental an issue. These votes were taken on June 11; on June 13, the Committee of the Whole reported the Randolph proposals, as amended, and the house (that is, the convention) postponed consideration of them until the following day. On June 14, however, on a motion by William Paterson of New Jersey, significantly seconded by Randolph, consideration was put off until June 15, and the house promptly adjourned. Then, on June 15, Paterson introduced what came to be known as the New Jersey (or small state) Plan. The convention now had two plans before it and the issue was fairly joined.[57]

Offered as a series of amendments to the Articles of Confederation, the New Jersey Plan would nevertheless have increased the powers of the general government in significant respects. For example, Congress would have been authorized to levy duties on imported goods, thus providing the government with a source of income independent of the requisitions on the states; to coerce payment of those requisitions; and to make rules regulating foreign and domestic commerce and to assess fines against anyone found to be in violation of them. Finally, the plan called for the establishment of a federal judiciary and a plural executive empowered to enforce federal law and to appoint "all federal officers not otherwise provided for."[58] If adopted, these amendments would have gone some distance toward remedying the defects of the Articles, but they would have left their principle (state sovereignty or quasi-sovereignty) intact. Their chief advantage over the Virginia Plan consisted in their "legality"; by adopting them, the convention would not be exceeding its authority. Paterson made much of this point.

Before going on to discuss the resolution of this conflict between these sharply different plans, it is necessary at least to mention other items on the convention's agenda. These included the method by which the chief executive was to be chosen, the length of his term of office, and, of course, the powers he was to exercise; the characteristics of the judiciary (one supreme court or, in addition, a complete system of federal courts); the qualifications of electors for the popular branch of the legislature; the size of the second branch and the qualifications of its members; the extent of the legislative powers, including the power to regulate the slave trade; and the methods of ratifying and amending the Constitution. These and other items provoked spirited and, in some cases, prolonged debate, but in none of them was the disagreement one of principle. Everyone agreed, if not in every case on the superiority then, at least, on the appropriateness of a republican form of government. "No other form would be acceptable to the American people." But they also recognized the temporary necessity to accommodate the Southern states on the slavery question. When debating the Virginia Plan, they agreed on the need to provide for legislative, executive, and judicial powers, and to separate them one from the other; in that context they also agreed that the legislature should consist of two houses. In addition to the slavery "interest," there were commercial, agrarian, small state, large state, and a variety of other "interests," but none that could not somehow be accommodated.

The one issue that embodied a difference of principle was that of representation. So grave were the differences on this issue, and so seemingly obdurate were the parties disputing it, that, as if in desperation, Franklin suggested daily "prayers imploring the assistance of Heaven." That was on June 28. Two days later, Gunning Bedford of Delaware delivered a long and bitter attack on the large state delegates, proponents of the Virginia Plan. "The little States," he said, "will meet the large ones on no ground but that of the Confederation." Referring then to the argument that this was America's last opportunity to establish good government, he indicated that he was under no apprehensions on this score. He said the large states dare not dissolve the confederation. "If they do the small ones will find some foreign ally of more honor and good faith, who will take them by the hand and do them justice."[59]

This speech marked the lowest point of the convention. Yet, by openly threatening a course of action that the other delegates had long feared as a possibility, Bedford, by his very recklessness, may have served the cause of compromise. At any rate, the compromise was not long in coming. Its terms are familiar and readily comprehended— one branch of the legislature would represent the people of the United States and the other the states as states—but its elements deserve to be elaborated.

It is not sufficient—to some extent it may even be inaccurate—to describe the dispute as a clash of "interests." What, besides large (or small) numbers, did the large (or small) states have in common that caused them to act in concert? "We might say, for example, that the 'interest' of the small states was to maintain a degree of influence in the affairs of the Union disproportionate to the number of people they contained; and that the 'interest' of the large states was to use their greater population to dominate the Union."[60] But as Madison was to point out, and as the subsequent history of the country attests, the states (and, indeed, the regions) were more divided by material interests than they were by the size of their populations; and an interest that divides some states may unite others, regardless of their size. Besides, the debate was not carried on in

102

those terms. The delegates did not speak of maintaining or acquiring political influence; they spoke the language of political principle, and there is no reason to believe that they were speaking dishonestly or disingenuously.

Roger Sherman of Connecticut (a small state) was opposed to the Virginia Plan, but not for selfish reasons. The powers granted to the national government by that plan were far in excess of what was needed by a government whose objects, in his judgment, were very few indeed: defense against foreign danger and against internal disputes and a resort to force, treaties with foreign nations, and "regulating foreign commerce, & drawing revenue from it."[61] He firmly believed that "all other matters civil & criminal would be much better in the hands of the States." This was a respectable and venerable argument. James Madison of Virginia (a large state) and the principal author of the Virginia Plan "differed from the member from Connecticut (Mr. Sherman) in thinking the objects mentioned to be all the principal ones that required a National Govt." Those were certainly important and necessary objects, "but he combined with them the necessity, of providing more effectually for the security of private rights, and the steady dispensation of Justice."[62] He then proceeded to make the argument—which he was to repeat in *Federalist* 10 and 51—that only in the large commercial republic would it be possible to control the effects of factions* and, with that control, provide the desired security for private

---

* "By a faction I understand a number of citizens, whether amounting to a majority or minority of the whole, who are united and actuated by some common impulse of passion, or of interest, adverse to the rights of other citizens, or to the permanent and aggregate interest of the community."[63]

rights. What divided Sherman and Madison was a disagreement as to the form of government best calculated "to secure these rights."

If, as the Anti-Federalists argued more cogently and fully during the ratification debates, rights could best be secured in a relatively small and essentially agrarian republic, where the government was kept close to the people by means of a fully democratic franchise, annual elections, and rotation of office, where manners would be kept simple and pure by means of moral education and the exclusion of foreigners as well as of foreign luxuries, then it followed that the principal seat of government would have to be the state. Someone of this persuasion would think of himself as first of all a citizen of his state and would stress the rights of states and the illegality of a plan depriving the states of their equal representation in the Confederation; and, because the objects of the Confederation were few, he would grant few powers to its government.

If, as Madison believed, rights could be secured only in a large republic, consisting of a wide variety of economic interests and religious sects, where it would be possible to prevent the formation of a majority faction, then it followed that the principal seat of government would have to be the nation. Someone of this persuasion—for example, James Wilson of Pennsylvania—would think of himself first of all as an American: "Among the first sentiments expressed in the first Congress one was that Virginia is no more. That Massachusetts is no [more], that Pennsylvania is no more etc. We are now one nation of brethren."[64] He would also argue—and Madison and Wilson did repeatedly argue—that the proponents of the New Jersey Plan were contending for a principle that was "confessedly unjust," contrary to the republican principle.[65] That principle required representation according to population.

But, of course, that principle was applicable only if it were true that the one nation had superseded the many colonies, and it was this that Paterson denied. "If," as he argued on June 16, "a proportional representation be right, why do we not vote so here?" Voting in the convention was by states because there was a Confederation governed by Articles that recognized the sovereignty of the states. And the Congress that governed that Confederation had called the convention for the limited purpose of revising the Articles. In the light of these instructions, the Virginia Plan was illegal, and Wilson's response—that the convention, while "authorized to *conclude nothing* [was] at liberty to *propose anything*"[66]—was clearly insufficient. Except that it begged the question, Randolph's response was better. He was not, he said, scrupulous on this matter of their authority. "When the salvation of the Republic was at stake, it would be treason to our trust, not to propose what we found necessary."[67] But what was it whose salvation was at stake, *the* republic or, as Paterson contended, the "league of friendship" among many republics?

Presumably, this issue was resolved when on June 19 the convention, by the comfortable margin of four votes (seven to three, with one state divided), rejected Paterson's New Jersey Plan and resolved to continue consideration of Randolph's Virginia Plan. Undeterred, however, Luther Martin of Maryland continued to protest that on the separation from Great Britain the states were placed "in a state of nature towards each other [and] would have remained in that state till this time, but for the confederation."[68] A week later, he launched a two-day harangue repeating the familiar legal objections to the Virginia Plan and warning of a dissolution of whatever union there was if the plan were to be adopted. Patiently, Madison explained that Martin's Maryland and the other small states had more to fear from dissolution than did his Virginia and the other large states:

> In a word; the two extremes before us are a perfect separation and a perfect incorporation, of the 13 states. In the first case they would be independent nations subject to no law, but the law of nations. In the last, they would be mere counties of one entire republic, subject to one common law. In the first case the smaller states would have everything to fear from the larger. In the last they would have nothing to fear.[69]

In the event, however, it was to be neither a perfect separation nor a perfect incorporation or union. It was, however, to be a "more perfect" union than that achieved under the Articles.

Madison's speech was followed by Franklin's call for daily prayers. Then, on the following day (June 29), William Johnson of Connecticut proposed the terms from which, two weeks later, the compromise was to emerge. Just as Franklin had urged delegates to acknowledge their need of divine assistance—which is to say, to recognize their fallibility—so Johnson now asked them to recognize the facts governing their situation. "The controversy must be endless whilst Gentlemen differ in the grounds of their arguments; those on one side considering the states as districts of people composing one political Society; those on the other considering them as so many political societies."[70]

Whatever the truth according to political theory or political history, in political fact the states were both districts *and* societies, and "the two ideas embraced on different sides, instead of being opposed to each other, ought to be combined; that in *one* branch the *people*, ought to be represented; in the *other*, the *States*." On that same day, the convention voted (six to four, with one state divided) that the "rules of suffrage in the 1st branch ought not to be according to that established by the Articles of Confederation." Oliver Ellsworth then moved that the rule of suffrage in the second branch should be that of the Articles. Like his Connecticut colleague Johnson, he urged the convention to accept this "compromise." We were, he said, "partly national; partly federal." Wilson, Franklin, and Madison, each in his own way, contributed to the movement toward compromise, but it was at this point that Gunning Bedford made his imprudent reference to the possibility that the small states might choose to form alliances with foreign powers. What happened next is best described in Storing's words:

> On the next working day [July 2], a vote was taken on the motion to allow each state an equal vote in the second branch. The result seems to suggest that Franklin's prayer for divine providence was not altogether fruitless, though human reason also played its part. The Maryland delegation was divided on this question, Daniel Jenifer being opposed to equal representation and Luther Martin in favor of it. Providentially, Jenifer was late in taking his seat that morning and Martin was thus able to cast the vote of Maryland in favor of the motion. The consequence of this was that when Georgia, the last state to be polled, was reached, instead of the question having been decided in

the negative, five states had voted in favor of the motion and five states against. Ordinarily the whole of the four-man Georgia delegation would have voted against equal representation, but it happened that two of the members were absent. One of the remaining Georgians was Abraham Baldwin, who was a native of Connecticut and is supposed to have come under the moderating influence of the Connecticut delegation. In any case, Baldwin apparently feared that the Convention would break up unless a concession was made to the small states. By chance or providence, the absence of two of his colleagues put in his hands the power perhaps to determine whether there was to be a Union or not. Voting, contrary to his convictions, in favor of equal representation in the second branch, Baldwin divided Georgia's vote, maintained the tie, and kept open the way for compromise.[71]

The question was then turned over to a committee, and the convention adjourned. Working on July 3 and reporting on July 5, this committee made the following proposals which were to be accepted as a package: each state to have an equal vote in the second branch of the legislature; all money bills to originate in the first branch and not to be amended in the second; and, in the first branch, each state to have one member for every 40,000 inhabitants, or, lacking that number, at least one member. This was followed by more discussion in the convention, and still more questions were referred to committees, from one of which came the provision that direct taxes as well as representation shall be apportioned among the states according to their number of inhabitants, counting a slave as three-fifths of a person for both purposes. Finally, on July 16, this so-called Great Compromise was accepted, five to four (with

Massachusetts, a large state, divided). The negative votes were cast by Pennsylvania, Virginia, South Carolina, and Georgia. In a note appended to his journal, Madison reports that the next morning "a number of the members from [these] larger states . . . met for the purpose of consulting on the proper steps to be taken in consequence of [this] vote."[72] Being unable to agree on the significance of giving the states an equal vote in the second branch— "time was wasted in vague conversation on the subject"— or on the course of action they might then follow, the large state delegates could do little other than to acquiesce in the outcome.

Another two months were spent working out the details of the other provisions, but with this vote on July 16 the crisis was reached and passed. The constitution that came out of the convention was partly national, partly federal, but without question it was more national than federal. It provided for a national government modeled, on the whole, on the Virginia Plan, which is why Luther Martin and Lansing and Yates of New York refused to sign it. Paterson, Bedford, and Read (all of whom did sign) got their way on second branch representation, and there was to be no national legislative negative on laws enacted by the states, but they won little else. (It can be doubted that they would have signed had they known that the national judiciary would possess such a negative.)[73] Ultimately, the small states had to admit that a more perfect union was a necessary condition of their continued existence as self-governing societies; they needed union more than the nationalists needed the states. In turn, while denying that constitutional change required the unanimous agreement of the states (the Articles of Confederation notwithstanding), and while their plan of a large commercial republic in no way depended on the continued existence of the states, the nationalists had to recognize their need of something close to unanimity if, as Storing puts it, they were to establish the principle for which they contended, which was, after all, *union*.

The point should be made again that the delegates were in complete agreement that government is instituted in order to secure the rights of man; they disagreed merely on how this might best be done. Strangely, perhaps, there was almost no discussion whatever in the convention of the necessity of a bill of rights;[74] for all we know, everyone agreed with what Hamilton was to say in the ratification debates, namely, that the Constitution was itself a bill of rights.[75] If so, they then agreed that rights are best secured in the very structure of a government that provides a "republican remedy for the diseases most incident to republican government."[76] The opponents of the Constitution—Patrick Henry prominent among them—seized on this absence of a bill of rights and exacted a promise from Madison to remedy this defect at the earliest opportunity. Madison honored this promise in the First Congress, when he introduced the amendments that became the Bill of Rights in 1791, after ratification by the required three-fourths of the states. In this connection, it should be mentioned, if only to indicate one of the ways in which this oldest of written national constitutions differs from those written in the twentieth century, not even the Bill of Rights makes specific reference to political parties, or to the rights to organize, strike, or work. Nor is there anywhere a reference to a ministry of culture, and considering what is sometimes done by governments under the label "culture,"

Americans can probably be thankful for this omission. Standing as they did at the beginning of the modern constitutional era, the Framers had a better opportunity, and perhaps a better reason, to weigh the advantages of classical political institutions. Thus, during the discussion of the structure of the second legislative branch, there were references to the institution of mixed government, or mixed regime. Why not, it was suggested by some delegates, add "weight" to the legislature by adding an element of aristocracy in the second branch, making it an American version of the British House of Lords? To which Charles Pinckney of South Carolina replied, because America does not have an aristocracy—"the materials for forming this balance or check do not exist"—and there is no prospect of its springing up out of a merchant class or, more generally, a commercial society.[77] If there was to be "weight" in the legislature, it would have to come not from great families but, as Madison made clear, from the smaller number of senators combined with the greater authority lodged in them.[78] The Framers knew they were constituting government for an egalitarian people; their problem was to devise institutions making equality compatible with liberty.

Because of the states and their functioning governments and societies, the convention was able to avoid making decisions on matters that are usually thought to be of a constitutional nature. Foremost among these was religion. Other than to include a provision (Article VI) forbidding religious tests as a qualification "to any Office or public Trust under the United States," the convention left religious matters to the states. The fact that, to one degree or another, and in one or another of its Christian varieties, over half the states had an established religion, undoubtedly

111

made it easy, if not necessary, to ignore the matter. Another was education. It was proposed that the new Congress be empowered to establish a national university and "seminaries for the promotion of literature and the arts and sciences," but nothing came of this, and to this day higher education remains under the control of the states and private institutions. As for elementary and secondary education, not only was the subject not discussed in the convention, but, to the extent to which such education existed at that time it was a private matter. In his *Notes on the State of Virginia*, Jefferson elaborated a plan for free public education, but it was to be years before any state established such a system.

Still another subject was the qualifications of voters. These varied from state to state, and, in the one case where specification was necessary, the convention simply turned the matter over to the states: the electors in each state of members of the House of Representatives "shall have the Qualifications requisite for Electors of the most numerous Branch of the State Legislature." Senators were to be chosen directly by the state legislatures. As for the president, some delegates favored election by the legislature, others favored election by the states (by way of the governors, the legislature, or electors chosen by governors or legislatures), but only Pennsylvania favored election by the "people at large." A long time was consumed before the convention settled on the electoral college system. Judges and other federal officers were to be appointed to office by the president with the consent of the Senate. Finally, the military, which plays so prominent a role in the politics of so many countries, was conspicuously absent from the Philadelphia convention. The president was made "Commander in Chief of the Army and Navy of the United States," but, at the time, there wasn't much of an army and very little of a navy. There were, in principle at least, state militias, and the president was given command of them "when called into the actual Service of the United States." As mentioned earlier, there were a variety of "interests" represented in the convention, but not one of them could be described as military.

Contemporary circumstances justify another word or two on voter qualifications. Contrary to what is sometimes said today, the Constitution does not and did not—never did—disfranchise anyone on account of race or sex; in fact, not a word had to be changed in it or added to it to qualify blacks and women to vote or, for that matter, hold *any* federal office. (The Fifteenth and Nineteenth amendments do not create a right to vote, or grant such right to blacks or women; they protect that right by forbidding its denial by "the United States or by any state.")

A brief word now on the convention's mode of procedure: the resolutions debated in the Committee of the Whole and, after being reported, adopted by the "house," were turned over to a five-man Committee of Detail; from these resolutions the Committee produced a constitutional draft, printed copies of which were furnished to each member on August 6.[79] The finished draft of the Constitution was the work of the Committee of Style and particularly Gouverneur Morris; printed copies of its report were furnished to members on September 12.[80] Several days were spent debating various provisions in the committee's draft, and a few significant changes were made in it. One of these had to do with the amending clause (Article V). As drafted, this clause provided for amendments to the Constitution to be proposed by the Congress, either on its own initiative or on the application of two-thirds of the states. Because there was apprehension on the part of some delegates that Congress might not respond to an application from the states, this provision was changed to require Congress, on such application, to call a convention for the purpose of proposing amendments. To the clause was also added a provision prohibiting amendments depriving a state, without its consent, "of its equal Suffrage in the Senate."[81] This took place on Saturday, September 15. Then, on September 17, after an eloquent Franklin speech (read for him by James Wilson) appealing to the delegates to overlook whatever they regarded as its faults, the engrossed Constitution was approved by a unanimous vote of the states (but not by a unanimous vote of the delegates).

The convention then resolved that "the preceding Constitution be laid before the United States in Congress assembled, and that it is the Opinion of this Convention, that it should afterwards be submitted to a Convention of delegates, chosen in each state by the People thereof . . . for their Assent and Ratification."[82] The significance of this lay in the decision to seek the "approbation" of the people ("the foundation of all power," as Madison put it when the question was being debated on August 31) and not of the Congress. The convention further resolved that, in its opinion, upon the ratification of (any) nine states, the Constitution should be considered in force among them. It then, after almost four months, adjourned *sine die.*

To James Madison goes the honor of pronouncing the authoritative judgment on the work of the convention:

114

But whatever may be the judgment pronounced on the competence of the architects of the Constitution, or whatever may be the destiny of the edifice prepared by them, I feel it a duty to express my profound and solemn conviction, derived from my intimate opportunity of observing and appreciating the views of the Convention, collectively and individually, that there never was an assembly of men, charged with a great and arduous trust, who were more pure in their motives, or more exclusively or anxiously devoted to the object committed to them, than were the members of the Federal Convention of 1787, to the object of devising and proposing a constitutional system which should best supply the defects of that which it was to replace, and best secure the permanent liberty and happiness of their country.[83]

RATIFICATION

The draft prepared by the Committee of Detail of the Constitution's Preamble began with the words, "We the people of the States of . . . ," followed by a list of all thirteen states. But the decision to have the new government begin operation upon ratification of the Constitution by at least nine states necessitated a change in this formulation. Who, in August 1787, could have predicted which states—or which nine states—would ratify? So the exordium was changed to read, "We the People of the United States." Once again the proponents of the states yielded to necessity what they would not concede in principle.

Both principle and the peculiar (confederal) condition of the United States in 1787 required ratification to be by the people rather than by the state legislatures. Madison made this point in a letter to Washington just prior to the convention. "To give a new system its proper validity and energy [he wrote], a ratification must be obtained from the people, and not merely from the ordinary authority of the Legislatures. This will be the more essential as inroads on the *existing Constitutions* of the States will be unavoidable."[84] In conformity with this, the convention suggested that the Congress submit the Constitution to specially convoked conventions in the several states, and the Congress, in turn, sent it on to the states with instruction that it be submitted "to a convention of Delegates chosen in each state by the people thereof."[85] This congressional resolution was adopted, in the absence of Rhode Island and over the opposition of New York, on September 28, eleven days after the convention adjourned in Philadelphia.

Again, it is worth reiterating that Madison was speaking the "common sense" of the matter when he articulated the reasons for going directly to the people for their consent. Here, from the countless examples one might offer to support this judgment, is one of the resolutions adopted by the Concord (Massachusetts) Town Meeting:

Resolved 2 That the Supreme Legislative, either in their Proper Capacity, or in Joint Committee, are by no means a Body proper to form and Establish a Constitution, or form of Government; for Reasons following. first Because we Conceive that a Constitution in its Proper Idea intends a System of Principles Established to Secure the Subject in the Possession and enjoyment of their Rights and Privileges, against any Encroachments of the Governing Part— 2d Because the Same Body that forms a Constitution have

116

of Consequence a power to alter it. 3d—Because a Constitution alterable by the Supreme Legislative is no Security at all to the Subject against any Encroachment of the Governing part on any, or on all of their Rights and privileges.[86]

Historians dispute the number of eligible voters as well as the number who actually participated in the elections in which convention delegates were chosen. As one might expect, hard evidence is hard to come by. Nothing better demonstrates the "popularity" of the Constitution, however—that is, its origins in the people—than the debates outside and preceding the various state ratifying conventions. This is especially true in the case of New York, in whose newspapers Hamilton, Madison, and John Jay combined under the name of Publius to write the eighty-five papers soon collected as *The Federalist*. Like their counterparts elsewhere, as well as the papers written by the Anti-Federalists (as they were now called), these were addressed to the *people*. In whatever numbers, it was the people who elected the delegates, and, therefore, it was the people on whose judgment everything ultimately depended. The significance of this may be glimpsed by comparing it with the Canadian Confederation Debates leading to the British North America Act of 1867, the Canadian Constitution. In the parliament of Upper Canada (Ontario), the objection was raised that members ought to consult opinion "out of doors," to which the response was, a decision respecting a constitution of government was not one for the people to make. (Thus, the enacting clause of the BNA read, in part, as follows: "Be it therefore enacted and declared by the Queen's Most Excellent Majesty.") It was otherwise

117

in the United States, in principle and, as well, in practice: the source of legitimate government was understood to be the people.

Beginning with Delaware on December 7, followed closely by Pennsylvania and New Jersey on December 12 and 18, respectively, the people of the United States in their various state conventions assembled began to ratify the Constitution. The process continued until 1788, when, on June 21, New Hampshire became the ninth state to ratify. (None had voted to reject the Constitution.) But no one had any illusions that the new government could now begin its operations, not as long as New York and Virginia remained outside. (North Carolina and Rhode Island were not seen as essential, and, indeed, the new government had been in operation for over a year before the latter state ratified on May 29, 1790.)

The debates in the Virginia and New York conventions were probably the most spirited and surely the most interesting. On June 2, 1788, 170 delegates convened in Richmond, Virginia's capital, and began the debate that went on for over three weeks. The Federalists, as they were now called, were led by Madison, George Wythe, John Marshall (one day to become chief justice of the United States), Henry Lee, Edmund Pendleton, and, once again, Edmund Randolph (who had refused to sign the Constitution). Their opponents were, at that time, equally famous and equally distinguished, especially George Mason and Patrick Henry. The June 27 vote to ratify was very close, eighty-nine to seventy-nine, with "recommendations" that Henry and his associates would have preferred to look upon as conditions. (These had mainly to do with adoption of a bill of rights.)

118

In New York, it was a contest between Alexander Hamilton and the followers of Governor George Clinton joined by a group of principled Anti-Federalists led by Melancton Smith. Hamilton was brilliant in debate, but Smith and company were able to respond with arguments well known to their classical republican predecessor in England.[87] They ended up voting for ratification, not because they were persuaded by Hamilton's substantive arguments but, more likely, because they knew there was substance to his argument that if New York did not ratify, its southern counties and its principal city would secede from the state and join the larger union. Hamilton saw to it that the news of Virginia's favorable vote reached Albany, the capital of New York, even as the convention was meeting there. Yet, with all these factors in favor of ratification, the July 26 vote margin was very narrow indeed (thirty to twenty-seven).

Upon being informed that the ninth state had ratified the Constitution, the Congress appointed a committee to "report an Act to Congress for putting the said constitution into operation." (This was on July 2, 1788, after Virginia's action had made it the tenth state to ratify.) On September 13, 1788, Congress resolved that "the first Wednesday in Jany. next be the day for appointing [presidential] Electors in the several states [and] that the first Wednesday in March next be the time and the present seat of Congress [New York City] the place for commencing proceedings under the said constitution—"[88] Washington took the oath as president on April 30, 1789, and in due course the new government was organized.

There have been many changes in the Constitution since 1789, changes both formal and informal, but the basic

119

structure remains intact. It is probably true to say that the men who framed it would have little difficulty recognizing it as their handiwork—and, what is more, find good reason to take pride in it.

Perhaps the most compelling evidence of the magnitude of the Framers' achievement (and also, one has to admit, of this country's good luck) can be seen in a quick glance at the history of the United States and of France since 1789. Since its revolution of that year, France has had, or has experienced, the First Republic, a Reign of Terror, a Directory, the Napoleonic dictatorship and then empire, the restoration of the Bourbon monarchy under first Louis XVIII (whose reign was interrupted by the brief return of Napoleon) and then Charles X, the July Monarchy under Louis Philippe, duc d'Orléans, the Second Republic, followed by the second empire under Louis Napoleon, the Third Republic, the World War II fascist regime under General Pétain, the Fourth Republic, and since 1958, the Fifth Republic. (And, as the old but updated joke has it, *il y aura une sixième.*) During that period, and ignoring for present purposes the Civil War, this country has governed itself under the Constitution of 1787.

That France's experience is more typical than ours can, in turn, be seen in the following statistics. Of the 160 countries in the world today, all but a handful have written constitutions—the exceptions are Great Britain, Israel, Libya, New Zealand, Oman, and Saudi Arabia—and of these all but a score have been written since World War II. In fact, 104 (of the 154) date from the beginning of 1970.[89] The United States is both the first and the oldest "new nation," and its durability can be attributed in good measure to the principles of its Constitution. Somehow that Constitution did what the Declaration of Independence says must be done and what the other constitutions have typically been unable to do: it instituted a government that secures human rights.

CHAPTER III

Constituting Democracy

||||

America's declaring of independence was not the only noteworthy event of 1776. The year also saw the initial publication of Adam Smith's *The Wealth of Nations*, a work destined to have a profound influence on the development of the United States and about which I shall have something to say in the next chapter, and the initial appearance in print of Jeremy Bentham, a political theorist who was to acquire some influence in Britain but—happily for this country—none or little in the United States. In this first book, *A Fragment on Government*, Bentham devotes some 150 pages to a largely captious critique of a couple of paragraphs from the introduction to the *Commentaries on the Laws of England* in which the author, William Blackstone, praises the British constitution as a mixture of monarchy, aristocracy, and democracy. To say nothing more, Bentham was not an advocate of "mixed government," but his purpose in this early book was merely to put an end to what he saw as the confusion and errors characterizing the political theory of his time and thereby to prepare the way for the principle that he announced in 1780 and that will probably be associated with his name forever, the principle of utility. According to this principle, or one version of it, the object of all legislation and, indeed, of government itself, is "the greatest happiness of the greatest number."

There is evidently something appealing in this principle, something, perhaps, to be found in its simplicity and apparent philanthropy; this may explain why there have been persons eager to appropriate it as a definition of democracy or as a formulation of the democratic principle. Does it not suggest the idea of one person, one equally weighted vote, to the end of allowing the majority to rule? What it lacks, of course, is any professed concern for those who are outvoted in the calculus, and in that respect it might even be said to be (assuming we are permitted to use the term) un-American. In truth, only someone indifferent to the idea of human rights could be much attracted by Bentham's principle, and only someone propelled by so overweening a vanity that he cannot imagine himself in a minority could knowingly agree to be governed according to its terms. The typical American might agree with Jefferson that the will of the majority is in all cases to prevail—the words are taken from Jefferson's First Inaugural Address—but only because, like Jefferson, he believes that to be rightful that will must be reasonable. As Jefferson went right on to say, the minority possess their equal rights, "which equal law must protect, and to violate would be oppression."

If he has been at all attentive to the rhetoric or, especially, the teaching of our founding documents, that American will know that human rights cannot be secured—or are not likely to be secured—by simply empowering the majority. A simply empowered majority will be a simple majority, and a simple majority is almost certain to be a "faction," to employ Madison's term. Factions are dangerous, and a properly constituted government is one that somehow secures "the public good and private rights" against the dangers they pose. This, in part, is what the Framers set out to accomplish, and a fair assessment would have to conclude that, on the whole, they were successful. They were successful because they could be said to have paid more attention to Adam Smith and William Blackstone and less (if any at all) to Jeremy Bentham, and for that we Americans are fortunate and ought to be grateful.

The Bill of Rights

At a time when so much attention is being paid to the subject of human rights and being focused especially on those countries that do not recognize or secure them, it is only to be expected that Americans would be conscious of their good fortune in this respect. Nor is it remarkable that they should attribute this to one feature of the Constitution, the Bill of Rights, in our day probably its most visible part, and to a judiciary with the power to enforce its provisions. Soviet citizens are not permitted to express their political opinions freely, but Americans have the First Amendment; Argentinians are (or were) brutally tortured, but Americans are protected by the Fifth Amendment's provision against self-incrimination; Cubans are held in jail without trial, but thanks to habeas corpus and the Sixth Amendment's right to a speedy and public trial, that sort of thing cannot happen in America. The list could be extended until it comprised all the privileges, immunities, and rights specified in the Constitution and the literally hundreds of corresponding cases where they have been upheld or enforced by the courts. How does the Constitution secure rights, and especially the rights of minorities? By delineating them in its text and empowering the courts to enforce them. That is the usual answer to our question.

It is, for example, the answer given in the *Citizen's Guide to Individual Rights Under the Constitution of the United States of America,* an official government publication prepared by the Subcommittee on the Constitution of the Senate Judiciary Committee.[1] After a brief (three-page) introduction of the sort appropriate to guidebooks and where, for example, the point is made that the original Constitution specified only a few privileges or rights and that still others have their bases not in the Constitution but in various statutes, the *Citizen's Guide* proceeds to list and then to elaborate the various constitutional provisions, most of them to be found in the first ten amendments. As then-Senator Birch Bayh of Indiana said in his preface to the volume, the "guarantees of individual rights found in our Constitution's Bill of Rights are the very foundation of America's free and democratic society."[2] This contention is not so much incorrect as it is inadequate or insufficient.

The Bill of Rights is an appendage to the Constitution, a set of ten amendments formally proposed by the First Congress in 1789 and declared ratified by the required three-fourths of the states in 1791; and it is not usual for an appendage to serve as the foundation of a structure. Of course, Bayh may be right in suggesting that while we owe our system of government to the body of the Constitution, we owe our liberty or our rights to its amendments. But if Bayh is right, the Framers were wrong. They expected the Constitution, even without amendments, to "secure the blessings of liberty," or, they could just as well have said, to secure the rights with which all men are by nature endowed.

What is beyond dispute is the purpose of the original amendments; they were adopted in order to limit the powers of the national government, not of the states. The Supreme Court so held in *Barron* v. *Baltimore* in 1833,[3] and anyone familiar with the debates in the First Congress, or with the political agitation that had led Congress to propose and the states to ratify the amendments, would have to agree that the Court was correct in so holding. It was Congress that was forbidden to make laws respecting an establishment of religion or prohibiting the free exercise thereof, Congress that was not to abridge the freedom of speech and press or infringe the right to keep and bear arms; the national executive that was not to quarter troops in a house without the owner's consent, or engage in unreasonable searches and seizures; the national judiciary that, to confine myself to the single example of the Eighth Amendment, was forbidden to require excessive bail, impose excessive fines, or inflict cruel and unusual punishments. Leaving aside the few provisions in Article I, section 10, it was not until after the Civil War that the Constitution was amended to contain specific limitations on the powers of the states.

What is also beyond dispute, although very little attention has been paid to it, is that during what is still the greater part of our history (1789–1925), the Bill of Rights played almost no role in the securing of rights. Prior to the *Gitlow* case in 1925,[4] which began the process of incorporation or absorption of the Bill of Rights into or by the Fourteenth Amendment (thereby making its provisions applicable to the states), there were few cases involving the first ten amendments and fewer still—in fact, only fifteen—in which a governmental action was held to be in conflict with one of them. There were only nine such cases during all of the nineteenth century, one of these being *Dred Scott* v. *Sandford* (scarcely a monument to liberty) and another being *Hepburn* v. *Griswold*, which was promptly overruled.[5] The religious liberty enjoyed by Americans owed nothing, absolutely nothing, to judicial enforcement of the First Amendment, and the same is true respecting the freedom of speech and press; not once during these first 136 years did the Supreme Court invalidate an act of Congress on First Amendment grounds. (This did not occur, in a speech case, until 1965 and, in a religion case, until 1971, if then.[6]) On one occasion the court invalidated a federal search and seizure,[7] but most of the pre-*Gitlow* cases involved one or another aspect of the Fifth Amendment.[8] The fact is, the Bill of Rights has served (and continues to serve) mainly to secure rights from abridgement by the states and not the federal government, the very opposite of the role the amendments were intended to play—or, more precisely, the very opposite of the role the Anti-Federalists expected them to play.

None of this would have surprised the authors of *The Federalist*, Hamilton, Madison, and Jay, or, for that matter, many of their associates in the party bearing that name. For reasons to be explained presently, they anticipated that the state and local governments would pose by far the greater danger to private rights. And for reasons too obvious to require explanation, it is politically much easier for the Supreme Court to invalidate state and local laws and ordinances than federal statutes enacted by a Congress representing national majorities. As we saw in the aftermath of *Brown* v. *Board,* the 1954 public school desegregation case, the Court was able to enforce its judgment even against the stubborn opposition of a united regional majority. But comparable examples involving congressional laws and majorities do not come readily to mind. It might be said that congressional majorities do not enact unconstitutional laws, which is true enough, or that the majorities assembled in Congress are not likely to be very determined or stubborn. Still, there have been occasions when the Court has been in conflict with the political branches, and it has not been often, to say the least, when the Court has emerged the winner. On the contrary, to cite the most notorious episode, President Franklin Roosevelt may have lost the 1937 "Court packing" battle when, in the effort to overcome the Supreme Court's opposition to his New Deal program, he proposed to increase its membership from nine to fifteen; but he and the Congress won the war. Whether or not it switched in time in order to save nine, as the wits had it, the Court did in fact give way before what would have been a national political majority determined to have its way.

On the whole, then, history has vindicated the Federalists who insisted that, as far as the federal government was the object of concern, a bill of rights would be either unavailing or unnecessary. As they saw it, the threat to rights would be posed mainly by popular majorities, and against such majorities bills of specified rights would prove (as in the states they had already proved) to be mere "parchment barriers."[9] It is, therefore, not surprising that as it came from the Philadelphia convention the Constitution did not contain a bill of rights, or that the word "right" (or "rights") appears only once in its text.[10] Yet, as Hamilton insisted, "the Constitution is itself, in every rational sense, and to every useful purpose, A BILL OF RIGHTS."[11] It is a bill of rights both because it is a statement or an expression of the people's natural right to govern themselves and because in its very structure it provides the means by which rights are secured. Those means are delineated in *Federalist* 9 and elaborated in subsequent numbers, beginning in the celebrated number 10.

The New Science of Politics

Federalist 9 begins with a bit of history leading up to a remarkable assertion. History, Publius asserts—and Publius here is Alexander Hamilton—seems to support the arguments advanced by "the advocates of despotism" that free republican government is an impossibility. There had been republics in the past, specifically the "petty republics of Greece and Italy"; and there had also been free governments, some of them "stupendous fabrics reared on the basis of liberty, which have flourished for ages." But the republics were unstable, wracked by "tempestuous waves of sedition and party rage," which caused them to fluctuate "between the extremes of tyranny and anarchy"; and the free governments, while stable and sometimes even "glorious," were not republican in form. Nothing in this history gives comfort to the friends of republican government—

among whom all Americans would have to be numbered[12]—and were it not for an unprecedented event in the world of science, they would be obliged to concede that the advocates of despotism were right: "The science of politics, however, like most other sciences, has received great improvement [lately]. The efficacy of various principles is now well understood, which were either not known at all, or imperfectly known to the ancients." By adopting these principles in its Constitution, America could succeed where all other nations had failed: it could combine liberty and order under a republican form. That, I would submit, is a remarkable assertion.

No less remarkable, perhaps, is the character of these newly discovered principles. They are decidedly not principles having to do with the education of citizens, or the preparation of persons for their role as citizens. Aristotle, the founder of the old political science, could assert confidently that the education of the young requires the special attention of the lawgiver, and that this education had to be adapted to the particular form of constitution, by which he meant that the democratic constitution, for example, required a democratic education for its young.[13] But there is no reference in *Federalist* 9 to the education of republican citizens or anything having to do with civic virtue and how it might be promoted or fostered. These were the concerns of the old political science, and, to some extent, they remained the concerns of the framers of state constitutions. The new political science, however, was concerned less with the political material and more with the structure of government; it provided the Framers of the federal Constitution with a model of "a more perfect structure," and did

130

so on the basis of principles "not known at all, or imperfectly known to the ancients."

The elements of this structure are familiar to all students of American government: "The regular distribution of power into distinct departments; the introduction of legislative balances and checks; the institution of courts composed of judges holding their offices during good behavior; the representation of the people in the legislature by deputies of their own election," and last but not least, "the EN-LARGEMENT of the ORBIT within which such systems are to revolve." These organizational principles are said to be the means "by which the excellencies of republican government may be retained and its imperfections lessened or avoided." As I said, a remarkable assertion or claim, at the time perhaps even extravagant, but not so when viewed from the perspective supplied by almost 200 years of unparalleled political prosperity. As employed in the Constitution, they provided a solution to the problem of popular government.

DISTRIBUTING POWERS

Not surprisingly, the Framers' most succinct statement of this problem can be found in what may well be the most frequently quoted passage in the *Federalist Papers:* "In framing a government which is to be administered by men over men," Madison wrote in *Federalist* 51, "the great difficulty lies in this: you must first enable the government to control the governed; and in the next place oblige it to control itself." It was the first of these difficulties that taxed the

131

ingenuity of Thomas Hobbes, for example, and his solution was an absolute ruler who, as described in the biblical text from which Hobbes took the name, if not the idea, was the Leviathan: "Upon earth there is not his like, a creature without fear. . . . He is king over all the sons of pride" (Job 41:33–34). But the Framers were firmly of the opinion that, given a people with sufficient virtue, control could be effected not through fear but through law to which the governed themselves give their consent. The trouble with the government under the Articles of Confederation—the "imbecility" of that government, as Hamilton described it in *Federalist* 15—was the incapacity of its laws to reach the people directly. The national government was required to legislate for the states, in their corporate or collective capacities, and not for the individuals "of whom they consist." This was not an effective method of controlling Daniel Shays, for instance, and his associates in the rebellion bearing his name. Under the new Constitution, however, Congress could make laws for the people of the United States, and the single, energetic executive was empowered to enforce them. Not only was Congress given the authority "to provide for calling forth the militia to execute the Laws of the Union," but the president was given command of that militia "when called into the actual service of the United States." Those troops have in fact been called forth and used on a number of occasions, from the time of the so-called Whisky Rebellion in 1794, when President Washington dispatched them to western Pennsylvania (and actually commanded them in person during the early stages of the march), again in 1894 when President Grover Cleveland sent them to Chicago to put down the Pullman strike, and more recently in 1957, when President Dwight D.

Eisenhower used them to integrate Little Rock's Central High School. On the whole, however, and contrary to the expectations of the Anti-Federalists to the effect that in a country so large as the United States the people would not be attached to the government and would not voluntarily obey its laws, this use of force has been the exception, not the rule.

The more difficult task was devising a system that would "oblige [the government] to control itself." Popular and regular elections are one means of effecting this control— "a dependence on the people is, no doubt, the primary control on the government"—but Madison goes right on to say that elections are not enough. They serve, or can serve, as effective checks on the performance of officeholders—they can be used to "throw the rascals out," as we say—but to the extent to which they are popular or democratic, they will promote the views of popular or democratic majorities, and it was this that gave rise to the Framers' apprehension, and this, moreover, that distinguished them from the Anti-Federalists.

To judge from their rhetoric alone, the Anti-Federalists feared aristocracy above everything else; feared it, saw elements of it everywhere in the Framers' Constitution, and proposed their alternatives with what at times appeared to be the single purpose of guarding against it.[14] The Framers, on the other hand, spoke openly of the "diseases most incident to republican government" and of the necessity of finding a "remedy" for these diseases. What made this task especially difficult was their insistence that it be a "republican remedy"—despite the charges leveled against them at the time and since, the Framers were not enemies of popular government—and, among other things, this required them

133

to find a substitute for, or to devise a purely republican version of, Montesquieu's system of separated powers.

Seemingly everyone, Federalists and Anti-Federalists alike, agreed on the need to separate the legislative, executive, and judicial powers. They agreed that the accumulation of these powers in the same hands "may justly be pronounced the very definition of tyranny," and, as the Federalists understood the case, this was so whether the government was "hereditary, self-appointed, or elective." Moreover, safety was not to be found in a system where these powers would be exercised by a "plurality of hands," as Jefferson put it, rather than "by a single one." Even power coming from the people and being exercised by their representatives had to be distributed among distinct departments, and distributed with a view to checking the legislative in particular, because the legislative is the strongest and the department most to be feared. Its tendency is to draw all power into its "impetuous vortex," and in government purely republican, "this tendency is almost irresistible."[15]

Unfortunately, the only model of a system of separated powers available to the Framers—that provided by "the celebrated Montesquieu" in his *Spirit of the Laws*—could not be adopted by them, not without adaptation. Montesquieu found his solution to the problem of tyranny in the English constitution (or what he saw fit to describe as the English constitution). In England, not only was the legislative power separated from and thereby (he said) independent of the executive, and the judiciary separated from each of the other branches, but the legislative was itself divided into two houses, one popular and the other representing the hereditary nobility. In this way, the division of the legislative power corresponded to the division in the so-

134

ciety: the House of Commons representing the common people and the House of Lords property and family. The balance between them would have been unstable (and, as we know, proved to be unstable) had it not been for the fortuitous presence of an hereditary monarch armed with the executive power, which, Montesquieu said, included an absolute veto. Belonging to neither of the two great parties and independent of both, he used this veto to maintain a balance between them. What came out of the legislature, then, was law applicable to everyone; the balance in the legislature, maintained by the veto or the threat of it, guaranteed the nonoppressive character of that law. The executive, separated from the legislature, had the job of enforcing this law against everyone; and the job of the independent judiciary was to see to it that it was the law, and only the law, that was being enforced. The *balance* of power prevented class oppression; the *separation* of powers prevented the oppression of the individual person. This, Montesquieu would have the reader believe, was the English constitution of the eighteenth century.[16]

In fact, his account, which he presented as a description, included a fair amount of prescription as well. Still, if these hereditary institutions had not existed in England, it would have been necessary for him to invent them or something like them; their absence in America, or their incompatibility with America, made it necessary for the Framers to invent or find a substitute for them. As described by Montesquieu, the English constitution offered a remedy for the diseases most incident to republican government, but not a republican remedy and, therefore, not a remedy that could be adopted without adaptation by the Framers. The American constitution had to be "strictly republican," not a mixture of democracy and aristocracy. Under it, government had to be "derived from the great body of the society, not from an inconsiderable proportion or a favored class of it."[17] In America, democracy could not be checked by being balanced against aristocracy, or weighed in the balance with it; to coin a phrase, it had to be constitutionalized.

It is worth remembering that the Federalists and Anti-Federalists, although divided on the question of whether the Constitution deserved to be ratified, agreed that the "general form and aspect of the government [had to] be strictly republican," as Madison put it in *Federalist* 39. "It is evident that no other form would be reconcilable with the genius of the people of America; with the fundamental principles of the Revolution; or with the honorable determination which animates every votary of freedom to rest all our political experiments on the capacity of mankind for self-government." There had to have been a general awareness—the Federalists certainly did their best to promote it—of the nature of that republican form and what it was designed to do. The people had to have known that the Constitution they were ratifying would impose restraints on the government and was intended to impose restraints especially on a democratic government; but the fact is they ratified it. They did so, presumably, because they were persuaded that rights—everybody's rights—would best be secured by a democracy that was constitutionalized.

Although there are now many constitutions and, as I pointed out in the previous chapter, almost all of them inscribed in formal written documents, it cannot be said that the world outside America has been much constitutionalized; since 1787 and especially since Tocqueville wrote in the 1830s, it has, however, been thoroughly if not "for-

136

mally" democratized. Today even nondemocratic and patently despotic governments claim to be democratic. (East Germans, for example, live behind a barrier consisting of high walls, barbed wire fences, mine fields, vicious dogs, and automatically triggered shotguns, but their government calls itself the German Democratic Republic.) And while there are, admittedly, a few kings left, and an occasional queen, none of them can be said actually to govern, and only a few of them govern even nominally. In no Western country is there a politically active nobility. Nations are no longer divided into "estates," as some of them once were; instead, they are divided into groups, some of them into tribal, ethnic, religious, or language groups. And whereas no modern constitution follows the example of the pre-revolutionary French monarchy by attempting to represent the estates of the realm, some of them attempt to resolve their diversity problems by recognizing that diversity in their texts, whether by assigning legislative seats to particular groups, as in the Egyptian constitution, or by protecting a minority's language rights, as in the Canadian, or by distributing offices on the basis of religious affiliation, as in the Lebanese. But, as this last example especially suggests, the granting of rights to groups in order to accommodate the differences between them is a good prescription for perpetuating those differences and probably for exacerbating them.

No such principle found its way into the Constitution of 1787. The closest thing to group representation is in the Senate, where—in the words of *Federalist* 39—the states "as political and coequal societies" are represented; but every effort to represent property or family, as a means of balancing democracy, to say nothing of sect, nationality, language, color, or gender, was soundly defeated in the constitutional convention. On June 7, for example, John Dickinson of Pennsylvania said "he wished the Senate to consist of the most distinguished characters, distinguished for their rank in life and their weight of property, and bearing as strong a likeness to the British House of Lords as possible." And the more of such men, apparently, the better. "He adhered," he said, "to the opinion that the Senate ought to be composed of a large number, and that their influence from family weight & other causes would be increased thereby." But his colleague from Pennsylvania, James Wilson, responded with the simple and telling observation that America lacked the "materials" for an aristocratic assembly. There were, and there would be, no great American families. "Our manners, our laws, the abolition of entails and of primogeniture, the whole genius of the people, are opposed to it." Both he and Madison were sympathetic with Dickinson's call for a Senate with "weight"—such a body was needed to balance the weight of democratic numbers in the House of Representatives—but it could not be achieved by multiplying the number of senators. In the absence of an hereditary nobility or a restricted franchise, the larger the number of senators, the more they would resemble their democratic constituents. So said Madison, and it was he who drew the conclusion: "When the weight of a set of men depends merely on their personal characters; the greater the number the greater the weight. When it depends on the degree of political authority lodged in them the smaller the number the greater the weight."[18] So it was that the Senate was kept small and the senators given longer terms and, in their authority to advise and consent to treaties and appointments, significantly greater power than that given the members of the House of Representatives. While wholly republican, such a Senate might be able to balance and check the more democratic House of Representatives. That, at least, was to be one of its functions, which is one reason why the Framers agreed to the resolution calling for a bicameral legislature "without debate or dissent."[19]

In summary, both systems featured a distribution of powers among the legislative, executive, and judiciary, but where Montesquieu limited the legislative power by dividing it between the people and the nobility, the Framers sought to limit it by means of a written document that specifies exceptions to it—"such for instance, as that it shall pass no bills of attainder, no *ex post facto* laws, and the like"[20]—but mostly by requiring that it be exercised in a formal manner. What the science of politics had discovered was the efficacy of these constitutional forms or "principles"—distribution of powers, checks and balances, an independent judiciary, the representation of the people in the legislature by deputies of their own election, and an enlargement of the orbit "within which such systems are to revolve." The most important of these, or the one on which the others depend, is representation.

REPRESENTATION

Who are to be represented? Or as Madison put the question in *Federalist* 57, "Who are to be the electors of the federal representatives?"

> Not the rich, more than the poor; not the learned, more than the ignorant; not the haughty heirs of distinguished

names, more than the humble sons of obscure and unpro-
pitious fortune. The electors are to be the great body of
the people of the United States.

For purposes of representation not only are the people not
divided into groups of any description—to repeat a point
made earlier—but they are represented in a way that distinguishes the American from the so-called constitutions of all
earlier republics, and specifically from those of Athens,
Sparta, Rome, Carthage, and Crete. These are the specific
references in *Federalist* 63 where Madison concedes that
the ancients were not completely unfamiliar with at least
the practice of representation; they knew about it, he writes,
but their knowledge of it was imperfect, and, as a consequence, they failed to take full advantage of it. Direct democracy, a system where the people assemble in person to
make the laws and otherwise to govern themselves, is obviously impracticable in any well-populated country; recognizing this, and apparently with some reluctance, the ancient
republics had to resort to electing representatives, in the
Spartan case, for example, Ephori, and in the Roman case
Tribunes. What they and the others failed to appreciate
were the positive benefits of representation. When properly instituted, representation can serve to refine and enlarge the public views by passing them through the me-
dium of a chosen body of citizens. Representative democracy
can be superior to direct democracy. "Under such a regulation it may well happen that the public voice, pronounced
by the representatives of the people, will be more consonant
to the public good than if pronounced by the people themselves, convened for the purpose."[21] America could enjoy
this benefit because, unlike the Athenians, Spartans, Ro-

mans, Carthaginians, and Cretans, in America, as Madison emphasizes, *"the people in their collective capacity"* have no share in the government.[22]

His meaning can be grasped by paying attention to the emphatic way in which he distinguishes the American from the earlier republics. Athens, he says, was for a time governed by "nine Archons, annually *elected by the people at large,"* and both the Spartan Ephori and Roman Tribunes were *"elected by the whole body of the people,* and considered as *representatives* of the people, almost in their *plenipotentiary* capacity." But under the Constitution of the United States no official and no collection of officials is elected by the people at large, or by the whole body of the people; because votes are not aggregated at the national level no federal official or collection of officials—neither the president nor any number of senators or members of the House of Representatives—can claim to represent, or can be said to represent, *"the people in their collective capacity."* The key to successful representation, or to use Madison's term, the pivot on which it turns, is this country's "extensive territory." As he says, "It cannot be believed that any form of representation could have succeeded within the narrow limits occupied by the democracies of Greece."

Within the limits of a small territory and a small population, representatives might become popular by practicing the "vicious arts by which elections are too often carried," and then use that popularity to betray the interests of the people. In saying this (in *Federalist* 10) Madison has in mind bribery and demagoguery. Or, on the other hand, they might simply serve as tools of local factions and prejudices, one of the "diseases" typical of direct democracies.

Representation will work well only in a large republic, or within the enlarged orbit, which compels districting and, moreover, lends itself to larger districts. With larger districts comes a larger number of fit candidates, thus making it more difficult for "unworthy candidates to practice with success [those] vicious arts"; and, moreover, the larger the district, the greater the variety of interests within it, thus reducing the representative's dependence on any particular one. And finally, the larger the country, the greater the variety of interests, thus making it "less probable that a majority of the whole will have a common motive to invade the rights of other citizens." In fact, districting can be said to be the key to the benefits of representation, and districting comes with size. If it does not prevent, it surely does inhibit the assembling of a simple majority of the whole people, the sort of majority that would then elect an American equivalent of the wholly dependent Archons, Ephori, or Tribunes. American majorities will be coalitions. Representation, which promotes such majorities, is intended to be a substitute for direct or "pure" democracy or any system approximating it. It is another way of constitutionalizing democracy.

Republican government requires the forming of majorities, and what is done by government—whether or not it abuses its powers—depends on the character of the majorities formed. What has to be found—"the great object to which our inquiries are directed," as Madison puts it in *Federalist* 10—is some way of securing "the public good and private rights" from a factious majority, and doing so while preserving "the spirit and the form of popular government." What he found was the "scheme of representation." Under this scheme, and distinguishing it from a "pure democracy," government is delegated to a small number of citizens elected by the rest and extends over a "greater number of citizens and greater sphere of country."

In a word, the purpose of representation is to promote or permit government by constitutional rather than simple majorities, majorities assembled not from among the people but from among their representatives. The elected are more likely than the electors to be persons with "enlightened views and virtuous sentiments [that] render them superior to local prejudices," and, seeing the great variety of interests represented in the Congress, they are more likely to be amenable to compromise. Moreover, the majority required to legislate will somehow have to be constructed, and there are rules of order governing this process, rules governing behavior as well as procedure. These rules encourage accommodation. For example, they require debate, which implies on the part of those participating in it a capacity and willingness to be persuaded, persuaded by another with an equal right to form the majority or to be part of it, with an equally legitimate interest, and, perhaps, with a superior argument. And it implies, and even encourages, the willingness to abide by the vote of the majority assembled. The importance of this cannot be exaggerated. Those who participate in this process are not permitted to overlook, because the rules require them to recognize, the right of every representative to be part of the majority, or to overlook the fact that the purpose of forming a majority is to govern. Free government especially is not a simple business, as representatives will come to realize as they seek the consent of those with different interests. This is calculated to affect the

143

speeches they make. Thus, representative government is characterized by speech whose purpose is to gain the consent of others.

This right to speak with a view to gaining consent is given constitutional protection in Article I: "For any Speech or Debate in either House," reads the relevant sentence in section 6 of the article, "they [senators and representatives] shall not be questioned in any other Place." Clearly, with this provision as well as with those directly affecting the election of members, the Framers hoped to put some distance—but some "republican" distance—between the people and their representatives.

Representation, chief among the discoveries of the new science of politics, made this possible; as I pointed out above, it was understood to be a substitute for simple, or "pure" democracy. It was also intended to be a substitute for ruling, but that is a subject to be pursued in the next chapter.

Conclusion

The fundamental soundness of this constitutional system has been demonstrated in and by our history, and nowhere more dramatically than on those occasions when it has failed. The single-issue division in 1798 between "Francophiles" and "Monocrats" produced the Alien and Sedition Laws, the latter of which especially is commonly held to be one of the most egregious denials of the freedom of speech and press ever enacted by Congress. The fact is that Congress's speech and press record is not as good as the absence of Supreme Court decisions might suggest. In 1835, President

144

Andrew Jackson called upon Congress to enact a criminal statute prohibiting "the circulation in Southern States, through the mail, of incendiary publications intended to instigate the slaves to insurrection." After a long and acrimonious debate, Congress refused to enact the bill, or the even more objectionable substitute measure introduced by Senator John C. Calhoun, but this proved to be only a nominal victory for First Amendment rights. Postmasters in Southern states simply refused to deliver antislavery newspapers, and no action was taken against them.[23] Then in the Civil War, when the division on the slavery issue threatened to divide the country permanently, newspapers were shut down, persons were held in jail without being brought to trial, civilians were tried by military courts, and, to mention one more example of a right abridged, property was confiscated.

These systemic failures have a common cause. The denial at the beginning of the black man's fundamental right not to be governed without his consent made it almost inevitable that he would later be denied his other rights, including his right to be represented in constitutional majorities. The consequence was that he remained a slave, and, as time passed, what was required to keep him a slave was the formation of a single-issue party. The consequences of this were felt by everyone.

All this might have been and could have been anticipated. In *Federalist 53*, Madison expressed his confidence that an increased intercourse among the different states would lead to "a general assimilation of their manners and laws," but it is only in our time that Georgia has come to resemble Pennsylvania, the Sun Belt, in essential respects, New England. Again, in *Federalist 56*, he predicted that the changes

145

of time on the comparative situation of the different states "will have an assimilating effect."

> The changes of time on the internal affairs of the States, taken singly, will be just the contrary. At present some of the States are little more than a society of husbandmen. Few of them have made much progress in those branches of industry which give a variety and complexity to the affairs of the nation. These, however, will in all of them be the fruits of a more advanced population; and will require, on the part of each State, a fuller representation.

That is, the states will, in time, come to resemble each other insofar as each state becomes economically more diverse. And when that happens, its representatives in Congress will each represent more than a single interest. What was required for the Framers' system to work was not only an "extensive territory," or, to refer once again to the formulation found in *Federalist* 9, an enlarged "ORBIT within which such systems are to revolve," but an industrialized territory, and especially an industrialized South. Only then might the South, and with it the nation, escape the curse of single-issue or factional politics. Only then would constitutional democracy be viable.

CHAPTER IV

Constitutionalism
and the
Religious Problem

‖‖

That truly eminent Victorian, Thomas Babington Macaulay, once had occasion to contrast the thought of Plato and that of Francis Bacon, taking the former as the exemplar of the old or premodern philosophy and the latter of the new or modern. He came up with this striking formulation: "The aim of the Platonic philosophy," he wrote, "was to raise us far above vulgar wants. The aim of the Baconian philosophy was to supply our vulgar wants. The former aim was noble; but the latter was attainable."[1] What he said of the Platonic might also be said of all premodern thought, philosophic and religious alike, by which I mean all thought that was not mathematical or scientific in the narrow sense in which we use that term today. Its focus was on the question of how one should live, or what is the good life, or what is happiness and how is it attained, or what is required for salvation or admission to the Kingdom of Heaven. In one form or another, and whether asked by Plato or Augustine, Aristotle or Aquinas, this was the question that animated serious inquiry up until the onset of modernity, and Macaulay suggests that it could not be answered, at least not to everyone's satisfaction. It had to do with the soul's needs, rather than the body's, for it was (and is) the soul that yearns for friends, for happiness, for salvation, or, to translate this into the language and world of politics, for justice, but the soul's needs are not manifest.

The body's needs or "wants" are otherwise—Macaulay is not unique in referring to them as "vulgar"—and whatever the case in the past, philosophy, particularly political philosophy, now knew how to satisfy them. The old philosophers described the path leading to the good and noble, which they defined in their various ways. As Macaulay says, they began in words and ended in words—even "noble words"—but they left the world "as wicked and as ignorant as they found it." The new philosophy, on the other hand, made it possible to build steam engines, to span great rivers, to conquer disease, to mitigate pain, to increase the fertility of the soil, and to light up the night "with the splendour of the day." Then, as if in response to one of the soul's demands, it promoted the cause of liberty or free government and, to that end, devised institutions facilitating the growth of the economy, it being understood by Adam Smith and others that material wealth not only was needed to supply the goods of the body but was a necessary (if not a sufficient) condition of achieving and maintaining that liberty. For example, it was understood to be a necessary condition of pursuing happiness with any prospect of success, and, for reasons related to the difference between the old philosophy and the new, this is a happiness that everyone defines and must define for himself. We modern, post-Baconian men want physical comfort, true, but we also want liberty, and mean by it mostly the right to be left alone by government. This is not what the ancients appeared to want; it is certainly not what was promised by their philosophy or delivered by their governments. For that difference—in our lives and in our politics—we can thank Francis Bacon and the more obviously political philosophers who followed him.

The difference is reflected even in our familiar political speech. We speak of the Reagan (Carter, Roosevelt, Lincoln, Washington) "administration" and eschew the use of the term "government," as in "Thatcher (Churchill, Baldwin, Gladstone, Pitt) government" or "Mitterand (Giscard, Pompidou, de Gaulle, Clemenceau) government"; and only somewhat hidden in that usage is the idea that we, unlike the subjects of governments founded originally on older principles, are not governed. We govern ourselves, and our public officials administer. "Government," as Professor Herbert Storing put it in his last published work, "[is] no longer seen as directing and shaping human existence, but as having the much narrower (though indispensable) function of facilitating the peaceful enjoyment of the private life. In this view, government and the whole public sphere are decisively instrumental; government is reduced to administration."[2] We do not admit to being governed, and we emphatically deny that we are ruled. That being the case, we no longer ask the old political question of who should rule. Our answer to that would be, no one; government is supposed to leave us alone.

But the old political science spoke without apology of governing or ruling. It did so partly because the political world it had to deal with was composed of rulers and would-be rulers; the various elements constituting that world—the people, the aristocracy, the royalty, the priests, or whatever—each claimed not a share of political power but the whole of it. Each claimed the right not merely to hold office in the society but to shape it (and shape the lives of the people composing it) and shape it according to its peculiar or characteristic view of justice. As the leading authority on this subject has written, "Ruling is what all governments did and admitted to before the modern doctrine of representation was born."[3] But the fact that they all did it does not imply that they all did it alike. Governments differed in their principles and, therefore, in the character of their rule, in the shape they imposed on their societies and in the kind of men they honored. An Athens ruled by kings differed radically from an Athens ruled by the people; Aristotle said simply it was a different city.

On the whole, these various regimes—democracy, oligarchy, aristocracy, monarchy—were incompatible one with another; they certainly could not readily be mixed or combined. Aristotle might delineate the elements of what he called a "polity," a form of government combining democracy and oligarchy, but actual regimes built on this model have seldom if ever been seen. In his sketch, it is not a balance of classes of the sort praised by Blackstone and elaborated by Montesquieu but, rather, a blending—accomplished by a modest property qualification, for example—of the rich and the poor, the few and the many. It is rule—or would be rule—by the middle class, who, it was hoped, would be more moderate than the partisan elements of which it is composed. Unlike an oligarchy, this middle-class polity would not be inclined to deprive the people of their liberty; unlike a democracy, it would not be inclined to deprive the rich of their property. Besides, its moderation causes it—or would cause it—to resemble, however faintly, an aristocracy or rule by the *aristoi*, the best.

Unfortunately, as I indicated above, "the properly mixed or balanced rule of partisans has seldom if ever appeared outside the pages of Aristotle,"[4] a fact duly noted by Hamilton in *Federalist* 9. The history—the real history—of the petty republics of Greece and Italy, he tells us, reveals occasional moments of "calm" and sometimes even of "felicity," but these moments are brief and are soon "overwhelmed by the tempestuous waves of sedition and party rage." And by party rage, Hamilton means the battle between these various and in practice unblendable partisans of oligarchy, monarchy, aristocracy, theocracy, or, and not to be overlooked, democracy. Precisely because each group claimed that its principle and only its principle was just, and on that basis claimed the right to impose its rule on the whole society, each group was a seditious group in any place where it was not in power. As Hamilton noted, partnership and sedition went hand in hand.

The new political science sought to rid the world of this sort of partnership—or of what Tocqueville was later to call "great parties"—and of the sedition, and of the strife and warfare that so frequently accompanied it. It hoped to do this by somehow persuading these partisans to give up their desire to rule the whole society in exchange for the right merely to be represented. As I indicated in the previous chapter, in addition to being a substitute for simple or "pure" democracy, representation was intended to be a substitute for ruling.

151

Seen in this context, representation is obviously connected to—in fact, derives from—the right of self-government. That right is fundamental because it is natural, and it is natural because, as we learn from Hobbes and Locke among others, nature itself provides no governor or ruler; contrary to the claims made in the past, by nature no one is entitled to rule another. It follows that everyone has an equal right to rule himself. The essential role or place of representation in the structure of constitutional government can be clarified (and emphasized) by restating this conclusion as follows: By nature everyone has an equal right *not* to be ruled, and representation is the way of securing it.

Persuading partisans to renounce ruling in favor of representation is not easy, but once accomplished the difference between the two systems is easily discerned: a representative government is one that leaves its people alone, but not in the sense of neglecting them. It leaves them alone by limiting itself to securing their rights without prescribing "how these rights should be exercised."[5] Ignoring for the moment the exceptions and qualifications, such a government will secure the property right without regard to the kind and amount of property acquired or the use to which it is put; it will secure the right to speak or publish without regard to what is said or printed; and it will secure the right to worship without regard to the forms of worship or its objects.

Because religious passions are the most difficult to harness, the right to worship has proved to be the most difficult to secure. It did not matter to Jefferson whether his neighbor said there are twenty gods or no God—it neither picked his pocket, he said, nor broke his leg[6]—but he had a hard time persuading his fellow Virginians to adopt the same generous view. And in this respect Virginians were not unique; religious enthusiasts could (and can) be found almost everywhere, and almost everywhere they are the most zealous of partisans. It is not in their nature to be satisfied with being represented; in Constantine's Rome or Calvin's Geneva, Belfast or Tehran, they want to rule.

THE RELIGIOUS PROBLEM

By Tocqueville's time, according to his own testimony, America had in fact largely succeeded in ridding itself of the kind of extreme partisanship that makes representative government impossible.* Americans were, in Jefferson's words, all republicans and all federalists, by which he meant, all members of that party to end parties. But this had not always been the case here; we had representatives before we had representative government and constitutions, even written constitutions, before we had constitutional government. The fact that a constitution is written is no guarantee that the government instituted by it is one of limited powers; proof of this is provided by the Soviet Union today and in 1621 by the "Ordinance and Constitution" written in London for the colony at Jamestown, Virginia. That ordinance required the colonial government to "initiate and followe" the example of the government in place in "the realme of England," and by no reasonable measure was the English government one of limited powers. Hence, the colony's "Counsell of State" and "Generall Assemblie" were charged and commanded to maintain the

* "Thus today [1835] there is no sign of great political parties in the United States."[7]

people of the colony "in justice and Christian conversation among themselves" and also to advance "the honor and service of Almightie God and the enlargement of His Kingdome amongste [the] heathen people."[8]

It was, of course, precisely this sort of proselytizing that led some Englishmen to become colonists in the first place, but the governments they themselves originally established here were typically not of limited scope or reach. When, for example, the eponymous William Penn settled his colony in 1682, he brought with him a "Preface to the Frame of Government" in which he explained the purpose to be served by his government. Viewed from the perspective of the convention that was to assemble in his city a century later, Penn's purposes may not have been antique or medieval, but they were surely not modern. As he saw it, government was "a part of religion itself, a thing sacred in its institution and end." His government was to be "shaped" by his ends, and his ends were shaped in part by "his theology of sin," as Kurland and Lerner put it.[9]

But a constitution of government properly so called can have nothing to do with sin. Of necessity, it will have to engage in what Penn called "the coarsest part" of governing—punishing "evil-doers"—but it will do so only if the evil they do is officially described as criminal behavior. It may not, however, follow Penn's instruction to "cherish those who do well," not as he meant this. To do so would require it to define doing-well, ultimately to define happiness and to act on the basis of that definition; and this, as I have emphasized more than once, it may not do—it may not properly do. Constitutional government leaves men alone to the extent that it can; it certainly does not meddle in their private lives, and it gives an extensive definition of what is properly private. Not so with governments claiming to rule by the grace of God: they meddle. Vestiges of such governments and their characteristic laws and ordinances were still extant in America in 1787, and, as Jefferson learned, to the extent to which those laws and ordinances were enforced or, worse, willingly obeyed, constitutional government was made difficult.

Whatever the case with the totalitarian "big brothers" of the twentieth century—Hitler and Stalin and his successors, for the conspicuous examples—the most officious meddlers have historically not been tyrants; tyrants, at least of the old-fashioned sort, were content to govern the bodies of their subjects, not their souls. They had no need or reason to govern souls. The most officious meddlers have traditionally been governments claiming a divine mission of one sort or another, and in the West that mattered for America the worst offenders were one variety or another of Christian (and the problem was exacerbated precisely because there was more than one variety): Charles I, who set off a half-century of civil war and revolution when he determined to impose the Book of Common Prayer and the Anglican episcopacy on the Scots; then the Puritan Lord Protector Oliver Cromwell; and finally James II, whose dream of a Roman Catholic Britain came to a bloody end in 1690 at the Battle of the Boyne, a battle whose repercussions can still be felt and (especially in the northern counties of Ireland) still suffered. Then there were Fifth Monarchy men, Rye House plots, and alleged "Popish plots"; there were Dissenters persecuted for refusing to worship in the prescribed manner and still others who were hanged for daring to defend the Dissenters; and worst of all, there was the notorious chief justice, George

Jeffreys, who denounced the sweet-souled Richard Baxter as a rogue, a schismatical knave, a hypocritical villain who hated the Anglican liturgy and "would have nothing but long-winded cant without book." Constitutionalism grew out of this experience and was intended to preclude its recurrence; its seventeenth-century sponsors intended it as the solution to what they saw as the religious problem.

Constitutional government requires an enlightened people, and enlightenment required, first of all, exposing the pretensions of those who claimed some God-given title to rule other men. By this time, thanks to the "[spreading] light of science," Jefferson was confident that this had been largely accomplished, at least (he thought) in America. Science had opened American eyes to the palpable truth "that the mass of mankind has not been born with saddles on their backs, nor a favored few [born] booted and spurred, ready to ride them legitimately, by the grace of God."[10] These words were made famous by Jefferson but they were not original with him; they were first uttered in 1685 by Richard Rumbold, a soldier in the religious wars (risings, plots, counterplots) that followed the Restoration of Charles II in 1660, and a victim—although not exactly an innocent victim—of James II, who did indeed claim to be booted and spurred by God to ride the likes of Rumbold. In fact, Rumbold uttered them* as he mounted the scaffold where he was hanged, drawn, and (after the fashion of the day) quartered. He was, of course, merely one of many thousands of the English, Scottish, and Irish who lost their lives in the religious wars that began when Charles I and

---

* "He never would believe that Providence had sent a few men into the world ready booted and spurred to ride, and millions ready saddled and bridled to be ridden."[11]

William Laud, the Archbishop of Canterbury, mounted their ill-conceived effort to force the Scots, for one, to worship in the Anglican manner. Ill-conceived and, as it turned out, ill-fated, but not illogical. Like the other kings and queens of England, Charles claimed to rule by the grace of God, and he exercised powers commensurate with that claim and with that terrible responsibility.

Successfully to rebut that claim—with the hope of defeating such projects—it is not enough to show, as Locke does in the *First Treatise*, that, contrary to the argument of Sir Robert Filmer, Adam had no dominion over the world, "either by natural right of fatherhood or by positive donation from God,"[12] or, if he had, that this authority had not been inherited by the Stuart kings of England. The essence of the problem for constitutionalism is not whether this or that king or queen rules by the grace of God, but whether God has provided rule for mankind. If He has, then even a democratically elected government is obliged to model its rule on God's providence; then every commonwealth, whatever its form of government, is properly a religious commonwealth, whether Jewish, Christian, or Muslim. And such commonwealths do not leave their peoples alone. To meet this problem, therefore, it was necessary to undermine the authority of revealed religion, which, in the Europe of the seventeenth century, meant the authority of Scripture and, especially, of the New Testament. There, as Locke said, "in the multitude of miracles he did before all sorts of people," is contained the proof of Jesus's authority, and where "the miracle is admitted, the doctrine cannot be rejected." And where the doctrine is accepted, the political consequences follow, among them the impossibility of constitutional government as we know it. And knowing that, it comes as no surprise to learn that the three most influential natural-right political philosophers of the seventeenth century, Hobbes, Locke, and Spinoza, each wrote a discourse on miracles, and each, like Locke's from which the passage quoted above is taken, is a critique intended to demonstrate that God cannot be known from miracles.[13]

How the religious problem was understood by the Framers a century later may be evident in this passage taken from a letter written by Madison to Jefferson shortly after the close of the constitutional convention:

> When indeed Religion is kindled into enthusiasm, its force like that of other passions is increased by the sympathy of a multitude. But enthusiasm is only a temporary state of Religion, and whilst it lasts will hardly be seen with pleasure at the helm [of state]. Even in its coolest state, it has been much oftener a motive to oppression than a restraint from it.[14]

And among the public documents addressed to this problem, none was of greater consequence than the Virginia Statute for Religious Freedom. Historian Bernard Bailyn, no mean authority on such matters, goes so far as to say it is the "most important document in American history, bar none." Drafted originally by Jefferson in 1777, debated but not adopted in 1779, and, thanks in large measure to the persistence of Madison, finally adopted in January 1786, the statute owes its ideas and even its principal formulations to John Locke's famous *Letter Concerning Toleration*. Journalists, and sometimes even a scholar or two, may question the extent to which Jefferson was indebted to Locke for his political theory,[15] but as S. Gerald Sandler writes,

"There can be little doubt of his indebtedness to Locke for his ideas on religious toleration." Jefferson had not only read Locke's *Letter*, but had taken careful notes on it—notes which have been preserved—and, as Sandler demonstrates, these notes, bearing Locke's teaching, found their way into the statute.[16]

Locke himself was a victim of the day's pervasive religious intolerance and, to escape it and to reduce the risk of his ending up on the gallows, he too fled to the continent. He knew Richard Rumbold and was later accused of being involved in the plot that led Rumbold to his death on the scaffold. That plot, or scheme, was hatched in Amsterdam by Scottish and English emigrants headed by the Earl of Argyle and the Duke of Monmouth. Even as they met to plan their military campaign against the Catholic James II, Locke was at work on the project that, in the course of time, would succeed where theirs would fail. In his account of these great events, Macaulay dismisses the military plans as "rash" but, despite this, says it is "remarkable that the most illustrious and the most grossly injured man among the British exiles stood far aloof [from them]." But there was nothing remarkable about this, unless, by "remarkable" Macaulay means, simply, worthy of being remarked. For the subject of his reference is Locke, and Locke's avoidance of violent methods, even violent methods of redressing the injustices committed against him, ought to have occasioned no comment. Locke was a notoriously careful man; prudent is the word customarily used to describe his character. Beyond that, he was a philosopher, not a partisan, and as such he was not a man to be blinded by personal resentment. Besides, as Macaulay writes, "He augured no good from the schemes of those who had assembled at Amsterdam; and he quietly repaired to Utrecht, where, while his partners in misfortune were planning their own destruction, he employed himself in writing his celebrated Letter on Toleration."[17]

It must be understood that Locke's ideas on religious toleration cannot be separated from his political theory; they are very much a part of his political theory, and of Jefferson's as well. If, today, we have difficulty seeing the connection, that is because Locke succeeded so well in separating religion and politics, and, following his directions, Jefferson and his colleagues succeeded so well in separating church and state. In the past, and especially in the seventeenth century, the two subjects were scarcely distinguishable, as Locke, "travelling on the Continent for his health," could readily appreciate.

Locke teaches that toleration is good policy—good for religion and even better for society—but, and of much greater consequence, he also teaches that toleration is founded on liberty of conscience, which, he writes, "is every man's natural right."[18] This is echoed by Jefferson in the Virginia Statute, where we read that "the rights hereby asserted are of the natural rights of mankind," and echoed again in his *Notes on the State of Virginia*. Complaining of the situation in that state prior to the adoption of the statute, and especially of the failure to abolish the practice of treating heresy as an offense punishable under the common law, Jefferson writes that "the error seems not sufficiently eradicated, that the operations of the mind, as well as the acts of the body, are subject to the coercion of the laws."[19]

Liberty of conscience is in fact one of those unalienable

rights to which the Declaration of Independence refers; indeed, since government is forbidden to define the happiness we all have an unalienable right to pursue, liberty of conscience may, in practice, be indistinguishable from the rights specifically mentioned in the Declaration. At any rate, Jefferson's statute and his Declaration are political documents, inspired or informed by the political theory set forth by Locke in the *Letter* and *Second Treatise* alike, and pointing in the direction of the constitution that separates church and state. Such a constitution will, for example, provide (as the American Constitution does in Article VI) that "no religious test shall ever be required as a qualification to any office or public trust under the United States," or, for another example, it will (as the American Constitution does in the First Amendment) forbid laws "respecting an establishment of religion, or prohibiting the free exercise thereof." Such provisions are required to secure the natural right or liberty of conscience; constitutional government, in turn, depends on that right being secured. The question is, by depending on that right, does it necessarily depend on Locke's understanding of that right? Much of consequence hangs on the answer to this question.

The modern constitutional state will not, and the United States does not, encourage anyone to act with a view to saving his soul, nor, in the typical case, does it prevent anyone from so acting. Contrary to what is implied in the title of a recent book, statecraft is not soulcraft, or not properly soulcraft. Which is to say, taking care of souls is not the business of constitutional government, certainly not of the American government, and most Americans would probably regard this as simply the common sense of the matter.

But was Locke expressing what they would regard as the common sense of the matter when he wrote that the "care, therefore, of every man's soul belongs unto himself"?[20]

To say this is to say more than that such care is not properly the government's, although, as the immediate sequel indicates, Locke employs one of his familiar rhetorical tricks to suggest that that is all he means to say.

> But what [he goes on] if he neglect the care of his soul? I answer: What if he neglect the care of his health or of his estate, which things are nearlier related to the government of the magistrate than the other? Will the magistrate provide by an express law that such a one shall not become poor or sick?

Passing a law making it a crime to become afflicted with smallpox, for example, may strike us, and would certainly have struck Locke's contemporaries, as absurd, but by drawing the analogy between heresy and smallpox (and laws respecting them), which is to say, by distracting us with this absurdity, he manages to avoid any mention of, or direct confrontation with, what was surely the prevailing opinion, or the dominant belief, of his time: that souls belong to God. That souls belong to God and that, in one way or another, He has revealed how they should be cared for.

There was, of course, no agreement then—nor is there now—as to the substance of that revelation, but among Christians (of all denominations), as well as Jews and Muslims, there was agreement respecting the fact of revelation. In one way or another—through the agency of Moses, Jesus, or the Archangel Gabriel (known in this case as Jibral)—God revealed His will or His law with respect to the caring of souls. Unlike the entities that seem to have become the object of our current cares ("selfs"), souls are not human artifacts; they are part of an order created by God. We may be responsible for their being good or bad, but we are not responsible for their being; and contrary to what is implied in Locke's statement, we are not simply free to do with them as we please.

Of course, we are free to disobey the law, but not with impunity. Locke may say that the care of a man's soul belongs to himself and, by clear implication, to himself alone, but his Anglican church—or the church to which he nominally belonged—held it otherwise. The eighteenth of the Thirty-nine Articles of Religion read then as it reads now: "They also are to be had accursed that presume to say, That every man shall be saved by the Law or Sect which he professeth, so that he be diligent to frame his life according to that Law, and the light of Nature. For holy Scripture doth set out unto us only the name of Jesus Christ, whereby men must be saved." In short, Scripture reveals God's law on the caring of souls, and salvation depends on obedience to that law; the disobedient "are to be had accursed."

His most Catholic Majesty Louis XIV would have agreed with that, differing only in the identity of the church through which salvation could be gained, and so, too, would his dependent (and the immediate cause of Locke's problems) James II. Louis and James believed that God had placed responsibility for the caring of souls in the priests of the Church, the "shepherds of souls," as they were called; the priests administer the sacraments and, by so doing and while so doing, serve as God's "conduits of grace."

What is true of Christianity is true as well of Judaism and Islam: salvation of souls is believed to have a dependent

163

character and that dependence is anchored in God. Only God can redeem souls: through acts of faith or through obedience to His law, which, in the case of every revealed religion, He has made known to us. The devout Jew, Christian, or Muslim simply cannot agree with Locke that the care of a man's soul belongs unto himself alone.

Nor, I think, can he agree with Locke that "liberty of conscience is every man's natural right."[21] That can only mean—or at least, it gives every appearance of meaning—that by nature man is under no law obliging him to act with a view to saving his soul. How could a devout Jew, Christian, or Muslim accept such a proposition? They may disagree on the means of salvation, but they agree that souls belong to God and that He has, in one way or another, provided the means by which they may be redeemed. To say that "liberty of conscience is every man's natural right" is to deny revelation; it is to say that God did *not* reveal the law to Moses, or did *not* reveal His word through Jesus and make it known to us in Scripture, or, by the archangel Gabriel, did *not* reveal the Koran to the prophet Muhammad. To say nothing more, Locke's argument for toleration is accompanied by a concealed attack on revealed religion. And the question raised a few pages back as to whether constitutional government necessarily depends on Locke's understanding of the natural right or liberty of conscience may now be restated, and restated more radically: If constitutional government depends on religious toleration, does religious toleration depend on disbelief?

At the outset it ought to be pointed out that, despite its title and nominal subject, Locke's *Letter Concerning Toleration* is not an argument for toleration. For an illustration of what it means to tolerate, one can do no better than to turn to the great English statute of 1689.[22] The Toleration Act, as it is known, abounds in contradictions and inconsistencies, but, as Macaulay correctly points out, it managed to remove "a vast mass of evil without shocking a vast mass of prejudice," achievements that can be credited precisely to its employment of those contradictions and inconsistencies.[23] No law based on a clear statement of principle could have succeeded, but, however dimly, the principle is there for those who seek it. For the first time, Macaulay writes, Protestant dissenters were "permitted by law to worship God according to their own conscience." They were forbidden to meet behind barred doors, but at the same time they were protected against hostile intrusion. Quakers, in turn, were not required to sign any of the Thirty-nine Articles of Religion, but the benefits of the act were extended to them nevertheless; they had only to make a general statement of faith accompanied by a sort of pledge of allegiance to King William and Queen Mary and a declaration of their abhorrence of that "damnable Doctrine and Position that Princes Excommunicated or Deprived by the Pope or any Authority of the See of Rome may be Deposed or Murthered by their Subjects or any other whatsoever." In practice, if not all that clearly, certain Protestant worshipers were tolerated; in practice and very clearly, Roman Catholics—to say nothing of "Jews, Turks, and Infidels"—were not.

To tolerate means to allow, to permit, to put up with, as we say; it derives from the Latin *tolero*, meaning to bear or to endure. In this last sense, it means to allow but not without some annoyance, discomfort, or reluctance. Still, one tolerates from a position of strength or confidence, and this is evident in the Toleration Act, which Macaulay praised as "very near to the idea of a great English law." It did not divest the Church of England of any of its offices or signs of its rank and authority; it did not in any way cast doubt on the validity of the established Articles of Religion or renounce the right to punish anyone who refused to subscribe to them. As Macaulay said, "The Toleration Act recognized persecution as the rule, and granted liberty of conscience only as the exception." It was a law in which the dominant Protestants expressed their willingness to indulge—and indulge is exactly the right word—certain other Protestants.

That the separation of church and state derives from an altogether different principle is, I think, clearly evident in George Washington's famous answer to the Address from the Hebrew Congregation of Newport, Rhode Island:

> It is now no more that tolerance is spoken of, as if it was by the indulgence of one class of people, that another enjoyed the exercise of their inherent natural rights. For happily the government of the United States, which gives to bigotry no sanction, to persecution no assistance, requires only that they who live under its protection should demean themselves as good citizens, in giving it on all occasions their effectual support. . . . May the children of the Stock of Abraham, who dwell in this land, continue to merit and enjoy the good will of the other inhabitants, while everyone shall sit in safety under his own vine and fig-tree, and there shall be none to make him afraid.[24]

Washington's is not a statement of toleration—as he makes explicit, indulgence doesn't enter into it—it is a statement of natural right. As he also makes clear, that right had been carried over into the Constitution, where, in two distinct provisions, it serves to separate church and state.

Originally, however, these constitutional provisions succeeded not in separating church and state but only church
and national state, or church and nation. And for the majority of the people who had anything to do with their
presence in the Constitution, this may have been all they
were intended to do. The proscription of religious tests
in Article VI applied (at that time) only to national office or national trust, and any attempt to broaden its
coverage to forbid state religious tests would almost surely
have failed. It would have failed because, whatever the
case with Jefferson, Madison, and Washington (who, in
his farewell address, said flatly that national morality depended on religious belief among the mass of the population but not, he implied, among those with "minds of
peculiar structure [and] refined education"), the people
and the politicians at the state level were not then disposed
to join in some Lockean statement of disbelief, however
disguised. It would have failed because the states, some
of them, continued to have religious tests and displayed
no willingness as yet to forsake them. Delaware, for example, required every person elected or appointed to public
office to subscribe to the following declaration: "I, AB,
do profess faith in God the Father, and in Jesus Christ His
only son, and in the Holy Ghost, one God, blessed for
evermore; and I do acknowledge the holy scriptures of
the Old and New Testament to be given by divine inspiration."[25] And Vermont, in its constitution of 1777, required
this declaration of persons elected to the state house of representatives: *I do believe in one God, the Creator and
Governor of the Universe, the rewarder of the good and
punisher of the wicked. And I do acknowledge the scrip-*

*tures of the old and new testament to be given by divine
inspiration, and own and profess the protestant religion.*"²⁶
Jews of Philadelphia would have no complaint against the
Constitution of the United States, but in 1783 they had
good reason to petition the Council of Censors of Pennsylvania to call a convention to revise the state constitution; that constitution required a declaration that only a
Christian could honestly make.²⁷

What was true of religious tests was also true of laws
"respecting an establishment of religion, or prohibiting the
free exercise thereof." Which is to say, the First Amendment, too, was intended to limit only the national government, and any attempt to broaden its coverage to forbid
state religious establishments and state laws inhibiting free
exercise would surely have failed. In fact, Madison made
such an attempt and it failed. One of his proposed amendments—and the one he regarded as "the most valuable . . .
in the whole list"—would have forbidden any state to "violate the equal rights of conscience," but after being adopted
in the House, it went down to defeat in the Senate.²⁸ Such
an attempt was altogether consistent with his judgment that
constitutional government could not readily be instituted at
the state level, where, for the time at least, politics would
be in the hands of simple (and probably factious) majorities. And most to be feared, because most volatile and po-
tentially violent, are factions "actuated by some common
impulse of passion."

With the Constitution firmly in place, dealing with such
factions posed no great difficulty at the national level. By
prohibiting religious tests and establishment, the Constitution would promote a multiplicity of religious sects, and,
as Madison emphasizes in *Federalist* 51, security for reli-

gious rights will be found in the fact of that multiplicity. Adam Smith explained the reason for this:

> The interested and active zeal of religious teachers can be dangerous and troublesome only where there is, either but one sect tolerated in the society, or where the whole of a large society is divided into two or three great sects; the teachers of each acting by concert, and under a regular discipline and subordination. But that zeal must be altogether innocent where the society is divided into two or three hundred, or perhaps into as many thousand small sects, of which no one could be considerable enough to disturb the public tranquillity. The teachers of each sect, seeing themselves surrounded on all sides with more adversaries than friends, would be obliged to learn that candour and moderation which is so seldom to be found among the teachers of those great sects, whose tenets, being supported by the civil magistrate, are held in veneration by almost all the inhabitants of extensive kingdoms and empires, and who therefore see nothing round them but followers, disciples, and humble admirers. The teachers of each little sect, finding themselves almost alone, would be obliged to respect those of almost every other sect, and the concessions which they would mutually find it both convenient and agreeable to make to one another, might in time probably reduce the doctrine of the greater part of them to that pure and rational religion, free from every mixture of absurdity, imposture, or fanaticism, such as wise men have in all ages of the world wished to see established.[29]

Not only would a particular sect not gain a majority, but the zeal of all would in time be cooled, and Smith goes on to suggest how that cooling process might be hastened. The study of science, the encouragement of "public diversions" or entertainment, and the "gradual improvements of arts, manufactures, and commerce": these are the means of correcting whatever is "disagreeably rigourous in the words of all the little sects," and the last of the three will have the additional benefit of destroying "the whole temporal power of the clergy [as well as that of the great barons]."[30] A people imbued with the spirit of commerce will be less zealous, less inclined to be partisans or to join what Tocqueville called "great parties," and, as a consequence, better fitted for constitutional government. Politically speaking, commerce is—or was intended by Locke, Smith, and some others, to be—a substitute for religion or, more precisely, a substitute for Hobbes's substitute for revealed religion.

The story is told that Hobbes was born prematurely when his mother took fright at the approach of the Spanish Armada to the English coast. As he said later on, "She brought forth twins—myself and fear." That was in 1588, and from that day to the time of his death in 1679 and beyond, there was much in his world to be afraid of: the strife leading up to the deposition and execution of Charles I, the Civil Wars under Cromwell, the confusion (to say nothing more) after Cromwell's death, the Restoration under Charles II, "and the constant struggle for power which continued between king and Parliament and among the various religious groups in England." As this one commentator says, "Hobbes witnessed it all," and if, unlike the thousands whose lives were lost in the widespread carnage that attended these events, he managed to survive—and to survive until his ninety-first year—that can be attributed in part to the "fear [that] lent wings to his feet" and kept him one step ahead of his enemies.

170

It was Hobbes who was persuaded—and who first persuaded those who mattered—that it was useless to protest that men ought not to pillage, plunder, or kill their neighbors, that it was equally useless to preach that they ought to respect the persons and property of others, or that they should love their neighbors even as they love themselves, or that they should model themselves on the Good Samaritan. As Hobbes saw it, preaching morality was part of the problem. For every Good Samaritan produced by preaching there was a score of religious zealots (Archbishop Laud, George Jeffreys, Oliver Cromwell—Hobbes's time was terrorized by such men) eager to do unto others what they understood God wanted done to them, but disagreeing as to what God wanted done. His immediate response to this was to reformulate the Golden Rule. His liberalized version reads as follows: *"Do not that to another, which thou wouldest not have done to thyself."*[31] In brief, leave them alone. Beyond that, he saw that peace and security for rights depended on purging men of their fear of "the power of spirits invisible," which fear caused them to do terrible things here on this earth, and replacing it with the fear of a very visible, temporal, and absolute sovereign, the Leviathan. To this terrible* sovereign men would yield their

---

* "His breath kindles coals, and a flame comes forth from his mouth.
In his neck abides strength, and terror dances before him.
The folds of his flesh cleave together, firmly cast upon him and immovable.
His heart is hard as a stone, hard as the nether millstone.
. . . .
Upon earth there is not his like, a creature without fear.
He beholds everything that is high; he is king over all the sons of pride." (Job 41:21–34)

171

rights, which it would secure by keeping the peace. The Leviathan was to be a substitute for moral teaching, or for old-fashioned (and ineffectual) morality.

And it was John Locke who, accepting Hobbes's premises concerning the nature of men, found the way to avoid his political conclusions. Their passions lead to war where their lives are "solitary, poor, nasty, brutish, and short"? Well, Locke taught, channel those passions and energies of men into safe activities, where they will compete not for dominion over others, not for glory, not for the blessings promised by competing gods, not for those things that cannot be shared, but for a share of the material wealth promised by the "godlike" prince whose laws of liberty encourage "the honest industry of mankind."[32] When this happens, the Leviathan can become more or less invisible; that is to say, he can leave men alone, at liberty. Best of all, he is transformed into the modern liberal state.

If, then, Hobbes's Leviathan was to be a substitute for old-fashioned morality, Locke's commercial society was intended as a substitute for the Leviathan and, as such, was a more benign substitute for morality. Before men could see its advantages, however, they had to be persuaded by Locke, Adam Smith, and the other new political scientists that what they have in common is more important than what divides them; that they share a common vulnerability and, therefore, a common need for peace or, as the Constitution's preamble puts it, for domestic tranquillity. They had to agree with Macaulay that "an acre in Middlesex is better than a principality in Utopia,"[33] especially because they cannot agree on where or what Utopia is. Less metaphorically, they had to agree with Locke that the "great and chief end . . . of men's uniting into commonwealths

172

and putting themselves under government is [merely] the preservation of their property."[34]

THE COMMERCIAL REPUBLIC

The Constitution does nothing directly to encourage Adam Smith's "public diversions," but it does much to promote the study of science and the improvement of the "arts, manufactures, and commerce." In these respects, it might have been written by Adam Smith. Not only does it secure to authors and inventors "the exclusive Right to their respective Writings and Discoveries," and does so precisely as a means of promoting the "Progress of Science and Useful Arts," but it gives Congress the power to regulate commerce—and, as Chief Justice John Marshall used to emphasize, to encourage commerce—"throughout this vast republic, from the St. Croix to the Gulf of Mexico, from the Atlantic to the Pacific."[35] The very size of the United States—great even then and expected to become even greater—instead of inhibiting or preventing the establishment of free republican government, as the old political science had taught, would facilitate it. This was one of the things discovered by the new science of politics. An "ENLARGEMENT of the ORBIT," to adopt Hamilton's phrase in *Federalist* 9, will serve to promote commerce and economic growth. And whatever may have been the case with Jefferson and those Anti-Federalists who attached virtue to husbandry and republicanism to a "sturdy yeomanry,"* the Framers—Madison,

---

* "Those who labor in the earth are the chosen people of God, if ever he had a chosen people, whose breasts He has made His peculiar deposit for substantial and genuine virtue. . . . Corruption of morals in the mass of cultivators is a phenomenon of which no age nor nation has furnished an example." Etc. Jefferson, *Notes on the State of Virginia,* query XIX.

173

Hamilton, Washington, and the rest—knew the importance of economic growth. Moreover, they claimed to know how to promote it; what it required was security for the property right.

Securing the property right meant protecting the right to acquire property and, along with the right, the various faculties required to exercise it effectively. These faculties are possessed unequally, but no matter. Americans at that time (before compassion came to be seen as the first of the cardinal virtues) were not hostile to the idea of private property and the right to acquire it. Madison was apparently so confident of this that he could write—and in a very public place, a newspaper—that the first object of government is "the protection of different and unequal faculties of acquiring property." From the protection of these different and unequal faculties would come (and as we know, did come) not only different kinds of property but "different degrees" of property. It is almost as if Madison—in this most celebrated of the *Federalist Papers* (number 10)— were arguing that the first object of government is to promote an unequal distribution of wealth.

Yet his statement is wholly in accord with the principle that the purpose of government is to secure the rights of all. Madison is acknowledging the fact that the only respect in which men are equal with one another is in their possession of natural rights; they are not equally endowed with intelligence, energy, diligence, pertinacity, or any of the other faculties from which, as he says, "the rights of property originate." To secure everyone's natural right to acquire property is to secure the rights of otherwise unequally endowed men, and thereby ensure that some become rich and that others remain poor, or relatively poor. But it also pro-

174

motes economic growth, and this was Madison's point. By assuring the "industrious and rational"—Locke's term[36]—that they may earn all they can and keep much of what they rightfully earn, the country inspires enterprise and stands to profit from it. In fact, it inspires almost everybody to be enterprising, causing a growth in the common wealth. The first thing that struck Tocqueville on setting foot in America, and the contrast with his native France must have been sharp, was the industriousness of the people. "Everybody works," he wrote his father, "and the mine is so rich that all those who work rapidly succeed in acquiring that which renders existence happy."[37] If Locke was right (and subsequent experience suggests or even proves that he was), an industrious people might increase the wealth of a nation by a factor of a thousand and more; compared with what might be accomplished by a "godlike" prince whose laws encourage "the honest industry of mankind," he concluded, God's original providence was "almost worthless."[38]

As is always and everywhere the case, this wealth would be unevenly distributed, but so long as the government secured the right—the right that clears the path for all, gives hope to all, and, in Lincoln's words, enterprise and industry to all—then our rich (unlike the rich of the past) would have no interest in keeping the poor down, and our poor (unlike the poor of the past) would have no interest in bringing down the rich. The exception to this, and it serves to prove the rule, would be in the feudal South, a fact observed by Tocqueville when he and his compatriot Gustave de Beaumont first crossed the river from Ohio to Kentucky. Writing again to his father, he remarked the difference between the free and the slave economies:

175

For the first time we have had a chance to examine there the effect that slavery produces on society. On the right bank of the Ohio everything is activity, industry; labor is honored; there are no slaves. Pass to the left bank and the scene changes so suddenly that you think yourself on the other side of the world; the enterprising spirit is gone. There, work is not only painful; it is shameful, and you degrade yourself in submitting yourself to it. To ride, to hunt, to smoke like a Turk in the sunshine: there is the destiny of the White.[39]

Tocqueville was mistaken about the amount of work being done in Kentucky—by no means was every white man riding, hunting, and smoking like a Turk in the sunshine—but that does not affect the larger point. In sharp contrast with the situation in Ohio and the free states generally, the life of the Southern white did depend on his being able to keep the poor down, and his destiny was to be brought down by those poor.

Conclusion

In addition to making it possible to realize the benefits of representation, the enlarged orbit would promote economic prosperity; it would do for the United States from the beginning what Western Europe, with its Common Market, has been trying to do for the last quarter century. It would enlarge the opportunities for the "industrious and rational" and might even cause "the quarrelsome and contentious"— again, Locke's term—to realize that they would be better off by going to work. Hamilton states this well in *Federalist* 12:

176

By multiplying the means of gratification, by promoting the introduction and circulation of the precious metals, those darling objects of human avarice and enterprise, [the prosperity of commerce] serves to vivify and invigorate all the channels of industry and to make them flow with greater activity and copiousness. The assiduous merchant, the laborious husbandman, the active mechanic, and the industrious manufacturer—all orders of men look forward with eager expectation and growing alacrity to this pleasing reward of their toils.

The prosperity of commerce, as Hamilton says in the same passage, "is now perceived and acknowledged by all enlightened statesmen to be the most useful as well as the most productive source of national wealth, and has accordingly become a primary object of their political cares." A few years before this was written Rousseau had deplored the fact that while the ancient political thinkers talked incessantly about morals and virtue, "those of our time talk only of business and money."[40]

Their reason for doing so was not, ultimately, to promote the material wealth of nations; their object, and the Framers' object, was constitutional or limited government. By taking government out of the business of promoting morals and virtue, to use Rousseau's terms, they expected material gratification, or comfortable preservation, to emerge as the primary object of men's passions. In the past, governments had in one way or another attempted to suppress these passions, but the commercial republic would be built on them. The authors of *The Federalist* had learned from Montesquieu (whom they repeatedly referred to as "the celebrated Montesquieu") that commerce cures destructive prejudices, that it "softens barbaric morals," that it causes

177

men to lose their taste for personal glory or conquest or desire for salvation, or any of the other things giving rise to disruptive factions.[41] It makes men "soft," but it makes constitutional government possible. The pursuit of wealth can, of course, divide a society between the rich and the poor, but when, thanks to the new political economy, every man has a reasonable expectation of achieving some measure of wealth and comfort, and the safety they bring, this traditional hostility will be muted. Men will be characterized by their interests, and these interests are not mutually incompatible. To state this in the language of *Federalist* 10, in the large commercial republic, the animosity of factions will become the competition of interests, and this competition will be peaceful.

There is one more point to make about property. Contrary to the loose talk heard on the left, and especially on the Marxist left, the property right is not a right possessed by property any more than the right to worship is a right possessed by God. Like the others, the property right is possessed by human beings; it is a *human* right because it is a human's right.

As the term was used by the Framers, however, property meant more than chattels, land, and buildings. "By property," Locke wrote, "I must be understood . . . to mean that property which men have in their persons as well as goods." While, in his account, as I pointed out above, men surrender their natural freedom and enter into commonwealths chiefly to preserve their property, Locke made it clear that by property he meant "their lives, liberty, and estates."

Madison conveyed this meaning exactly when he wrote that, in its larger sense, property "embraces everything to

178

which a man may attach a value and have a right, and *which leaves to every one else the like advantage.*" In a word, he went on, "as a man is said to have a right to his property, he may be equally said to have a property in his rights." And again, like Locke, Madison said government "is instituted to protect property of every sort: as well that which lies in the various rights of individuals, as that which the term particularly expresses."[42]

With all this said, however, it was generally understood at the time of our founding as a nation that property in the narrow sense was intended to play a special role under a government instituted "to secure these rights." Property in this narrow sense was a sort of metaphor serving to remind us of our rights in general and, therefore, serving to protect them all in practice. It is, "Cato" wrote in 1721, "the best Support of that Independency, so passionately desired by all men." The person who can say "this is mine" or "I have a legal right to this" has one of the qualities essential to citizenship in a constitutional democracy. This is so because a right to property—a parcel of land, a house, a room of one's own, or whatever—is a tangible reminder (and for most of us, the most effective reminder) of other rights and, therefore, of the proper limits of government. Those limits are defined by our rights, and without the property right, the entire structure of rights might collapse. Stalin and his successors understood this very well indeed. If government can take that which we can feel, taste, smell and hear, that from which we derive our physical sustenance, why can it not rightly deprive us of other, less tangible goods? That is the point, and that was a point well understood by the Framers of the Constitution.

Religious toleration does not, then, depend on an open

179

and official declaration of disbelief; certainly no such declaration has ever been issued in this country. But if our experience can be generalized, it probably does depend on a way of life from which at least weakened belief follows as a consequence. That, surely, is one of the consequences of a life devoted to commerce. Rather than being a whole way of life, religion, in the commercial republic, becomes merely a part of life, in most cases, a part consigned or relegated to one day (or one morning) a week. Commerce—business, if you will—leads men, perhaps imperceptibly, away from the continuous concern with those issues characteristic of life in a preconstitutional age.

CHAPTER V

Constitutionalism
as Such

||||

Pure democracies, said James Madison, societies where the people assemble and administer the government in person, have been patronized by "theoretic politicians [who have] erroneously supposed that by reducing mankind to a perfect equality in their political rights, they would at the same time be perfectly equalized and assimilated in their possessions, their opinions, and their passions." Madison thought this to be a mistake. As long as men are free to form opinions and to act in accordance with them, even a democratic society—indeed, especially a democratic society—will be divided into interests and parties, and, by allowing the majority to rule, a pure democracy offers no means of protecting the weaker party from the stronger. "Hence it is that such democracies have ever been spectacles of turbulence and contention; have ever been found incompatible with personal security or the rights of property; and have in general been as short in their lives as they have been violent in their deaths."[1]

A constitutional democracy, on the other hand, is a democracy subjected to constitutional limitations or confined in its exercise of power by constitutional forms or formal requirements. Its purpose is not as President Jimmy Carter and other "theoretic politicians" would have had it—"to make government as good as the people"—but to make it better than the people; to do this, as Madison said, while at the same time preserving "the spirit and the form of popular government."

FORMS AND FORMALITIES

By persuading the people to respect constitutional forms— not readily done, according to Tocqueville—America achieved popular government without populism. "Men living in democratic centuries," Tocqueville writes, "do not readily understand the importance of forms and have an instinctive contempt for them." Forms, he adds, arouse their disdain "and often their hatred." This is unfortunate because democracies "by their nature" need forms more than other regimes, and, in his judgment, this need would become greater. Forms serve to protect the rights and liberties of persons from the governing power, he says, and it is in the nature of democracy for that power to grow stronger and for those persons to become weaker with the passage of time. As he puts it, "Forms become more important in proportion as the sovereign is more active and powerful and private individuals become more indolent and feeble."

These passages appear at the end of the second volume of

Democracy in America, in the chapter following his discussion of the sort of despotism democracy has to fear, a juxtaposing that serves to emphasize the importance of the subject and, of course, our need to understand it. That task is not made easy by Tocqueville's failure to provide so much as a single example of what he means by a form, or by a translator's practice of writing "formality" and "formalities" where Tocqueville had written *forme* and *formes,* even though there is (and was) a very common French word *formalité* that Tocqueville could have used if this is what he meant to say.² The distinction is subtle but not unimportant. It is not easy to understand the political importance of a formality, especially when what is implied is "mere formality." (Why not be disdainful of a mere formality?) The typical student today can accept Tocqueville's argument as to the political importance of aristocratic customs and manners—how they served to moderate the "social power" and by so doing protected individual liberty—and he has little trouble understanding the importance of finding a substitute for them, but he is not ready to believe that what stands between him and despotism is something on the order of good table manners.*

Of course, the student is right about this, but the suggestion is not quite so ridiculous as it might at first appear. Forms and good manners, even good table manners, have something more in common than the fact that Tocqueville sees reason to discuss them both in a book about modern

---

* On at least one occasion in our history, bad manners were declared unconstitutional. This happened in a case of a black woman who was convicted of contempt of court because, a witness in a criminal trial, she refused to respond to the prosecutor's questions so long as he addressed her only by her first name. The Supreme Court reversed the conviction, and did so summarily. *Hamilton* v. *Alabama,* 376 U.S. 650 (1964).

183

democracy. The formal way and the well-mannered way are the less efficient ways and, almost for that reason alone, are understood to be the proper ways. Soup, for example, can be efficiently drunk directly from bowl or cup rather than sipped from the side of a spoon, but by sipping it we mark the difference between ourselves and the beasts. Criminals can be lynched rather than indicted and then tried according to the cumbersome processes of law, but by indicting and trying them we mark the difference between civilized and barbarous practice, or due and undue process. Good manners and forms are barriers between ourselves and the objects of our desires, and there is much to be said for barriers of that sort; at a minimum, they restrain us or force us to act indirectly. Constitutionalism has much in common with acting indirectly.*

While similar in their purposes, forms and manners differ in the source from which they derive. "Manners, speaking generally, have their roots in mores [*moeurs*],"[3] Tocqueville writes, and by "forms" he means ways prescribed in law and especially in constitutional law. They are ways of doing properly what has to be done politically: choosing officials, empowering them, making and enforcing the law, and so on, and, since in a democracy no one derives political power from the facts of his birth, these ways have to be set down in law. As Tocqueville emphasizes, forms serve "as a barrier between the strong and the weak, the government and the governed." They are intimately related to constitutionalism.

Constitutionalism is limited government, government lim-

---

* The day before this was being written a group calling itself Direct Action accepted responsibility (or as they would say, claimed credit) for the bombing of a Paris police station. Direct action is the opposite of formal action and, not accidentally, is the way of terrorists.

ited mainly by its forms. It is limited not only by what it is specifically forbidden to do—for example, to deprive someone of his freedom of worship—but also by the manner in which it does what it has to do. Constitutional government is above all government by due or formal process, process governed by rules. Two examples follow, one legal and the other legislative.

There is nothing in the Constitution forbidding government to deprive a person of his life or liberty, but it may do so only with due process of law. It may do so only after a trial at which the defendant is entitled to be represented by legal counsel—by which the Constitution means *effective* legal counsel—and is not required to testify against himself, but may call witnesses on his own behalf and must be given the opportunity to confront the witnesses called against him; a trial in which the government is required to prove guilt beyond a reasonable doubt; and all this (and more) in public and before a jury of his peers. It follows from this, of course, that some criminals or so-called criminals will be acquitted, but that is a risk that must be accepted because that is an outcome that is not unacceptable.

The rules, or the "legal technicalities," as they are sometimes called by persons disgusted with a particular outcome, are not devised solely with an eye to ascertaining guilt or punishing the guilty; that could be done expeditiously with the thumbscrew and very efficiently and inexpensively in our pharmacological age with one sort of drug or another. But as Professor Mansfield has recently written, "Respecting the rights of a criminal is more important than convicting him."[4] The reason for this is not hard to find. The forms of due process may protect the criminal, but, more importantly, they also protect the innocent. The govern-

185

ment that believes it is more important to convict the criminal than to respect his right to a fair trial will adopt means that will surely threaten the innocent and, from time to time, convict him as well. In other words, the rights of the innocent are not severable from, or independent of, the rights of the criminal. One can even go further and say that the rights of everyone are dependent on the rights of the criminal being respected. Which is to say, rights are interdependent, something Americans have long understood, apparently. "The American man of the people," Tocqueville notes, "does not attack [the rights] of others, in order that his own may not be violated."[5] The government that finds it convenient (and is allowed) to deprive the criminal of his right to a fair trial will, on other occasions but with similar excuses, find it convenient to deprive other persons of their right to property, for example, or of their right to speak or worship. Doing what is convenient or expeditious—acting directly, if you will—is habit forming, and it is a dangerous habit.

There is also nothing in the Constitution forbidding government to take property, but it may do so only with due process of law, or with "just compensation" when the taking is for a "public use," or, finally, in the form of taxes. But it may tax only with the consent of the taxed, which is to say, with the consent of the governed. That consent is given formally by a constitutionally defined legislative majority in which the person taxed must be represented—"no taxation without representation," as we said at the beginning—and to levy or collect a tax without obtaining that consent is to deprive the person of his right to property. What is important here is that the process by which that consent is given (or withheld) can be formalized, or governed by rules that must be obeyed if the law enacted is to have the force of law.

This is one reason why John Locke chose to differ from Thomas Hobbes respecting the identity of the authority to which men, when leaving the state of nature and forming civil society, surrender the powers, the liberties, or the natural rights they possess (but do not necessarily enjoy) in that state. In Locke's account, they are surrendered not, as Hobbes would have it, to a Leviathan, a living human (and not merely institutional) sovereign executive, but, rather, to the legislative: "into the hands of the community in all cases that exclude him not from appealing for protection to the law established by it." The implication is that men would be irrational to surrender their natural liberties, or resign their natural powers, to any civil society other than one that promises to govern by means of law and not executive fiat. The community, Locke writes, comes to be governed by "settled standing rules" or "standing laws," or "promulgated established laws," or, as he finally puts it, by "antecedent, standing, positive laws."[6] That point is made time and again. Locke emphasizes law and, in effect, the sovereignty of law instead of the sovereignty of a Hobbesian Leviathan, because in his view there is safety in law, and there is (or can be) safety in the process by which law is made.

This is especially true when the laws are made in an assembly. Despotic or arbitrary government is not so much to be feared, Locke argues, "where the legislative consists, wholly or in part, in assemblies which are variable, whose members, upon the dissolution of the assembly, are subjects under the common laws of their country, equally with the rest."[7] There is, of course, safety in requiring the lawmakers to be subject to the laws they make. But that is not all. Assemblies will have to adopt rules governing the process by which they make the laws—formal rules respecting quorums, time, place, and manner of debates, and the like—and there is safety to be had in these rules. Then, unlike Hobbes's sovereign, the legislative power can be divided between two assemblies, and between the assemblies and a separately established executive; Locke was in fact the first to delineate the elements of what we know as the separation of powers, probably the most formal of constitutional forms. And there will have to be rules governing the working relations between the two assemblies as well as between the assemblies and the executive, formal rules that must be followed if the law is to be law or to have the force of law. Furthermore, as the Supreme Court has reminded the Congress on two recent occasions, statutes requiring or permitting action in violation of the constitutional rules are not law and cannot be enforced. In one of these cases especially, the argument was made that contemporary conditions required Congress to do what it had done, to which the chief justice, writing for the Court, replied as follows: "Convenience and efficiency are not the primary objectives—or the hallmarks—of democratic government,"[8] by which he meant (and should have said) constitutional government. As amended, it is a perfect statement of constitutionalism.

The Constitution is above all a formal document, a compendium of the sort of forms Tocqueville had in mind but neglected to specify. By adopting it and the various amendments comprising the Bill of Rights, the Americans of the Founding generation demonstrated either that they were not yet a thoroughly democratic people or that, in matters

188

of great moment at least, they were capable of acting in a manner that Tocqueville said was uncharacteristic of "men living in democratic centuries." They certainly did not then display an instinctively democratic contempt for (or hatred of) formalized government.

Conclusion

It was Tocqueville's assessment that a democratic people would be disposed to mutter or worse when "legal technicalities" allowed criminals to go unpunished, and that they would become annoyed or worse when their projects were impeded, delayed, or obstructed by constitutional forms or, as they might say, formalities. But just as Americans of the Founding generation were willing to adopt the Constitution with all its formalities, Americans of subsequent generations have been willing to accept its restraints; in fact, sometimes they are more willing to accept the restraints than the judges are to impose them.[9]

Put another way, Americans generally continue to identify constitutionality not only with legitimacy but, to the distress of Justice Felix Frankfurter on one occasion, with wisdom. Dissenting in the 1943 flag salute case, Frankfurter complained that the "tendency of focusing attention on constitutionality is to make constitutionality synonymous with wisdom, to regard a law as all right if it is constitutional." Such an attitude, he went on, "is a great enemy of liberalism."[10] Well, perhaps. Certainly wisdom is not *synonymous* with constitutionality, or foolishness with unconstitutionality, but it is not foolish—at least, it is not simply foolish—to confuse them. In each case, a connection of some

189

sort exists, and constitutionalism requires the people to believe in the existence of those connections, to believe that constitutionality and wisdom and unconstitutionality and foolishness are somehow related.

Madison was concerned about this even before the Constitution was ratified. It was this concern that led him to take public issue with his friend and colleague Thomas Jefferson, who, in his draft of a constitution for the state of Virginia, had suggested that questions of constitutionality be turned over to the people themselves. Madison acknowledged that the plan was consistent with republican theory, that, as constitutions derive from the people, it is appropriate that the people determine whether their terms have been violated; nevertheless, and despite the great authority attached to the name of its author, Madison felt obliged to state his objections—his "insuperable objections"—to it. It was both impracticable, he said, and dangerous, and dangerous because, among other reasons, it would undermine the stability of the government. "As every appeal to the people would carry an implication of some defect in the government," he wrote, "frequent appeals would, in great measure, deprive the government of that veneration which time bestows on everything, and without which perhaps the wisest and freest governments would not possess the requisite stability."[11]

Frankfurter was right to think that a preoccupation with constitutionality tends to cause the people to identify it with wisdom—"to regard a law as all right if it is constitutional"—but he was wrong to complain about it. They will be inclined to make that identification as long as they respect the Constitution, and it is one of the duties of the Supreme Court when it makes decisions and when it *ex-*

190

plains the decisions it makes to promote that respect. It must explain why it is right (or wise) to reverse a criminal conviction obtained in violation of a constitutional rule; why it is right (or wise) to forbid legislative vetoes, even though their use is very convenient; and why it is right (or wise)—even in the face of a federal debt of some $2 trillion and an annual budget deficit on the order of $200 billion—to refuse to allow the Congress to confer executive powers on an officer of the legislative branch.

CHAPTER VI

Deconstructing
America

||\|

The Constitutional Convention had some difficulty settling on the rule governing the size of the House of Representatives. During the debates on August 8, 1787, James Madison is recorded as objecting to fixing the ratio at one representative for every 40,000 inhabitants. "The future increase of population if the Union shd. be permanent, will render the number of representatives excessive." To which Nathaniel Gorham of Massachusetts replied as follows: "It is not to be supposed that the Govt will last so long as to produce this effect. Can it be supposed that this vast Country including the Western territory will 150 years hence remain one nation?"[1] Now, 200 years later, it is appropriate both to marvel at the republic's longevity and to inquire into the state of its health. Has the Constitution succeeded in doing what the Framers intended? To what extent does it remain in place? And to what extent has the Supreme Court remained its "faithful guardians"?

James Madison and the other Framers promised, here in words found at the end of *Federalist* 10, that under the Constitution a "rage for paper money, for an abolition of debts, for an equal division of property, or for any other improper or wicked project, [would] be less apt to pervade the whole body of the Union than a particular member of it." Even after 200 years, one would have to say that on the whole they were right. Those "wicked" projects have been advanced here as they have been elsewhere, but never successfully; alone among the Western democracies, the United States has never known a sizable Socialist party, for instance, to say nothing of a sizable Communist party, and has never had reason to expect that anything resembling a British Labour government might gain control in Washington. In a state, perhaps, and in a city here and there, surely, but never (or not yet) in Washington. The Socialist party slogan in the 1940 presidential election was, "The masses are eager for Thomas and Krieger," but that proved to be something of an exaggeration, to say the least. Besides, as Alexis de Tocqueville may have been the first to note, there is no American "mass" or "masses." "Why is it," he asked, "that in America, the land par excellence of democracy, no one makes that outcry against property in general that often echoes through Europe?" His answer was, "because there are no proletarians in America."[2] Some of the credit for that must surely be given to the Constitution.

That Constitution has, admittedly, been somewhat "democratized" since 1787 and 1791, when the Bill of Rights

193

was added to it. Senators are now elected directly by the people of the states rather than chosen by their legislatures; Congress now has the power to levy a tax on incomes "from whatever source derived"; and the voting rights of not only blacks and women but of eighteen year olds and those without the price of a poll tax have been granted constitutional protection. Given the strength of democratic sentiment throughout our history and the ready appeal of its ideological slogans—"government as good as the people," for example—the wonder is that the constitutional changes have not been more numerous and more radical. For, in truth, while there have been no Marxist masses, no proletariat, America has never been without partisans with a "passion [for] pure democracy," as Madison characterized them, partisans who in time came to be known as populists. The populist remedy for the diseases most incident to republican government is, quite simply and unabashedly, more democracy. To achieve it, they agitate against those constitutional forms that, in their judgment, impede, delay, or obstruct the will of the people.

As Madison could have predicted, however, they have had most of their success at the state level, and especially in the Western states where the various institutional devices of direct democracy are a feature of state and local government. South Dakota (1898) and Oregon (1902) were pioneers in the use of such devices, and not surprisingly, it was Senators James Abourezk of South Dakota and Mark Hatfield of Oregon who proposed to inaugurate an element of direct popular rule at the national level. Their constitutional amendment (first introduced by Abourezk in 1977) would have permitted 3 percent of the voters in a presidential election to put an "initiative" on the ballot at the next election to be voted up or down without amendment, thus bypassing Congress and president alike. Had it been adopted, we would have gained some experience on a continental scale of the sort of direct democracy Jean-Jacques Rousseau proposed for places about half the size of Monaco.

Nothing came of the proposal. In spite of a good deal of favorable publicity and, according to a Gallup poll, the support of 57 percent of the adult population, the Abourezk-Hatfield resolution never even reached the floor of the Senate. A victim of exactly the sort of formal rules it was designed to supplant, the resolution was tied up and eventually died in committee.

On the whole, then, and especially when compared with other places and other times, the Madisonian promise of general prosperity has been fulfilled. Of course there is poverty in America, a disproportionate amount of it among blacks where it lingers as a vestige of slavery and its aftermath; but there is also a growing black middle class, just as there has always been a growing white middle class. Once, when asked for an autobiographical statement in connection with his having been nominated for the presidency, Abraham Lincoln replied that it was a great folly to make anything out of him or his early life. "It can all be condensed into a single sentence," he said, "and that sentence you will find in Gray's *Elegy:* 'The short and simple annals of the poor.' That's my life, and that's all you or anyone else can make of it." But, of course, that was not all there was to his life, even his early life.

At about the time of his reference to Gray's *Elegy,* Lincoln composed a statement in which he attributed "our great prosperity" to the principle expressed in the Declaration of Independence and embodied in the Constitution, the

195

principle of "liberty to all." This principle, he went on, "clears the *path* for all—gives *hope* to all—and, by consequence, *enterprize*, and *industry* to all." That Lincoln was sustained by that principle is, I think, obvious; and that Americans even today are sustained by it is the point of a story told by a former Democratic congressman (and now federal judge). Running hard for reelection in 1972, he encountered and asked for the support of someone who appeared to be a typical factory worker. The worker said he could not vote for a Democrat that year because of the "soak the rich tax" proposed by the head of the ticket, George McGovern. Somewhat nonplussed by this response, the congressman hesitated before suggesting that the tax probably would not affect the worker one whit. "Yes," replied the worker, "but it might hit my kids."

Also in *Federalist* 10, Madison expressed the Framers' confidence that the republican remedy for the diseases most incident to republican government was to be found in the "extent and proper structure of the Union." The influence of "factious leaders" would be confined to their localities, he wrote, and there was some reason to hope that in time, and with the diversification of the local economies, they would cease to gain control even in their localities. In any event, he said, while a religious sect might "degenerate into a political faction" in one part of the Union, "the variety of sects dispersed over the entire face of it must secure the national councils against any danger from that source." That was the promise and that promise too has been kept: no sect, no religious group, no self-styled "Moral Majority" has come close to imposing its will on the nation as a whole. The country has had its share of self-righteous zealots who burn draft cards with homemade napalm or pour lamb's blood on the walls of the Pentagon and has suffered an occasional religious fanatic; but no fanatic has come close to seizing power. The consequence is, the country has enjoyed and continues to enjoy religious liberty.

Having long been accustomed to it, most of us might take this for granted; but the Framers could not take it for granted because the world that preceded theirs had little or no experience of it. That world had known neither the separation of church and state nor the peace that depends on religious toleration. Hobbes, Locke, Jefferson, and the rest might speak of the fundamental right of conscience, but they all knew that securing that right took some doing. It took more than the written guarantees of the First Amendment; securing that right depended on their being able to subordinate religion to the private sphere. They had to persuade us to agree with Jefferson that whether our neighbors said there was one god or twenty, or even no god at all, was of no concern to us or to the government.

But securing that right also depended on the Founders being able to secure the republic dedicated to securing the right. To some of them this meant that when subordinating religion, or consigning it to the private sphere, care had to be taken not to abolish it or neglect it to such an extent that it would languish and die. This concern became evident during the course of the debates in the first Congress on the proposed bill of rights when, clearly, not everyone agreed with Jefferson that it was a matter of indifference whether their neighbors said there was no god at all. Said one member with reference to the First Amendment, we must, of course, forbid Congress to make laws respecting an establishment of religion or prohibiting its free exercise, but we must be careful to avoid any formulation of

197

the amendment that "might be thought to have a tendency to abolish religions altogether."[3] George Washington stated the reason for this in his farewell address. "Of all the dispositions and habits which lead to political prosperity," he said, "religion and morality are indispensable supports." And he had no illusions that morality could be sustained without religion. "Whatever may be conceded to the influence of refined education on minds of peculiar structure, reason and experience both forbid us to expect that national morality can prevail in exclusion of religious principle."

It would appear that most members of the first Congress were of that opinion. Madison's efforts to impose First Amendment restrictions on the states failed in the Senate, and there can be no doubt that a majority of the House understood the amendment as adopted to leave room for state and local support of religious organizations and activities on a nondiscriminatory basis. Indeed, the states were left free to engage in a wide variety of activities forbidden to the national government. They might engage in public education, for example, including public moral education; by way of supporting what we have come to call the nuclear and extended families, they might forbid or inhibit divorce, punish infidelity, require within the family the care of infants, children, parents, and even grandparents, penalize illegitimacy, and forbid the publication of obscene materials; in addition, they might do what George Mason wanted the federal government to be permitted to do: enact sumptuary laws. On August 20 and again on September 13, even as the Convention was about to adjourn *sine die*, he called for such authority. "He moved to enable Congress 'to enact sumptuary laws.' No government [he said] can be maintained unless the manners be made consonant to it." And three weeks later he renewed the appeal. "He had not lost sight of his object," he said.

> After descanting on the extravagance of our manners, the excessive consumption of foreign superfluities, and the necessity of restricting it, as well with economical as republican views, he moved that a Committee be appointed to report articles of Association for encouraging by the advice[,] the influence[,] and the example of the members of the Convention, economical frugality and american manufactures.[4]

The committee was duly appointed, but there is no record of its ever having reported.

Sumptuary laws, frugality, the danger of foreign manners and luxuries: this was the language of the Anti-Federalists, and after leaving the Convention, Mason became one of them. Mercy Warren, perhaps the wisest among them, said later on that it would have been better for the United States to have erected "a defence around her seaboard" and a *"Chinese wall"* along the Appalachian ridges, this to prevent the people from becoming "corrupted by wealth, effeminated by luxury, impoverished by licentiousness, and . . . the *automatons* of intoxicated ambition."[5]

Typically, this was not the language of the Framers; they spoke of rights and the institutional means by which they were to be secured: separation of powers, checks and balances, representation, an independent judiciary, and an extended commercial republic—no Chinese walls for them—and they said little or nothing about moral or civic education. True, when preferring to leave the presidency, Washington called for the establishment of a national university "where the youth from *all parts* of the United States might receive the polish of erudition in the arts, sciences, and belles-lettres," and there was a time when Jefferson would have supported him in this effort; as it happened, however, that university, or at least Jefferson's university, was built in Virginia. Was this the way it was supposed to be? That is, did the Framers expect the states to be concerned with the education of citizens and, more generally, the conditions of republicanism? Whatever the answer, and to the extent that these matters were anyone's business, they were the business of the states, the states and their old-fashioned laws.

The point is important because, with the nationalization of the Bill of Rights by way of the Fourteenth Amendment, these old-fashioned laws came before the Supreme Court, where they were weighed in the balance with the new-fashioned principles, so to speak, and were found wanting. In the process, the Court became a political institution, causing its critics to charge it with making law and its friends to praise it for the sort of law it made. Unnoticed (or unremarked) by critics and friends alike was the inappropriateness of making laws by "creating" rights. Not only is this an abuse of the independence granted the Court by the Constitution, but "unalienable" rights cannot be secured by "creating" rights that have no foundation other than a court's *ipse dixit*.

An Independent Judiciary

Tocqueville's analysis of the national legislative and executive powers in America is confined to a general chapter on the Constitution, a chapter in which he also had some things to say about the federal courts and their jurisdiction. But because the "political power" entrusted by Americans to the courts was, he said, "immense," and to his European readers probably unfamiliar, he thought it right to "devote a separate chapter to the power of the judges."[6] The basis of that power was their right "not to apply laws which they consider unconstitutional," and it was this power, unique in his time, that Tocqueville thought had to be explained.

We call it judicial review, and while the point has frequently been disputed, sometimes fiercely, there is really no question but that the Framers intended the judges to exercise it. What is in doubt is whether this was understood to be a political power, and that depends on how "political" is understood. Tocqueville thought it political because, by refusing to enforce popular but unconstitutional laws, the courts put limits on the power of the people, who, he said, accepted this restriction only because of the manner in which it was imposed: not as part of the political or legislative process but, rather, as part of the judicial or legal process, a process that was nominally not at all political. The antidemocratic restraints were somehow camouflaged or, as he put it, concealed in the judicial power.[7]

Interestingly enough, the system praised by Tocqueville was not the one promoted assiduously and persistently by some of the most prominent of the Constitution's framers, Madison, James Wilson, Gouverneur Morris, and a few others. They would have given the judiciary an openly political role under the Constitution.

The so-called Randolph or Virginia Plan, largely written

by Madison and formally presented to the Constitutional Convention on the first day of substantive business, May 29, 1787, included the following provision:

> Res[olve]d. that the Executive and a convenient number of the National Judiciary, ought to compose a council of revision with authority to examine every act of the National Legislature before it shall operate, & every act of a particular [*i.e.*, state] Legislature before a Negative thereon shall be final; and that the dissent of the said Council shall amount to a rejection, unless the Act of the National Legislature be again passed, or that of a particular Legislature be again negatived by _____ of the members of each branch.

The resolution was debated on June 4 (when the Convention voted to give the executive alone a qualified veto) and again on June 6, when Wilson (with Madison's second) moved to include "a convenient number of the national Judiciary" in the exercise of this power. The motion having been defeated, Wilson and Madison tried again on July 21 and again without success. It is a measure of their determination that on August 15 they made still another effort and, after another debate, were once again defeated.[8]

There was no dispute concerning the appropriateness of judges exercising what has come to be known as judicial review; that the courts would have this *judicial* power seems to have been assumed during the course of debate on this measure. And there was a general agreement on the necessity to impose a political check on the legislature. "All agree," asserted Nathaniel Gorham of Massachusetts, "that a check on the Legislature is necessary." Without a check, said Madison, the legislature will "absorb all power into its vortex."[9] There was, furthermore, agreement on the appropriateness of putting this power in the hands of the chief executive. What concerned Madison and Wilson was that the executive alone would be unwilling or unable to use it.

The difficulty, they thought, would arise from the nature of republican government, "which could not give to an individual citizen that settled pre-eminence in the eyes of the rest, that weight of property, that personal interest agst. betraying the National interest, which appertain to an hereditary magistrate." Personal merit alone might allow a person to gain the presidency of a republic, but it would not sustain him in a contest with the legislature. His firmness would need support; Gouverneur Morris wondered whether even the British monarch did not depend on judicial support when he vetoed acts of Parliament.

These arguments proved unavailing for one simple reason: most delegates were unwilling to give the judges any political power. Elbridge Gerry of Massachusetts said it was quite foreign to the office to make them judges of the "policy of public measures"; his Massachusetts colleague, Rufus King, agreed. Judges, he said, should be able to expound the law "free from the bias of having participated in its formation." Luther Martin of Maryland came closer to expressing Tocqueville's concerns when he said that their role as constitutional guardians made it essential that Supreme Court justices have the confidence of the people. "This will be lost," he went on, "if they are employed in the task of remonstrating agst. popular measures of the Legislature." Charles Pinckney of South Carolina came closer still when he said that "the interference of the Judges in

203

the Legislative business . . . will involve them in parties," a point repeated by Roger Sherman of Connecticut, who "disapproved of Judges meddling in politics and parties."[10]

So it was that the veto power came to be lodged in the presidency alone and the judicial power confined to the courtroom.[11] There, under the provisions of Article III, the judges are not authorized to declare laws unwise or ill advised; they are not even directly authorized to declare them unconstitutional. The only power given them is to decide certain designated "cases" and "controversies." The power to declare laws unconstitutional is derivative; it derives from the necessity to decide a case or controversy in which one party is relying on the law and the other party is relying on the Constitution, and where the law and the constitutional provision are in conflict. This was said by Chief Justice John Marshall in 1803 in the celebrated case of *Marbury* v. *Madison* and has been settled doctrine ever since.[12]

It could scarcely be otherwise. It would certainly violate the most fundamental of republican principles were these judges given the authority to make political decisions. Federal judges serve for life. Because they never have to submit themselves to public scrutiny, they have no right to decide public or political questions. And they were given this independence from the voters precisely because they were expected to make decisions respecting private rights. The judges were expected to stay out of the one area and the public was expected to stay out of the other.

Marshall drew this distinction in his opinion for the Court in the *Marbury* case. "The province of the court," he said, "is, solely, to decide on the rights of individuals. . . . Questions in their nature political, or which are, by the constitution and laws, submitted to the executive, can never be made in this court." Madison especially ought to have appreciated this; he made the same distinction in *Federalist* 10 when he spoke of the need to "secure the public good and private rights . . . and at the same time to preserve the spirit and the form of popular government." Federal judges were denied the power to decide questions about the public good because, under the terms of republican government, such questions can be decided legitimately only with the consent of the governed. The public and their representatives were denied the power to decide questions about private rights because such questions can be decided legitimately only by some impartial body. When deciding questions about the public good it is relevant—indeed, in most cases it is essential—to exercise discretion and to weigh consequences; but discretion and the weighing of consequences may not properly enter into decisions respecting private rights. A court will have to decide whether the right exists—in the Constitution or in a statute—and, if so, what it is; but at that point inquiry ceases. What a person does with the right—for example, how he worships, what he says, or what he does with the money he earns or inherits—is none of the public's business (unless, of course, what he does is "adverse to the rights of other citizens, or to the permanent and aggregate interests of the community," to quote *Federalist* 10 once again).

The public good describes that area where the judges may not intrude, the area where what is done may be done *only* with the consent of the governed. Private rights describe that area where the public may not intrude, the area where what is done may be done *without* the consent of the governed. The situation is confused today because the judges, and more precisely, the Supreme Court justices, have taken upon themselves the authority to *create* rights, and with every right created they have narrowed the range of that public or political area. The constitutional right to privacy, for example, was not written in the Constitution; it was created by being discovered in 1965 in "penumbras, formed by emanations" from the First, Third, Fourth, Fifth, and Ninth amendments.[13] Eight years later, although not sure whether this "fundamental" right was located in the Ninth or the Fourteenth Amendment, the Court said it was "broad enough to encompass a woman's decision whether or not to terminate her pregnancy."[14] By creating rights—and, moreover, by acting as if this were a traditional prerogative of the judiciary—the Supreme Court has narrowed the range of public questions over which the public might exercise its authority.

It did more than that. It began to treat the Constitution in the way the currently most fashionable literary critics treat a work of literature, as a text to be "deconstructed" and then, in a way, "reconstructed," but not interpreted because it has no "determinate" or "decidable" meaning; or better, as a text that can be interpreted but not misinterpreted. The job of the Supreme Court is not to expound its meaning but to provide it with meaning. Its highest function, so the argument goes, is a political function: to keep the Constitution up to date or in tune with the times. "The genius of the Constitution," says Justice William J. Brennan, Jr., "rests not in any static meaning it might have had in a world that is dead and gone, but in the adaptability of its great principles to cope with current

206

problems and current needs," and the Court is in charge of this adaptation.[15]

In a more recent speech, Brennan presented his version of the frequently made argument that this notion of a living Constitution can be traced back to John Marshall, and unlike many another commentator making the same attribution, Brennan cited his source: Chief Justice Charles Evans Hughes. According to Hughes, Marshall said in the *McCulloch* case, "We must never forget, that it is a *constitution* we are expounding . . . a constitution intended to endure for ages to come, and, consequently, to be adapted to the various *crises* of human affairs."[16] This notion that the Constitution is adaptable is at odds with Marshall's well-known statements that the "principles" of the Constitution "are deemed fundamental [and] permanent" and, except by means of formal amendment, "unchangeable."[17]

The discrepancy is real enough, but it derives from the fact that Hughes (and following him many others), by joining two sentences separated by eight pages in the original, simply misquotes Marshall. Marshall did not say that the Constitution may be adapted to "the various crises of human affairs"; he said the legislative powers granted by the Constitution are adaptable to meet those crises. The first statement, in which Marshall admonishes us to remember that we are expounding a constitution, is part of his argument that a constitution cannot specify "all the subdivisions of which its great powers will admit"; if it attempted to do that it would "partake of the prolixity of a legal code."[18] In the second statement, appearing eight pages later, Marshall's subject is the necessary and proper provision of Article I, section 8. "This provision," he says, "is made in a constitution intended to endure for ages to come, and consequently, to be adapted to the various crises of human affairs."[19] The immediate sequel makes it even clearer that he is talking about legislative powers, not the Constitution itself: "To have prescribed the means by which the government should, in all future time, execute its powers, would have been to change, entirely, the character of the instrument, and give it the properties of a legal code." His meaning is put beyond any doubt in an essay he subsequently published in the *Alexandria Gazette* in which, with specific reference to his *McCulloch* statement concerning adaptation, Marshall says this: "Its [the statement's] sole object is to remind us that a constitution cannot possibly enumerate the means by which the powers of government are to be carried into execution."[20] It was not Marshall's view that the Constitution must be kept in tune with the times; on the contrary, his view was the Framers' view that the times, to the extent possible, must be kept in tune with the Constitution. Why, otherwise, have a constitution?

Admittedly, Marshall's task was considerably easier than Brennan's. Not only was the Constitution shorter, with fewer specific prohibitions of state action especially, but the few prohibitions it did contain were stated in what would appear to be much more precise language. There is not much doubt about a clause forbidding states to "grant Letters of Marque and Reprisal," which may be one reason why no state has ever granted one. There would appear to be considerable doubt about a clause forbidding states to deny "the equal protection of the laws," which may be one reason why so many states have so frequently done so. Much the same thing can be said, or apparently can be said, of the clause forbidding states to abridge the "privileges and immunities of citizens of the United States" and of the clause forbidding them to "deprive any person of life, liberty, or property without due process of law." In short, it is the Fourteenth Amendment, and specifically its first section, that has given rise to problems of interpretation and, following in their train, the extraordinary growth of judicial power.

THE FOURTEENTH AMENDMENT

The Civil War was followed immediately by the adoption of the Thirteenth and Fourteenth amendments to the Constitution. The first of these outlawed slavery, and the second—by declaring that "[all] persons born or naturalized in the United States, and subject to the jurisdiction thereof, are citizens of the United States and of the State wherein they reside"—incorporated black persons into that body known as "the people of the United States."

"Who," to repeat the question Madison asked at the beginning, "are to be the electors of the federal representatives?"

> Not the rich, more than the poor; not the learned more than the ignorant; not the haughty heirs of distinguished names, more than the humble sons of obscure and unpropitious fortune. The electors are to be the great body of the people of the United States.[21]

What Madison did not say in 1788 was, "not the white, more than the black," a deliberate omission the Fourteenth Amendment attempted to repair. Now, clearly, blacks were eligible to become part of the people of the United States, in short, citizens; and those born in the United States were declared to be citizens. As such, they were entitled to be represented in the lawmaking process where their rights would be protected. There they might be outvoted, but that is a prospect shared by everybody. At least now, having been officially incorporated into the body politic, they would be governed not, as in the past, as slaves or subjects, but with their consent.

That was the promise, and on the face of section 2 of the amendment it appeared to be a serious promise: any state denying that right to vote and be represented was to be deprived of its congressional representation just so much. The sanction was clear and, apparently, mandatory. Congress by law would simply reduce the number of members to which the offending state would otherwise be entitled; or perhaps the House of Representatives would simply refuse to seat a proportion of the state's representatives equal to the proportion of persons disfranchised. As it turned out, however, although many a state denied or abridged the right, no serious effort was ever made in Congress to impose the sanction.[22]

Nor did Congress make a serious effort to exercise the other major power granted it by the Fourteenth Amendment, that of enumerating the privileges or immunities belonging to national citizenship. Although it has been a subject of considerable dispute, the power to provide that enumeration or specification seems to be crystal clear in the language of the amendment, especially when read in the light cast by one of its related provisions. Article IV of the unamended Constitution speaks of the privileges and immunities of *state* citizenship, and the language carries the presumption that enumeration of these privileges and immunities would be provided by the respective states. Would it not follow, having now for the first time prescribed the conditions of *national* citizenship, and having elevated national citizenship over that of the states, and having then, in the next sentence, spoken of the privileges or immunities of this national citizenship, that the Constitution intended to give Congress the authority to provide their substance? Specifically, if New York may, by law or constitutional provision, declare that one of the privileges of New York citizenship is to sue in its courts, would it not seem an appropriate exercise of the power granted in section 5 of the Fourteenth Amendment for Congress, by law and in the course of time, to declare that one of the privileges of national citizenship is to attend a nonsegregated public school? (A privilege that may not be abridged by "any law" of any state?) As I said, however, Congress never made a serious effort to provide that enumeration, and this, combined with a ridiculous decision of the Supreme Court in 1873, had the effect of rendering the clause a practical nullity.[23]

These failures on the part of Congress—indeed, on the part of the political branches of the government—had consequences that extended into our own time and will extend beyond it. Although now formally a part of the people of the United States, black Americans remained politically isolated, unrepresented in the constitutional majorities that governed the country. This meant that their rights would not be secured by the institutions of representative government, and the problem this presented festered until, almost of necessity and certainly not unjustly, the Supreme Court intervened. Unfortunately, the instruments available to and employed by the Court—especially the equal protection

211

clause—were not well adapted to the use to which they were put, and using them caused them to be deformed. More than that, their use contributed to the deformation of the Constitution.

Read literally, the due process clause of the Fourteenth Amendment imposes restrictions not on state legislatures or on the kind of laws they may enact but on state courts.* It forbids those courts "to deprive any person of life, liberty, or property, without due process of law"; which is to say, when imposing punishments or penalties on *any* person, the state courts are now under a national constitutional obligation to follow the accepted processes of law.[24]

And the equal protection clause of the Fourteenth Amendment, again when read literally, says nothing to the state legislatures, but it says something of real importance to the state executives. They are now forbidden to "deny to [*i.e.*, withhold from] any person within [their] jurisdiction the equal protection of the laws." Governors and sheriffs and the rest were now, for the first time, under a *national* constitutional obligation to provide the protection of the laws to any person within the jurisdiction of their states or counties, whether resident or visitor, citizen or alien, black or white, adult or child, male or female.

Only by distortion of their terms could either of these clauses be made a measure of the constitutionality of state legislation. But in the absence of congressional definitions

---

* Section 1 of the Fourteenth Amendment reads as follows: "All persons born or naturalized in the United States, and subject to the jurisdiction thereof, are citizens of the United States and of the State wherein they reside. No State shall make or enforce any law which shall abridge the privileges or immunities of citizens of the United States; nor shall any State deprive any person of life, liberty, or property, without due process of law; nor deny to any person within its jurisdiction the equal protection of the laws."

212

of privileges or immunities, this is what the Supreme Court began to do toward the end of the nineteenth century.

One of the first so-called substantive due process cases illustrates the point. Louisiana had enacted a statute forbidding the purchase of insurance from out-of-state companies and had sought to recover a sum of $3,000 from a New Orleans cotton merchant who had insured a shipment with a New York company. Whatever might be said against the purpose or *substance* of this statute, Louisiana had not violated legal *process* by adopting or enforcing it. The Supreme Court nevertheless declared it to be a violation of due process. It said the liberty protected by the clause included the liberty to enter into contracts and then proceeded to say, in effect, that the states were forbidden to deprive any person of this liberty no matter what process, due or undue, it followed.[25] Again, to refer to two later cases, there is nothing in the language of the clause enabling judges to distinguish between miners and bakers, or, more precisely, between a law limiting the hours of employment of miners and a law limiting the hours of employment of bakers. The Supreme Court, nevertheless, upheld the miners law and struck down the bakers law, and it did so for reasons having nothing whatever to do with the *process* of law.[26]

In these and a host of similar cases, the judges were exercising a power that had been explicitly denied them in the convention of 1787: they were passing judgment on "the mere policy of public measures." Of necessity, and no doubt out of conviction as well, they cast these judgments in constitutional terms, but the time came when the people (led by the politicians) were not persuaded of the connection. By 1937, having long been "employed in the task of remonstrating agst. popular measures of the Legislature"—

the words are those of Luther Martin in the 1787 convention—they were on the verge of losing the confidence of the people, and it was on this confidence that their power ultimately depended. Hence, when President Franklin Roosevelt threatened to undermine their authority by "packing" the Court with new members of his choosing, they gracefully withdrew from the field. From that time forward, public economic policy would be made by officials constitutionally and nominally qualified to make it; at a minimum, it would henceforth be made with the consent of the governed. What became true of economic policy, however, would prove not to be true of social policy; and with respect to racial policy especially, it would prove to be emphatically untrue.

GOVERNMENT BY JUDICIARY

The "switch in time saved nine" and also preserved the principle of judicial independence, but it could not by itself repair the damage done over the years to the Constitution. Thanks in large part to the Court's Fourteenth Amendment jurisprudence, the Constitution came to be seen not as the embodiment of fundamental and clearly articulated principles of government but as a collection of hopelessly vague and essentially meaningless words and phrases inviting judicial construction. In other words, it came to be understood as no more than an invitation to these insulated judges to make constitutional law and, when necessary, remake it.

For a time after 1937, the Court was disposed to decline that invitation and to defer to the judgments made in the political branches of government, both state and national. To a far greater extent than in the immediate past, statutes were to be presumed to be constitutional or, at least, not unconstitutional; this was stated as a principle in a famous footnote in an opinion handed down in a 1938 case.[27] In that same footnote, however, the Court indicated that it would not necessarily be governed by that principle in all categories of cases. One of the exceptions, it said, might be cases involving statutes directed at "racial minorities."

What followed is too familiar to require elaboration: housing in formerly restricted neighborhoods was made available to black buyers; public schools and then public facilities generally were desegregated; and, to mention merely one more example, the various barriers to black voting were removed. All this and more was accomplished by the courts directly or, in some cases, as the result of their initiative; and it was done because the states, governed by white majorities, had failed to act and because Congress had done nothing to cause them to act. But, again, the instrument employed was ill adapted to the task. The Court's treatment of racially restrictive real estate covenants is one case in point. The covenants—private agreements entered into with a view to excluding (in this case) blacks from certain neighborhoods—were discriminatory but not, the Court acknowledged, illegal. Unlike other legal contracts, however, these were held to be unenforceable: "In granting judicial enforcement of the restrictive agreements in these cases, the States have denied petitioners the equal protection of the laws."[28] But this was by no means evident, and nothing the Court said made it evident. The blacks were surely the victims of *private* discrimination, but if anyone was being denied the equal protection of the laws it was

215

the white covenantors. They had entered into legal contracts, reprehensible but legal nevertheless, and they were denied access to the courts, where, alone, those contracts might be enforced. In short, they were denied the right to claim the protection of the laws, which, Chief Justice Marshall said many years ago, is "the very essence of civil liberty."[29]

No more persuasive was the Court's rationale in *Brown* v. *Board,* the public school desegregation case. The black school children were surely being denied a privilege that ought to have been enjoyed by all citizens, but, as even the most venerable opponents of racial discrimination have admitted,[30] the Court did not make it evident that they were being denied the equal protection of the laws. The Court might have meant that for a state to separate by race is to treat races differently and, therefore—although the conclusion is by no means obvious—unequally; but what it said was that "separate educational facilities are inherently unequal,"[31] a logical absurdity that evoked no comment from persons blandly contented with the result but hoots of derision from logicians and hostile white Southerners. Nothing in the Court's opinion could persuade them that the decision was rooted in, or issued from, the Constitution.

To prove its nonconstitutional origins, the state of Virginia sponsored a project culminating in the publication of a sizable volume of over 700 pages containing the legislative history and the debates in the post-Civil War Congress on the Thirteenth, Fourteenth, and Fifteenth amendments. Careful study of these materials would enable "judges, lawyers, teachers, and students" to determine for themselves whether decisions such as that in *Brown* v. *Board* "comport with the reconstruction amendments as originally

216

understood and intended."[32] The project was, of course, naive in its conception and barren in its consequences. By this time the prevailing view was that Supreme Court justices could not be bound by the original understanding of a constitutional provision or by the intent of its framers, even if that understanding or intent could be unearthed from the rubble of those old words. The good judge, according to this view, does not engage in the hopeless and, more to the point, irrelevant task of trying to ascertain the "true" meaning of the equal protection clause, for example. He does what Justice William O. Douglas was praised for doing: he raises the question of what is good for the country and seeks "to translate his answers . . . into constitutional law."[33] The instruments he employs—the equal protection clause or whatever—cannot be said to be ill adapted, not to *this* task; on the contrary, the (presumed) vagueness of those clauses affords him the freedom he requires to do his job, which is to make public policy. "Interpreting those five little words ["equal protection of the laws"] is hardly a question of law in the ordinary sense," said Joseph Rauh, a one-time Supreme Court clerk and long-time Court watcher. "It is a matter of highest public policy based on history, custom and current public morality."[34]

As those "five little words" had come to be understood, Rauh was surely correct; interpreting them is not a matter of constitutional exposition. Read literally, the clause means that every "person" within the jurisdiction of a state—regardless of race, gender, age, nationality, social status, or whatever—is entitled to the protection of the laws, whatever they are. There is nothing in its language (or, for that matter, in its legislative history) that can serve as a measure of the constitutionality of the laws themselves.

One law distinguishes between blacks and whites, another between men and women, and still others between children and adults, aliens and citizens, the sick and the well, criminals and law-abiding persons, homosexuals and heterosexuals, bastards and (to use Shakespeare's term) "honest madam's issue." Not all these laws have been declared unconstitutional; the Court has not yet held that states are forbidden to make *any* distinctions among classes of persons or are required to treat *all* persons or *all* classes equally. Some distinctions are forbidden, some are not, but there is nothing in the equal protection clause to help the Court decide which are forbidden and which are not. To make that decision nevertheless—declaring some laws unconstitutional and others not unconstitutional—is a political act beyond any committed by the judiciary in Tocqueville's time; it is policy making, and Rauh admits as much when he goes on to say that the "Supreme Court is part of our nation's political process, and the sooner this is accepted as inevitable the better." It has become, against the expressed will of the Framers, a council of revision, except that the president does not serve on it and, because the Court casts them in constitutional terms, its revisions or policy decisions cannot be overridden or reversed.

In his Pulitzer Prize–winning book on the *Dred Scott* case, Professor Don E. Fehrenbacher says that, while the decision in that case represented an effort on the part of the Supreme Court to turn back the clock of civilization, "in at least one respect it had a distinctly modern ring." Like its successor today, the *Dred Scott* Court was not content to play the role of constitutional censor of "public policies fashioned by other hands"; it attempted to do what the contemporary Court has succeeded in doing, namely, in becoming the initiator of social change. "Government by judiciary is now, in a sense, democracy's non-democratic alternative to representative government when the latter bogs down in failure or inaction."[35] Not surprisingly, its most avid friends are of the opinion that government by judiciary is not a "non-democratic alternative," that, in fact, the judiciary is more truly representative than even the Congress and, therefore, that the judges are under no obligation to wait for the other branches of government to "bog down."

Why wait when, according to Harvard law professor Abram Chayes, the judicial process is superior in all respects to the way things are done (or not done) in the legislative and executive branches. Chief among its presumed advantages is that it is governed by lawyers, and lawyers are governed by a "professional ideal of reflective and dispassionate analysis of the problem before [them] and [are] likely to have some experience in putting this ideal into practice." Not only that, but it is a judge who presides over the process, a judge whose "professional tradition insulates him from narrow political pressures."[36] Which is to say, the judge, unlike members of Congress, is insulated from the voters and, for that reason, is better able to govern.[37] As Chayes would have it, the Framers provided a system of representative government because they failed to see the advantages of government by judiciary—either that or they thought the lawyers of their day to be unprepared to assume the responsibilities of statesmanship. Perhaps they thought them to be incapable of disinterested actions. Nothing, of course, could be further from the truth.

In theory, the country was indeed founded by self-interested men who acted in order to secure their private rights; in practice, however, these same men pledged "to each other [their] Lives, [their] Fortunes and [their] sacred Honor." In theory, the country was founded by men claiming rights against each other; in fact, they were men closely associated in families, churches, and a host of other private institutions. In their books, government is created by men who had been living in a state of nature and are seeking to escape its miseries; in fact, the American government was created by men whose characters had been formed under the laws of an older and civilized politics.

Moreover—and it is precisely here that the modern Supreme Court has shown its incapacities for governing—although the Framers (including all the lawyers among them) knew that their principles forbade the use of the laws directly to generate virtuous habits, they did not regard it as improper for the laws, and in practice this meant the laws of the states, to support the private institutions in which these habits had been generated and were to be generated. They apparently took it for granted that states would use the law to support the institution of the family, for example; on at least one occasion even the Supreme Court acknowledged its *political* importance. Here is John Marshall writing for the Court in an 1823 case:

> All know and feel . . . the sacredness of the connection between husband and wife. All know that the sweetness of social intercourse, the harmony of society, the happiness of families, depend on that mutual partiality which they feel, or that delicate forbearance which they manifest towards each other.[38]

No such sentiment, no such appreciation, ever surfaces in a modern family case; not, that is, at the Supreme Court level.

With a view to supporting the institution of the family, and in a variety of ways, the states punish and seek to inhibit illegitimacy; but the Court, starting "from the premise that illegitimate children are not 'nonpersons,' " that they are in fact "clearly 'persons' within the meaning of the Equal Protection Clause of the Fourteenth Amendment," strikes them down one and (almost) all.[39] Only once did the Court, by the narrowest of margins, uphold such a statute—this one prohibiting an illegitimate child from sharing equally with legitimate children in the estate of a father—and here Justice Brennan, speaking for the four dissenters, complained that the majority had acted "to uphold the untenable and discredited moral prejudice of bygone centuries."[40]

Tocqueville, the greatest of democratic educators, could write powerfully of the importance of the woman who, in the family, shapes the morals/manners by which democracy lives, who is allowed to choose her husband and is taught that "the springs of happiness are inside the home," and whose chastity as a young girl is protected not only by religion but by an education that limits her "imagination";[41] but not a trace of these lessons appears in today's Supreme Court decisions. The old-fashioned state laws proscribing obscene—to say nothing of pornographic—publications, are regarded as narrow-minded comstockery that, by inhibiting the liberty to "express oneself," are held to be in flat violation of the Fourteenth Amendment. And with these appeals to the imagination came the "publification of sex," as I have put it,[42] and with the publification of sex comes—well, whatever it is, it is of no relevance and, therefore, of no concern to the modern Supreme Court. Except to Justice Douglas who was of the opinion that obscenity was good for us and quoted a Universalist minister in support of that judgment.[43] One could never suspect from a reading of the Court's opinions in these censorship cases that, as Allan Bloom once wrote, "during the greater part of recorded history disinterested, that is to say, philosophic, men were of the opinion that republics required the greatest self-imposed restraints whereas tyrannies and other decadent regimes could often afford the greatest individual liberties."[44]

Tocqueville again, even more powerfully than Washington in his farewell address, could argue the importance of religion in a democratic regime. "When any religion has taken deep root in a democracy," he wrote, "be very careful not to shake it, but rather guard it as the most precious heritage from aristocratic times."[45] But such a concern is foreign to the modern Supreme Court. Nominally, at least, it allows statutes supporting religious institutions if their purpose is "secular," but in case after case the Court has managed to find that, whatever the purpose of the statute, its "primary effect" is to aid religion, and that cannot be permitted. Government must be neutral not merely between religions but between religion and irreligion, which, although the Court proceeds in blissful ignorance of it, is not at all what the First Amendment meant to the men who added it to the Constitution.

It is not possible to point to a single statement proving that the Framers expected the states to provide the sort of civic or moral education required of citizens in a republican regime, but there is ample evidence that they were aware of the requirement. And it is an incontestable fact that, from the very beginning, the states were aware of it and attempted to meet it, if only by supporting the private institutions whose business it was to provide that education.

By the same token, it is not possible to point to a single statement proving, or even suggesting, that the Framers of the Fourteenth Amendment in the Thirty-ninth Congress intended it to be used as it is now being used—that is, to call into question the validity of state laws providing or encouraging that sort of education. For example, there is no indication whatever that the Thirty-ninth Congress intended to do what the First Congress explicitly refused to do, namely, to forbid *state* as well as federal laws respecting an establishment of religion. Such laws are certain to inhibit somebody's freedom, or somebody's idea of freedom, if only by depriving that somebody of his "right" to attend a public school where teachers are not required to "announce that a period of silence, not to exceed one minute in duration, shall be observed for meditation."[46] But, sadly, when these laws are tested under the rubric of the Fourteenth Amendment as it is now interpreted, the Court tends to expand the rights of republican citizenship but ignore altogether what Washington, for one, saw as its conditions or preconditions.

Nowhere is this more evident than with the so-called right of self-expression. This new right has nothing to do with representative government in general or with the gaining of consent in particular. By this right one may "express" himself (or his *self*) by wearing obscene jackets in courthouse corridors, uttering the foulest of language in schoolboard meetings or publishing it in student newspapers, hanging the American flag upside down or wearing it on the seat of one's trousers or, under some circumstances, by burning it.[47] All forms of political expression, no doubt, but not the sort of *speech* that is calculated to elicit consent, nor, for that matter, is it uttered with that intention.

On the contrary, it is a way of expressing contempt: for fellow citizens, for the country (Amerika), and for the very idea of representative government. "Those who are 'into' self-expression," as one authority put it recently, "do not care whether they gain a point by persuading a majority."[48]

But to persuade a majority, or demonstrate a willingness to join one, is the constitutionally prescribed way of exercising the most basic of human rights, the right to consent to government, or the right to govern oneself. It is the most basic right because, as we know from the Declaration of Independence, without a government to which we give our consent no rights are secure. By "creating" this new right of self-expression, then, and thereby encouraging persons intent on exercising it to the limit described in these decisions, the Supreme Court has—unwittingly no doubt—contributed to the weakening of that basic right, thereby putting at risk the sort of representative and constitutional government that depends on it.

Success in the legislature is measured by the extent to which one's interest is accommodated in the law adopted by the majority, and to achieve that success it is necessary to display a willingness to be accommodating oneself. Immoderate and outrageous demands especially are not likely to be successful, which explains why immoderate politicians are disdainful of legislative assemblies. "Take away that fool's bauble," Oliver Cromwell shouted, the bauble being the mace symbolizing the authority of the House of Commons.

Success in the Courts, however, is now measured by having one's interest *declared* a right, and with the right comes the freedom to be immoderate because, as I pointed out earlier, the right defines an area where the public may not enter. And the modern Supreme Court has done little to discourage interests that are immoderate to begin with. When the Court looks into those "penumbras, formed by emanations" from a potpourri of constitutional provisions and manages to find a "right" to terminate a pregnancy, it is almost inevitable that it will be asked to look again and see if it cannot come up with a right to engage in consensual sodomy.[49] And had the Court succeeded in finding it—and it came within one vote of doing so—it would have inevitably been asked to look one more time and see if it could not find hidden somewhere in those shadows the "fundamental right" to be incestuous. After all, as one law professor said back in 1973, the Constitution protects all fundamental rights, sexual expression is a fundamental right, and sexual intercourse between "blood relatives" is one form of that expression.[50]

But what foundation is there for any of these new "rights"? This nation began by declaring certain rights to be unalienable or natural, and natural because they are grounded in the nature of man. Many an American at the time was familiar with the philosophical works purporting to prove this. Then, because there was a general agreement that these rights were indeed fundamental, we the people were able to institute a government designed to secure them. This was well stated by Justice William Paterson in a case decided on circuit back in 1795.

> It is evident [Paterson said], that the right of acquiring and possessing property, and having it protected, is one of the natural, inherent, and unalienable rights of man. Men have a sense of property: Property is necessary to their subsistence, and correspondent to their natural wants and desires; its security was one of the objects, that induced

them to unite in society. No man would become a member of a community, in which he could not enjoy the fruits of his honest labour and industry. The preservation of property then is a primary object of the social compact, and, by the late Constitution of *Pennsylvania*, was made a fundamental law.[51]

In the literal sense of the word, we were able to *found* a government on what was understood to be fundamental. It is not possible to believe that we could have founded a government on the right to terminate a pregnancy or the so-called right to engage in consensual sodomy, even if some judge or some law professor were solemnly to assure us that they were fundamental. Besides, what could possibly be the basis for such an assurance or such a declaration?

Justice Harry A. Blackmun, whose most enduring legacy to the American people will be his opinion in *Roe* v. *Wade*, the leading abortion case, wrote the principal dissent in the sodomy case. He began by protesting that, contrary to what was said in the majority opinion, the case did not concern a fundamental right to engage in homosexual sodomy but, rather, the fundamental right "to be let alone." But, of course, that argument carries no weight whatever. There is, and can be, no general constitutional right to be let alone. Let alone to do what? To worship? Absolutely. To read? Yes. To waste time? Even that. But to rob a bank? To counterfeit money? To "utter" checks? To make noise? To refuse to be vaccinated? To shoot heroin? To manufacture it? To make child pornography films? In countless ways the law invades privacy, even (with a warrant) the privacy of the home. So it is not enough to speak abstractly of a right to be let alone, and, implicitly at least,

Blackmun acknowledges this in the very next sentence when he says that the Georgia statute at issue "denies individuals the right to decide for themselves whether to engage in particular forms of private, consensual sexual activity."[52] So the question is, what is the foundation for *this* so-called right? And the answer is, no more than the interest that some persons have in being let alone to engage in that form of sexual activity. To say nothing more, not everyone shares that interest—which explains why those who do share it make their appeal to the courts rather than the Congress—and, when it comes to securing rights, that is a fact to be reckoned with.

Strictly speaking, our rights may have their foundation in nature or in a duly enacted statute, but for their security they depend ultimately on the support not only of public official but of public opinion. As I said immediately above, we Americans were able to found a government on the rights to life, liberty, and the pursuit of happiness because there was general agreement that these rights were indeed fundamental, the gift of nature's God; that, we declared, was a self-evident truth. We have also been able to enforce the various provisions of the 1964 Civil Rights Act because, again, there was a general agreement that discrimination on the basis of race or gender was simply unjust. Precisely because they come out of a Congress where all interests are represented, such rights are likely to enjoy the kind of support that makes securing them relatively easy. We have not yet been able, and we may never be able, to secure the judicially created right to affirmative action precisely because it lacks that kind of support; to many Americans, affirmative action is nothing but reverse discrimination.

Thus, a right for which there is no general support may be readily "created" but not readily enforced, and a right that is created in the teeth of profound opposition may divide the community into warring camps. (That much we ought to have learned from our experience with the abortion issue.) All of which explains why the Framers founded representative government rather than government by judiciary.

The Court is undoubtedly under pressure from the jurisprudence currently in fashion in the prestigious law schools to take rights seriously. Fair enough. But contrary to the purveyors of this fashion—in the press as well as in the schools—this does not require the Court to grant interests the status of rights, as if by natural right a person consents to government on condition that his interests be satisfied. This is absurd because it is impossible, and it is impossible because not all interests can be satisfied. For example, it is a fact that the interests of the pro- and anti-abortion groups cannot both be satisfied. Indeed, by making abortion a right, the Court brought into being an organized and frequently violent anti-abortion interest. And that is likely to happen whenever the Court declares an activity to be a fundamental right when it is demonstrably—because it has no basis in nature, in convention, or in contemporary opinion—not a fundamental right. The professor who set out to take rights seriously proceeded to find, in a model of government of his own devising, a fundamental right to disobey the law,[53] which, if exercised by a significant number of persons, would return us to the state of nature where we could enjoy that "right" to our hearts' content—to our hearts' content but within the limits of a life that, if Hobbes was right, will be "solitary, poor, nasty, brutish, and short." And that is the direction in which the Court's decisions have been taking us.

No government, not even the most liberal or generous, can promise to satisfy all wants or interests. What it can fairly promise, if it is properly organized, is security for those rights that are understood to be unalienable or fundamental, which in practice will mean the right to be governed only with one's consent. Under the Constitution's system of representative government, this becomes the right to be part of a governing majority. Such majorities cannot be constructed out of the variety of hostile single-interest groups that have been generated by the Supreme Court's recent holdings under the Fourteenth Amendment, an amendment adopted in order to make one people where there had previously been two.

CONCLUSION: *Quis custodiet ipsos Custodes?*

Who indeed will guard the guardians themselves? The extravagance of the power now claimed by some members of the Court especially is nowhere better seen than in Justice Brennan's actions in a women's rights case decided during the period when the so-called Equal Rights Amendment, having been proposed by the required two-thirds vote in each House of Congress, was awaiting ratification by the required three-fourths of the states (a ratification it never received). The issue in the case, *Frontiero* v. *Richardson*,[54] or more precisely, the issue on which the justices were divided, was whether sex, like race, should be treated as a suspect classification. If so, states would be required to bear a heavier burden when attempting to justify the distinctions drawn in the statute.

> Brennan circulated a draft opinion on the limited grounds, and then he sent around an alternative section that proposed a broad constitutional ban, declaring classification by sex virtually impermissible. He knew that his alternative would have the effect of enacting the Equal Rights Amendment, which had already passed Congress and was pending before the state legislatures. But Brennan was accustomed to having the Court out in front, leading any civil rights movement.[55]

The authors of this account conclude by quoting Brennan as being of the opinion that there "was no reason to wait several years for the states to ratify the amendment"—no reason other than the fact, which Brennan knew to be a fact, that the Constitution *as then written* would not support the decision he wanted the Court to render. Unable to persuade Justice Potter Stewart to join the coalition he had put together, Brennan lamented to his law clerks that he had come "within an inch of authoring a landmark ruling that would have made the Equal Rights Amendment unnecessary."

No statement is more revealing of the contemporary liberal's view of the Constitution and the powers of the Court respecting it. It says, in effect, that Brennan and any four of his colleagues are entitled to do in private—in the privacy of the Court's conference room—what may be done in public only by extraordinary majorities of the states and of the House and Senate. It says, in effect, that the Constitution may be amended in two ways, one difficult and the other easy; one public and the other private; one by following the procedures delineated in Article V of the Constitution and the other by vote of William J. Brennan, Jr., joined by four other Supreme Court justices. Assigned the task of being its "faithful guardians," these justices fancy themselves its parents.

CHAPTER VII

Taking
the Constitution
Seriously

|||

Unlike the first federal judges, whose formal legal education was likely to have been very limited indeed—John
Marshall was largely self-educated in the law and John
Jay, the first chief justice, learned his in an office—today's
judges come from schools where they are formally instructed in the various branches of the law, including constitutional law. There is probably not a law school in the
country that does not offer that particular instruction or
many that do not make it part of the required curriculum.
There is, however, good reason to doubt that many, or
even any, offer a course in the Constitution. It is in fact not
unusual to encounter constitutional law courses that begin
with the Fourteenth Amendment, a practice that is defended on the ground that, after all, the schools are in the
business of training practitioners and the great bulk of an

attorney's constitutional law practice will be in the area of the Fourteenth Amendment.

The situation is only marginally better in the colleges. Jefferson advised students interested in the law to read Adam Smith's *Wealth of Nations*, "the best book extant" on political economy; Montesquieu's *Spirit of the Laws*; Locke's little book on government, "perfect as far as it goes"; and, "descending from theory to practice there is no better book than the Federalist."[1] Such advice is rarely given today, and almost never as part of a curriculum in constitutional government. Undergraduates will be offered courses in constitutional law, but in the typical political science department that is likely to involve the study of judicial behavior or, at best, civil liberties. And there, as in the law schools, that means the study of Fourteenth Amendment rights, with the consequence that there, again as in the law schools, constitutional government comes to mean government within the limits prescribed by the judiciary and only nominally by the Constitution, or by a Constitution kept "up to date"—which is to say, revised—by the judiciary.

The prince of revisionists is, of course, Justice William J. Brennan, Jr.; as might be expected, he is also a speaker much favored by academic audiences—or, at least, by the professors who decide who shall speak to the academic audiences. It was before one such audience that Justice Brennan suggested that the Fourteenth Amendment was "perhaps our most important constitutional provision," more important than the "original basic document itself"; and it was before another such audience that he ridiculed the idea that the Constitution can be taken seriously—the

Constitution as written, that is. Someone had recently suggested that, when interpreting constitutional provisions, the justices ought to be bound by the "intentions of the Framers"; this, said Brennan, is a "view that feigns self-effacing deference to the specific judgments of those who forged our original social compact [but in truth] is little more than arrogance cloaked as humility." Indeed, he went on, there is some doubt as to whether it makes sense to speak of original intention in connection with a document that is jointly drafted. "Typically, all that can be gleaned [from the records they left] is that the Framers themselves did not agree about the application or meaning of particular constitutional provisions, and hid their differences in cloaks of generality."[2]

But Brennan was not being as candid as he would have had his audience believe. The last seven or eight pages of this address were given over to talk about human dignity—he's for it—and, in his only reference to a specific constitutional issue, he amplified its meaning by discussing capital punishment. He is against it; not only that, he insisted here as he has on the bench that it is unconstitutional.

The following litany appears in literally scores of memorandum decisions where Brennan and his closest colleague, Justice Thurgood Marshall, are in dissent: "Adhering to our views that the death penalty is in all circumstances cruel and unusual punishment prohibited by the Eighth and Fourteenth Amendments . . . we would grant the application for stay, the petition for writ of certiorari and vacate the death sentence in this case."[3] But the Constitution is not obscure on the death penalty. This could not be said to be one of those subjects where the Framers, being unable to agree, "hid their differences in cloaks of gen-

234

erality." On the contrary, the constitutional text is crystal clear. It permits capital trials when preceded by a "presentment or indictment of a Grand Jury"; it permits a person to be "put in jeopardy of life," provided it not be done twice "for the same offense"; it permits both nation and states to deprive persons of their lives with but not "without due process of law"; and, in addition to these various Fifth (and Fourteenth) Amendment provisions, in Article II, section 2 (1) it empowers the president "to grant reprieves." The Constitution *as written* permits capital punishment; it can be said to forbid it only if time has somehow worked some strange alchemy on the text. And that is Brennan's contention.

The question is not, he says, what *did* the words mean but, rather, what *do* they mean in our time? "For the genius of the Constitution rests not in any static meaning it might have had in a world that is dead and gone, but in the adaptability of its great principles to cope with current problems and current needs."[4] This is easily said—which is one reason why it is so frequently said—but not so easily done, and not so easily done because there is typically no agreement on what is required to deal with the problems or meet the needs. All sorts of Americans—in the electorate, Congress, state legislatures, White House, statehouses, and courts of all descriptions—have ideas as to these matters, but they do not always or usually agree. Supreme Court justices do not always agree, which gives rise to a small problem. Assuming, for the moment, that the Constitution is to be adapted rather than formally amended, then, surely, the justices should have some say in the matter. But which justices? Here is how they voted in a recent case having to do with health care for handicapped infants:

235

BURGER, C.J., announced the judgment of the Court and delivered the opinion of the Court with respect to Parts I and II, in which BRENNAN, MARSHALL, BLACKMUN, POWELL, REHNQUIST, STEVENS, JJ., and O'CONNOR, joined, and an opinion with respect to Part III, in which POWELL and REHNQUIST, JJ., joined. BLACKMUN, J., filed an opinion concurring in part. STEVENS, J., filed an opinion concurring in part and concurring in the result. O'CONNOR, J., filed an opinion concurring in part and dissenting in part, in which BRENNAN and MARSHALL, JJ., joined. WHITE, J., filed a dissenting opinion.[5]

Time, perhaps, will tell who on the Court is right respecting the problems and prescient respecting the needs; but when "time" and not the constitutional text provides the standard by which judicial decisions are to be measured, the inevitable consequence is a Constitution that can be interpreted but not misinterpreted, construed but not misconstrued. Why, then, bother with a constitution at all? What good is it?

The Framers had a better grasp of these matters. They provided for a Supreme Court and charged it with the task, not of keeping the Constitution in tune with the times but, to the extent possible, of keeping the times in tune with the Constitution. To repeat the words of the great chief justice, John Marshall, the principles of the Constitution "are deemed fundamental [and] permanent" and, except by way of formal amendment, "unchangeable." He was emphatic about this because he had a keen appreciation of constitutional properties, or of the principles on which the entire structure rested. The Constitution derives its binding authority—binding on the governed and the government alike—

only from the fact that it is an act of the people in their constituting capacity. According to Alexander Hamilton, this was common knowledge at the beginning, an opinion shared by all the "friends of the proposed Constitution." Only the people may ordain and establish a constitution, and only the people may "alter or abolish" a constitution already established—and they may do so only when acting in a "solemn and authoritative" manner. That, said Hamilton, is a "fundamental principle of republican government."

By what right would the Supreme Court "adapt" a Constitution that owes its authority to the fact that it was adopted by the people? It is astonishing how seldom this obvious question is addressed by the friends of judicial adaptation. When pressed, they refer to Marshall's opinion in *McCulloch* v. *Maryland*, but, as I demonstrated in the previous chapter, they misunderstand that opinion because they misquote it. By what right would Brennan and Marshall, in the face of those crystal clear provisions, five of them, change the Constitution to have it forbid capital punishment? They say that time has changed our notion of what is cruel and unusual, that as a people we are less sanguinary than we were in 1787, but even assuming its relevance, there is no evidence of this. The polls show, and show consistently, strong majorities in favor of the death penalty. Again, in *Bowers* v. *Hardwick*, Justice Harry Blackmun lacked one vote of being able to speak for the majority of the Court. So, to repeat the question, and this time more radically: By what right does a bare majority of the Court "adapt" or revise the Constitution to make homosexual sodomy a "fundamental right"? Blackmun provided an answer (of sorts) in what proved to be the dissenting opinion: "Like Justice Holmes, I believe that '[i]t

237

is revolting to have no better reason for a rule of law than that so it was laid down in the time of Henry IV. It is still more revolting if the grounds upon which it was laid down have vanished long since, and the rule simply persists from blind imitation of the past.' " But Holmes was talking about the common law—judge-made law—and not about the Constitution. The powers of a judge under the two systems are, to say the least, not the same, and it is "revolting" that a Supreme Court justice does not know this. "It is still more revolting" if he knows it but chooses to ignore it.

But enough; the remarkable thing about the Constitution is how little it has had to be changed or, for that matter, adapted. Since the adoption of the Bill of Rights, the Constitution has been formally amended sixteen times, and only six or seven of those could properly be regarded as amendments to the text (and one of those, the twenty-first, being an amendment of an amendment). Consider the facts:

• Slavery was abolished by constitutional amendment, but, to do that, not one word of the preexisting text had to be amended or deleted.

• Constitutional amendments were required to remove state barriers to black and female suffrage, but not a word of the Constitution had to be changed to *allow* blacks and women to vote.

• Women now serve in House and Senate, on the Supreme Court, and will, almost surely, soon be elected vice president and eventually president, but to accomplish this not one word of the Constitution had or will have to be changed.

• No constitutional change was required to allow "Jews, Turks, and infidels" to vote or hold political office.

That list could be extended but the point has been made. As my colleague Robert Goldwin has written recently, the original Constitution did not speak of white and black, white and slave, men and women, or Christian and Jew; its terms were "electors," "citizens," "members," "inhabitants," "officers," "persons," and "representatives." Contrary to what Justice Brennan tells his academic audiences, the Constitution has not had to be rewritten for our world precisely because it was not written for a "world that is dead and gone."

During the time of its existence, the government has grown astronomically, exceeding the growth of the territory and even that of the population. The population has grown by a factor of sixty—from just under 4 million to approximately 240 million—and the federal budget is now more than 100,000 times larger than it was at the beginning. (The first budget, prepared by a committee of the House of Representatives and reported by Elbridge Gerry on July 9, 1789, called for expeditures in the amount of $8,285,603; in fiscal year 1987 the national government will spend about $990 billion, or just less than $1 trillion.) The Framers might be appalled by such numbers, and might very well object to some of the ways that money is being spent; but they might also find some satisfaction, and take some pride, in the fact that the structure of the government is still recognizably their handiwork.

And were they to investigate the subject, they would discover that that constitutional structure continues to secure the civil and religious rights of the people who live here. In *Federalist* 51, Madison said that in a free government the security for civil rights must be the same as that for religious rights: "It consists in the one case in the multiplicity of interests, and in the other in the multiplicity of sects." Safety, he said, would lie—and it does lie—in preventing the formation of "oppressive combinations of a majority," and that was to be accomplished by means of those institutions discovered or improved by the new science of politics. Those institutions are embodied in the constitutional text, and there is nothing obscure about that text, or nothing so obscure as to defy a search for its true meaning. What is true of the Fourteenth Amendment provisions respecting "privileges or immunities," "due process of law," and "the equal protection of the laws" (and that only because, as I suggested in the previous chapter, we have never given that text its literal reading), is not true of the original and unamended Constitution, and especially not true of those provisions respecting the basic structure of government. Conservatives will want to protect that structure, just as liberals are inclined to tamper with it.

In fact, tampering with it is part of what might be called the liberal agenda. Some liberals, at least, are as eager to abolish the electoral college or the separation of powers as most of them are to abolish capital punishment, censorship, and an unequal distribution of wealth.

But to speak of a conservative agenda is almost a contradiction, an oxymoron. Conservatives certainly cannot simply take stands opposite to those taken by liberals. They cannot, for example, adopt a program favoring primogeniture, laws of entail, titles of nobility, a social class structure,

240

an established church, drawing and quartering, or any other traditional (but cruel and unusual) form of punishment. These causes are denied to conservatives by the Constitution; or better, the Framers of the Constitution deprived Americans of much, if not all, of a traditional conservative agenda. These terms, "liberal" and "conservative," derive from the Enlightenment and French Revolution, and measured by those events the Constitution of the United States is—clearly and overwhelmingly—liberal. The only appropriate agenda for conservatives is to defend the liberal Constitution—if necessary, to defend it from the liberals—because by that Constitution rights are secured.

This knowledge—that, at least so far as the national government is concerned, security for rights is found in the structure elaborated in that text—could be one of the happy lessons learned in this bicentennial season. In a world where constitutions come and go with discouraging regularity, the fact that ours has survived for 200 years should cause us not only to celebrate but to search for the reasons for our almost singular success. Such a search must begin with a study of the constitutional text—"the original basic document itself" that Brennan would subordinate—and of the works, such as *The Federalist*, where that text is elucidated. The occasion calls for instruction in constitutional government rather than in the constitutional law of our times, and there is no better place to begin that study than in the words and deeds of the Founders, including among the Founders the first Supreme Court justices, who, as Ralph Lerner reminded us some twenty years ago, consciously acted as statesmen-teachers, or, as Lerner put it, as "republican schoolmasters" to the nation.[6]

241

Appendix

The substance of Garry Wills's argument in his widely acclaimed book, *Inventing America*, is that there is not one Declaration of Independence but three: the one written by Jefferson, the one adopted by the Continental Congress on July 4, 1776, and the one we know today, which, he claims, is largely a product of Lincolnian imagination. Jefferson's Declaration was "philosophical and nonpolitical," Wills asserts; it was only by tampering with it that the Congress managed to come up with one that was "mainly political." And it was only by romanticizing it that Abraham Lincoln could make it a statement characterizing the nation and marking its birth. Lincoln said, "All honor to Jefferson, to the man who, in the concrete pressure of a struggle for national independence by a single people, had the coolness, forecast, and capacity to introduce into a merely revolutionary document, an abstract truth, applicable to all men and all times," but Wills insists this is nonsense. It was not Jefferson's purpose to proclaim timeless truths, he says, or attempt to set down the principles of popular government. According to Wills, what Lincoln saw fit to praise in the Declaration is not to be found in it, not in the one written by Jefferson.

But Jefferson did not disown the Declaration of Independence as we know it; on the contrary, he wanted to be remembered as its author and, to that end, issued instructions for this epitaph to be carved on his gravestone:

"Here was buried Thomas Jefferson Author of the Declaration of American Independence [,] of the Statute of Virginia for religious freedom & Father of the University of Virginia." [B]ecause by these, as testimonials that I have lived, I wish most to be remembered.

Wills cannot deny that Jefferson composed this epitaph—the original is in his own handwriting—or that it does indeed appear on his gravestone; all Wills can say is that the words do not mean what they appear to mean. Jefferson was not, he insists, expressing pride in his authorship of the Declaration of American Independence, the Declaration adopted by the Continental Congress on July 4, 1776. Not at all. He was expressing pride in, and wanted to be remembered as the author of, his private nonpolitical Declaration, the Declaration before it was "tampered with" by the Congress. "Jefferson's epitaph," Wills says, "is famous for its semi-private character, for its exclusion of [references to] official things like the presidency." And in this "famous" list of what Wills absurdly calls unofficial actions—writing a state law and founding a state university—"Jefferson's own Declaration fits better than the congressional one."[1]

And we know that Jefferson's purpose in the Declaration was precisely to "proclaim timeless truths" concerning the principles of popular government; we know this because he said as much in a letter of June 24, 1826, to Roger C. Weightman, the last letter he is known to have written. He had been invited to join the citizens of the nation's capital in "their celebration on the fiftieth anniversary of American Independence," but illness prevented him from accepting. He said he would have been delighted to meet with

> the small band, the remnant of that host of worthies, who joined with us on that day [July 4, 1776], in the bold and doubtful election we were to make for our country, between submission or the sword; and to have enjoyed with them the consolatory fact, that our fellow citizens, even after half a century of experience and prosperity, continue to approve the choice we made.

As for the Declaration issued that day, he went on,

> May it be to the world, what I believe it will be, (to some parts sooner, to others later, finally to all,) the signal of arousing men to burst the chains under which monkish ignorance and superstition had persuaded them to bind themselves, and to assume the blessings and security of self-government. That form which we have substituted, restores the free right to the unbounded exercise of reason and freedom of opinion. All eyes are opened, or opening, to the rights of man. The general spread of the light of science has already laid open to every view the palpable truth, that the mass of mankind has not been born with saddles on their backs, nor a favored few booted and spurred, ready to ride them legitimately, by the grace of

244

God. These are grounds of hope for others. For ourselves, let the annual return of this day forever refresh our recollections of these rights, and an undiminished devotion to them.

Then, as if to make it almost impossible for his countrymen to forget his special connection with the Declaration, Jefferson (and, remarkably if not providentially, John Adams as well) proceeded to die on July 4, 1826, the fiftieth anniversary of its adoption. How could any American deny his connection with the Declaration or, more to the point, want to sever it?

Why, to be still more precise, should anyone today want to detach the name of Thomas Jefferson from the Declaration of Independence and, beyond that, America from the principles of 1776? What cause would be served by this? Chief Justice Taney's motives for distorting the Declaration in *Dred Scott* v. *Sandford* were clear enough; given its literal meaning, its reference to the natural equality of all men "would seem to embrace the whole human family"—including, Taney was quick to add, members of the "enslaved African race"—and he could not admit that. That is to say, his political program for the expansion of slavery into the Western territories could not admit that by nature blacks were endowed with the same rights as whites; therefore, he and the other justices in the *Dred Scott* majority had, in effect, to read blacks out of the human race. And Alexander Stephens's reasons for denouncing Jefferson were clear enough. Stephens was vice president of the Confederate States of America, the first government in the history of the world, he said, to be based on the "physical and moral truth [that] the negro is not equal to the white man." He acknowledged that Jefferson and his colleagues at the beginning were of the opinion that "the enslavement of the African was in violation of the laws of nature," but they were wrong, Stephens said, "fundamentally wrong," and had to be renounced.[2] But, to repeat, what cause of our time is served by detaching the country from the principles of 1776?

The answer to this question is by no means unambiguous. The Declaration speaks of unalienable rights and by so doing directs our attention back to John Locke and, behind him, to Thomas Hobbes, the first political philosopher to speak of natural rights. In fact, one could say that Hobbes was the founder of the natural or human rights school, and in our day everyone speaks favorably of human rights. But Hobbes has never enjoyed a good reputation among moralists. His seventeenth-century contemporaries suspected him (and with good reason) of being an atheist. Be that as it may, there is surely nothing sublime in his teaching that the purpose of life is the avoidance of death, that the fear of violent death at the hands of other human beings is the strongest of all the passions, that this fear is the source of the fundamental and unalienable right of self-preservation, that from this right is derived "the first, and fundamental law of nature [which is] to seek peace," and that from this first law is derived the second, which requires men to give up their rights to an absolute sovereign who uses the fear of death—or, one might say, the fear of the hangman—to keep the peace. Edmund Burke, a favorite of present-day conservatives and moralists, had descendants of Hobbes in mind when, in 1790, he said, "In the groves of *their* academy, at the end of every vista, you see nothing but the gallows."[3] Even Locke referred to Hobbes as that "justly decried author," and "Hobbist" has always been a pejorative term.

But Locke himself no longer enjoys an unsullied reputation. Jefferson thought Locke to be one of the three greatest men ever to live, and it used to be customary to refer to him as "America's philosopher"; but that is no longer true—or at least, that designation no longer goes unchallenged. The reason for this change in his status among us has something to do with property and its ill repute in some contemporary circles. To speak of rights in a Lockean context is to conjure up thoughts of property and, what is thought to be worse, a dynamic rather than a static property: not merely a right to possess and use but a right to acquire. That is what Locke meant by the property right, and fully to secure it is certain to create significant disparities of income and wealth, disparities that are unacceptable to modern egalitarians. Nor is that all that is thought to be wrong with Locke: to secure the right to acquire would seem to promote acquisitiveness, which bears a certain resemblance to covetousness, a mortal sin according to traditional Christian doctrine. To disconnect Jefferson and with him America from John Locke is, for the typical left-wing critic, a moral as well as an intellectual necessity.

This may explain why Garry Wills says there is no evidence that Jefferson ever read Locke's principal political work, the so-called *Second Treatise of Government*, and why he insists there is not even an "echo" of the *Treatise* in any of Jefferson's writings. In fact, of course, there is much more than an "echo" of the one in the other. The Declaration speaks of "a long train of abuses," for example, a phrase taken word for word from section 225 of the

Treatise, and of "mankind [being] more disposed to suffer," which, in section 230 of the *Treatise* reads, "the people, who are more disposed to suffer." Rather than serving to disconnect Jefferson from Locke's *Treatise,* even a cursory comparison of their texts tends to connect them. Evidently, Jefferson had read the *Treatise,* and probably had studied it as carefully as we *know* he had studied Locke's *Letter Concerning Toleration.*[4] What is more, we know that he recommended that it be required reading at the University of Virginia Law School. Faced with this sort of evidence, what sort of argument is left to the anti-Lockean?

He might renounce Jefferson, after the fashion of Alexander Stephens, or emphasize the distinctions between Jefferson's works and Locke's. He might, for example, make what he can of the fact that the Declaration speaks of life, liberty, and the pursuit of happiness, whereas Locke spoke of life, liberty, and property. Failing that, he might adopt a modern version of the Confederates' case for secession: the United States was created by the states, either in 1788 when the Constitution was ratified, or in 1781, when the Articles of Confederation were ratified, or perhaps in 1777, when, in the Continental Congress, the Articles were adopted. It was *not* created in 1776, when independence was declared and certain principles espoused. To recognize 1776 as its date of birth would be to associate America with those principles. Hence the argument that independence was declared not by one people but by thirteen, or, in order to take account of New York's tardiness, by twelve new nations on July 4, with the thirteenth coming in on July 15.

By 1860 this argument had become pernicious—leading as it did to what was by far the bloodiest of our wars—

but today it is merely absurd. Contrary to the Confederates, past and present, there was in 1776 a strong disposition toward union, as well as a widespread inclination of persons to think of themselves as "Americans." Wills complains of Lincoln's "biblically shrouded" figure in the Gettysburg Address, "four score and seven," because that takes us back to 1776, "the year of the Declaration, of the self-evident truth that all men are created equal." Lincoln, he says, was mistaken in his assumption that it was one people that acted in 1776; on the contrary, July 4, 1776, "produced twelve new nations (with a thirteenth coming in on July 15)." And what is his evidence in support of this? "All thirteen original colonies subscribed to the Declaration with instructions to their delegates that this was *not* to imply formation of a single nation."[5] This is simply not true. Indeed, the opposite is true. Except for North Carolina, which was silent on the issue of union, and New York, which issued no timely instructions whatever, every colony in one way or another instructed its delegates to vote for "union" or "confederation." Here, for a conspicuous example, are the Virginia instructions issued on May 15, 1776, calling for a "confederation of the Colonies":

> *Resolved unanimously,* That the Delegates appointed to represent this Colony in General Congress be instructed to propose to that respectable body to declare the United Colonies free and independent states . . . and that they give the assent of this Colony to such declaration, and to whatever measures may be thought proper and necessary by the Congress, for forming foreign alliances, and a confederation of the Colonies, at such time and in such manner as to them shall seem best; provided that the power of forming Government for, and the regulation of the in-

ternal concerns of each Colony, be left to the respective Colonial Legislatures.

On June 14, Connecticut authorized "a regular and permanent plan of Union and Confederation of the Colonies"; New Jersey spoke of America and authorized action to promote a "Confederation for union"; Maryland spoke of the "liberties of *America*"; Pennsylvania of the "liberty, safety, and interests of *America*"; South Carolina of the "welfare of this Colony in particular and of *America* in general"; Delaware of "the happiness and safety of their constituents in particular, and *America* in general"; Georgia of a cause that is "not Provincial, but Continental"; Rhode Island authorized action to promote "the strictest union and confederation between the said United Colonies"; New Hampshire wanted to declare the "thirteen United Colonies a free and independent state"; and lastly, Massachusetts authorized its delegates to vote for independence and to take "such further measures as shall to them appear best calculated for the establishment of right and liberty to the *American* Colonies."[6] In accordance with these instructions the various delegates representing this "one people" voted for independence on July 2 and, on July 4, declared the causes which impelled them "to assume among the powers of the earth, the separate and equal station to which the Laws of Nature and Nature's God entitle[d] them."

To speak much within compass—the phrase is John Locke's—Wills is mistaken; even his own evidence shows him to be badly mistaken. Rather than pursue the matter any further, however, I shall allow Jefferson himself to have the last word:

But with respect to our rights, and the acts of the British government contravening those rights, there was but one opinion on this side of the water. All American Whigs thought alike on these subjects. When forced, therefore, to resort to arms for redress, an appeal to the tribunal of the world was deemed proper for our justification. This was the object of the Declaration of Independence. Not to find out new principles, or new arguments, never before thought of, not merely to say things which had never been said before; but to place before mankind the common sense of the subject, in terms so plain and firm as to command their assent, and to justify ourselves in the independent stand we are compelled to take. Neither aiming at originality of principle or sentiment, nor yet copied from any particular and previous writing, it was intended to be an expression of the American mind, and to give to that expression the proper tone and spirit called for by the occasion. All its authority rests then on the harmonizing sentiments of the day, whether expressed in conversation, in letters, printed essays, or in the elementary books of public right, as Aristotle, Cicero, Locke, Sidney, etc. The historical documents which you mention as in your possession, ought all to be found, and I am persuaded you will find, to be corroborative of the facts and principles advanced in that Declaration.[7]

Notes

CHAPTER I

1. Martin Diamond, *The Founding of the Democratic Republic* (Itasca, Ill.: F. E. Peacock, 1981), p. 2.

2. This was first brought to my attention by Professor Harry V. Jaffa.

3. James Madison to Nicholas P. Trist, February 15, 1830, in Gaillard Hunt, ed., *The Writings of James Madison* (New York: Putnam, 1900–1910), vol. 9, p. 355.

4. John Locke, *Two Treatises of Government*, II, secs. 6, 7, 8.

5. Ibid., sec. 87.

6. In this account I have drawn freely from my article, "Natural Rights and the Constitution," in Leonard W. Levy, Kenneth L. Karst, and Dennis J. Mahoney, eds., *Encyclopedia of the American Constitution* (New York: Macmillan, 1986).

7. Alexis de Tocqueville, *Democracy in America* (Garden City, N.Y.: Doubleday, 1969), p. 238 (vol. 1, pt. 2, ch. 6).

8. *Country Reports on Human Rights Practices for 1984*, Report submitted to the Committee on Foreign Relations, U.S. Senate, and Committee on Foreign Affairs, U.S. House of Representatives, by the Department of State, 99th Cong., 1st sess., Senate Report 99–6 (February 1985), p. 1235.

9. Locke, *Treatises*, I, secs. 86–87.

10. Hannah Arendt, *On Revolution* (New York: Viking, 1965), p. 36.

11. See, generally, William H. Nelson, *The American Tory* (Oxford: Clarendon Press, 1961); and Robert McCluer Calhoon, *The Loyalists in Revolutionary America 1760–1781* (New York: Harcourt Brace Jovanovich, 1973). Charles Inglis, *The True Interest of America Impartially Stated* (Philadelphia, 1776); Jonathan Boucher, *A View of the Causes and Consequences of the American Revolution* (London, 1797); Massachusettenis (Daniel Leonard), *Letters to the Inhabitants of the Province of Massachusetts-Bay* (Boston: *Massachusetts Gazette*, 1774–1775).

12. *Cherokee Nation* v. *Georgia*, 5 Peters 1, 17 (1831).

13. *Elk* v. *Wilkens*, 122 U.S. 94, 103 (1884).

14. 43 *Statutes at Large* 253. For a comprehensive historical account of the legal status of Indians, see Francis Paul Prucha, *The Great Father: The United States Government and the American Indians*, 2 vols. (Lincoln: University of Nebraska Press, 1984).

15. *Montana* v. *United States*, 450 U.S. 544 (1981); *Merrion* v. *Jicarillo Apache Tribe*, 455 U.S. 130 (1982); *Santa Clara Pueblo* v. *Martinez*, 436 U.S. 49 (1978).

16. Carl L. Becker, *The Declaration of Independence: A Study in the History of Political Ideas* (New York: Vintage Books, 1942), p. 5.

17. Worthington C. Ford, ed., *Journals of the Continental Congress, 1774–1789* (Washington, D.C.: Government Printing Office, 1904), vol. 2, pp. 177–183 (July 13, 1775). The following paragraphs can be found on pages 180–181:

Brothers, thus stands the matter betwixt old England and America. You Indians know how things are proportioned in a family—between the father and the son—the child carries a little pack—England we regard as the father—this island may be compared to the son.

The father has a numerous family—both at home and upon this island.—He appoints a great number of servants to assist him in the government of his family. In process of time, some of his servants grow proud and ill-natured—they were displeased to see the boy so alert and walk so nimbly with his pack. They tell the father, and advise him to enlarge the child's pack—they prevail—the pack is increased—the child takes it up again—as he thought it might be the father's pleasure—speaks but few words—those very small—for he was loth to offend the father. Those proud and wicked servants finding they had prevailed, laughed to see the boy sweat and stagger under his increased load. By and by, they apply to the father to double the boy's pack, because they heard him complain—and without any reason said they—he is a cross child—correct him if he complains any more.—The boy entreats the father—addresses the great servants in a decent manner, that the pack might be lightened—he could not go any farther—humbly asks, if the old fathers, in any of their records, had described such a pack for the child—after all the tears and entreaties of the child, the pack is redoubled—the child stands a little, while staggering under the weight—ready to fall every moment. However he entreats the father once more, though so faint he could only lisp out his last humble supplication—waits a while—no voice returns. The child concludes the father could not hear—those proud servants had intercepted his supplications, or stopped the ears of the father. He therefore gives one struggle and throws off the pack, and says he cannot take it up again—such a weight would crush him down and kill him—and he can but die if he refuses.

Upon this, those servants are very wroth—and tell the father many false stories respecting the child—they bring a great cudgel to the father, asking him to take it in his hand and strike the child.

This may serve to illustrate the present condition of the king's American subjects or children.

18. Thomas Jefferson, *Notes on the State of Virginia* (New York: Harper Torchbook, 1964), query VI, pp. 55–64, 56–59; query X, p. 90; app. 1, p. 184.

19. St. George Tucker, *A Dissertation on Slavery* (Philadelphia: Mathew Carey, 1796), p. 89.

20. Herbert J. Storing, "Slavery and the Moral Foundations of the American Republic," in Robert H. Horwitz, ed., *The Moral Foundations of the American Republic*, 2nd ed. (Charlottesville: University Press of Virginia, 1979), pp. 229–230.

21. Winthrop D. Jordan, *White Over Black: American Attitudes Toward the Negro, 1550–1812* (Chapel Hill: University of North Carolina Press, 1968), p. 548.

22. Patrick Henry to Robert Pleasants, January 18, 1773, in Robert Douthat Meade, *Patrick Henry: Patriot in the Making* (Philadelphia: Lippincott, 1957), pp. 299–300.

23. "Letter from The Yeomanry of Massachusetts," *Massachusetts Gazette*, January 25, 1788, in Herbert J. Storing, ed., *The Complete Anti-Federalist* (Chicago: University of Chicago Press, 1981), vol. 4, p. 224.

24. See Max Farrand, ed., *The Records of the Federal Convention of 1787* (New Haven: Yale University Press, 1911–1937), vol. 2, pp. 443, 453–454, 601–602, 628.

25. Ibid., vol. 3, p. 210.

26. Storing, *The Complete Anti-Federalist*, vol. 5, p. 150.

27. David Brion Davis, *The Problem of Slavery in the Age of Revolution 1770–1823* (Ithaca: Cornell University Press, 1975), pp. 166, 169, 174; Jordan, *White Over Black*, p. 436.

28. Jefferson, *Notes on the State of Virginia*, query XIV, pp. 132–139.

29. Jefferson, "Autobiography," in Adrienne Koch and William Peden, eds., *The Life and Selected Writings of Thomas Jefferson* (New York: Modern Library, 1944), p. 51.

30. Ford, *Journals of the Continental Congress, 1774–1789,* vol. 1, p. 112.

31. See Robert V. Wells, *The Population of the British Colonies in America Before 1776* (Princeton: Princeton University Press, 1975).

32. Article XI of the Articles of Confederation speaks of the possibility of Canada being admitted into the Union by "acceding to this confederation," but adds that no other colony shall be admitted "unless such admission be agreed to by nine states."

33. Arthur Zilversmit, *The First Emancipation: The Abolition of Slavery in the North* (Chicago: University of Chicago Press, 1967), pp. 55, 83.

34. Jordan, *White Over Black*, p. 545.

35. Zilversmit, *The First Emancipation*, p. 222.

36. Jordan, *White Over Black*, p. 548. This began to change in the 1820s, when the American Colonization Society came to be dominated by defenders of slavery; and in the 1830s the leading abolitionists—William Lloyd Garrison, James Gillespie Birney, Theodore Dwight Weld, Sarah Grimké, *et alia*—had all cut their ties with colonization organizations. See William M. Wiecek, *The Sources of Antislavery Constitutionalism in America, 1760–1848* (Ithaca: Cornell University Press, 1977), pp. 127 ff., 154.

37. Henry N. Sherwood, "Early Negro Deportation Projects," *Mississippi Valley Historical Review* 2, no. 4 (March 1916): 495.

38. Ibid., pp. 495–496.

39. James Sullivan to Jeremy Belknap, June 29, 1795, Massachusetts Historical Society, *Collections*, 5th series, vol. 3, p. 414.

40. W. E. Burghardt Du Bois, *The Suppression of the African Slave-Trade, 1638–1870* (New York: Russell & Russell, 1898; 1965), p. 98. Du Bois devotes the whole of chapter 8 to the 1807 act. The events referred to in the text may be found in *Annals of Congress*, vol. 16, pp. 167–190, 220–228, 231–244, 270–274, 477–478, 487, 528; vol. 17, pp. 854–855.

41. *The Josefa Segunda, Roberts et. al., Claimants*, 10 Wheat. 312 (1825). Section 4 of the statute (printed in the margin on page 315 in the Wheaton Reports) reads in part as follows: The illegally

imported slaves shall be "subject to any regulations not contravening the provisions of this act, which the legislatures of the several states . . . at any time hereafter may make, for disposing of any such negro, mulatto or person of colour." 2 *Statutes at Large* 426.

42. James Madison to Robert Walsh, November 27, 1819, in *Writings*, vol. 9, pp. 1–13.

43. U.S. House of Representatives, *Annals of Congress*, December 12, 1820, vol. 37, pp. 636, 638.

44. Ibid., February 13, 1821, p. 1134. The provision in question originated in the Committee of Style (on which Pinckney did not serve) and was modeled on Article IV of the Articles of Confederation, where the term is "privileges and immunities of free citizens."

45. William Wirt, "Rights of Free Negroes in Virginia," November 7, 1821, in *Opinions of Attorneys General*, vol. 1, p. 506.

46. Act of March 26, 1790, ch. 3, 1 *Statutes at Large* 103.

47. "Letters of Agrippa," December 28, 1787, in Storing, *The Complete Anti-Federalist*, vol. 4, pp. 85–86.

48. U.S. House of Representatives, *Annals of Congress*, February 3–4, 1790, vol. 1, pp. 1109, 1118, 1112, 1114.

49. U.S. House of Representatives, *Annals of Congress*, December 22, 1794, vol. 4, pp. 1005–1006.

50. Ibid., January 1, 1795, vol. 4, pp. 1034–1035.

51. James Kent, *Commentaries on American Law* (New York: 1826–1830), vol. 2, p. 63.

52. William Lancaster, North Carolina Ratifying Convention, July 30, 1788, in Jonathan Elliot, ed., *The Debates in the Several State Conventions*. . . . (1888; rpt. New York: Burt Franklin, n.d.), vol. 4, p. 215.

53. Paul Leicester Ford, ed., *The Writings of Thomas Jefferson* (New York: 1904–1905), vol. 1, p. 71, as quoted in Morton Borden, *Jews, Turks, and Infidels* (Chapel Hill: University of North Carolina Press, 1984), pp. 14–15.

54. Borden, *Jews, Turks, and Infidels*, pp. 69, 74.

55. The subject was thoroughly treated in what is in effect the concluding chapter of the first volume of *Democracy in America*, the chapter entitled, "Some Considerations Concerning the Present State and Probable Future of the Three Races that Inhabit the Territory of the United States."

CHAPTER II

1. *Federalist* 1.

2. New Hampshire was the first to act. Its constitution was adopted on January 6, 1776, six months before the Declaration of Independence. It is said to be the first written constitution "drawn

up by an English colony without consultation with or the approval of the crown or Parliament." Massachusetts, the last state to act during this period, adopted its constitution in 1780. Connecticut and Rhode Island governed themselves until 1818 and 1842, respectively, under their royal charters but "stripped of their monarchical components and reinterpreted as republican constitutions." See Willi Paul Adams, *The First American Constitutions: Republican Ideology and the Making of the State Constitutions in the Revolutionary Era,* trans. Rita and Robert Kimber (Chapel Hill: University of North Carolina Press, 1980), pp. 5–6, *passim.*

3. *Federalist* 1.

4. Patrick Henry, Virginia Ratifying Convention, June 4, 1788, in Herbert J. Storing, ed., *The Complete Anti-Federalist* (Chicago: University of Chicago Press, 1981), vol. 5, p. 211.

5. Charles C. Tansill, ed., *Documents Illustrative of the Formation of the Union of the American States,* 69th Congress, 1st session. House Doc. No. 398 (Washington: Government Printing Office, 1927), p. 46.

6. See above, p. 24.

7. John Locke, *Two Treatises of Government,* II, sec. 119.

8. Ibid., sec. 4.

9. Pittsfield Petitions, May 29, 1776, in Oscar and Mary Handlin, eds., *The Popular Sources of Political Authority: Documents on the Massachusetts Constitution of 1780* (Cambridge: Belknap Press/ Harvard University Press, 1966), p. 90. See also Harold C. Syrett et al., eds., *The Papers of Alexander Hamilton* (New York: Columbia University Press, 1961–1979), vol. 3, pp. 550–551.

10. Locke, *Treatises,* II, secs. 96–98, 132.

11. Ibid., sec. 132.

12. This point is made explicitly in *Federalist* 47.

13. Locke, *Treatises,* II, sec. 93.

14. Robert P. Kraynak, "John Locke: From Absolutism to Toleration," *American Political Science Review* 74, no. 1 (March 1980): 56–59.

15. Locke, *Treatises,* II, secs. 141, 137, 142.

16. John Trenchard and Thomas Gordon, *Cato's Letters,* no. 60 (January 6, 1721), no. 62 (January 20, 1721), in David L. Jacobson, ed., *The English Libertarian Heritage* (Indianapolis: Bobbs-Merrill, 1965), pp. 117–118, 130–131.

17. This phrase is taken from section 91 of the British North America Act of 1867, 30 & 31 Victoria, c. 3.

18. "The great and penetrating mind of Locke seems to be the only one that pointed towards even the theory of this great truth [namely] that the supreme, absolute and uncontrollable authority, *remains* with the people." James Wilson, Pennsylvania Ratifying

Convention, Dec. 4, 1787, in John Bach McMaster and Frederick D. Stone, eds., *Pennsylvania and the Federal Constitution: 1787–88* (Lancaster: Historical Society of Pennsylvania, 1888), p. 316.

19. James Madison to Thomas Ritchie, September 15, 1821, in Gaillard Hunt, ed., *The Writings of James Madison* (New York: Putnam, 1900–1910), vol. 9, p. 72.

20. "The Impartial Examiner," *Virginia Independent Chronicle*, February 20, 1788, in Storing, *The Complete Anti-Federalist*, vol. 5, pp. 175–177. Italics in original.

21. Tom Paine, *Rights of Man*, in Sidney Hook, ed., *The Essential Tom Paine* (New York: Mentor Books, 1969), pp. 203, 246 ff.

22. James Morton Smith and Paul L. Murphy, eds., *Liberty and Justice: A Historical Record of American Constitutional Development* (New York: Knopf, 1958), p. 215.

23. James Monroe, "Views of the President on the Subject of Internal Improvements," May 4, 1822, in James D. Richardson, comp., *A Compilation of the Messages and Papers of the Presidents, 1789–1897* (New York: Bureau of National Literature, 1897), vol. 2, p. 718.

24. See Harry V. Jaffa, *Crisis of the House Divided: An Interpretation of the Issues in the Lincoln-Douglas Debates* (Garden City, N.Y.: Doubleday, 1959).

25. Abraham Lincoln, Message to Congress in Special Session, July 4, 1861, in Roy P. Basler, ed., *Abraham Lincoln: His Speeches and Writings* (Cleveland: World, 1946), pp. 603–604.

26. Worthington C. Ford, ed., *Journals of the Continental Congress* (Washington, D.C.: Government Printing Office, 1904–1937), vol. 2, pp. 195–199.

27. In a recent and excellent study of the politics of the Continental Congress, Jack N. Rakove points out that the debates on the Articles of Confederation failed to provoke in Congress a great discussion of the nature of the Union. Yet, as he demonstrates, there was at least an implicit agreement that the Union existed prior to the Articles. For example, in 1777 Thomas Burke of North Carolina proposed a bicameral legislature for the Confederation, thereby acknowledging the existence of an American nation (to be represented in one house) as well as the states (to be represented in the other house). See Jack N. Rakove, *The Beginnings of National Politics: An Interpretative History of the Continental Congress* (New York: Knopf, 1979), p. 173, *passim*.

28. Max Farrand, ed., *The Records of the Federal Convention of 1787* (New Haven: Yale University Press, 1911, 1937), vol. 1, p. 250.

29. Richard Henry Lee to _____, April 28, 1788, in Storing, *The Complete Anti-Federalist*, vol. 1, p. 17.

30. Continental Congress, "Letter Transmitting Proposed Articles of Confederation," in Jonathan Elliot, ed., *The Debates in the Several State Conventions on the Adoption of the Federal Constitution*, 2d ed. (1888; rept. ed. New York: Burt Franklin, n.d.), vol. 1, p. 69.

31. Alexis de Tocqueville, *Democracy in America* (New York: Vintage Books, 1945), vol. 1, p. 176.

32. Richard Henry Lee to George Mason, May 15, 1787, in Robert A. Rutland, ed., *The Papers of George Mason* (Chapel Hill: University of North Carolina Press, 1970), vol. 3, p. 877.

33. Richard Henry Lee to Samuel Adams, March 14, 1785, in James Curtis Ballagh, ed., *The Letters of Richard Henry Lee* (New York: Macmillan, 1911–1914), vol. 2, pp. 343–344.

34. Lee to Mason, May 15, 1787, in Rutland, *The Papers of George Mason*, p. 877.

35. Melancton Smith in the New York ratifying convention, in Storing, *The Complete Anti-Federalist*, vol. 1, p. 18.

36. George Washington to John Jay, August 1, 1786, in John C. Fitzpatrick, ed., *The Writings of George Washington from the Original Manuscript Sources, 1745–1799* (Washington, D.C.: Government Printing Office, 1931–1944), vol. 28, p. 502.

37. George Washington to James Warren, October 7, 1785, in ibid., p. 290.

38. Albany Plan of Union, July 10, 1754, in Leonard W. Labaree, et al., eds., *The Papers of Benjamin Franklin* (New Haven: Yale University Press, 1959–   ), vol. 5, pp. 387–392.

39. Franklin, "Reasons and Motives for the Albany Plan of Union," in ibid., p. 400.

40. Ibid., p. 417.

41. Ford, *Journals of the Continental Congress*, vol. 1, pp. 49–51.

42. Washington, "Circular to the States," June 8, 1783, in Fitzpatrick, *The Writings of George Washington*, vol. 26, p. 486.

43. Benjamin Rush to Richard Price, October 27, 1786, in L. H. Butterfield, ed., *Letters of Benjamin Rush*, Memoirs of the American Philosophical Society, vol. 30, pts. 1–2 (Princeton: Princeton University Press, 1951), pt. 1, p. 408.

44. *Federalist* 6.

45. Tansill, *Documents Illustrative of the Formation of the Union*, pp. 39–43.

46. Ibid., p. 46.

47. Ibid., pp. 55–84. The relevant sentence in the Virginia statute reads as follows: "BE IT THEREFORE ENACTED by the General Assembly of the Commonwealth of Virginia that seven Commissioners be appointed by joint Ballot of both Houses of assembly who or any three of them are hereby authorized as Deputies from

this Commonwealth to meet such Deputies as may be appointed and authorized by other states to assemble in convention in Philadelphia." Ibid., pp. 69–70.

48. On September 5, the convention voted unanimously to request Congress to pay "the Secretary and other officers of this Convention such sums in proportion to their respective times of service, as are allowed to the secretary & similar officers of Congress." Farrand, *Records*, vol. 2, p. 510. The officers referred to, presumably, were Nicholas Weaver, Messenger, and Joseph Fry, Door Keeper. Ibid., vol. 1, p. 2.

49. See Harvey C. Mansfield, Jr., "The Forms and Formalities of Liberty," *The Public Interest*, no. 70 (Winter 1983).

50. "Mr. King objected [to a proposed rule that was not adopted] authorizing any member to call for the yeas and nays and have them entered on the minutes. He urged that as the acts of the Convention were not to bind the Constituents it was unnecessary to exhibit this evidence of the votes; and improper as changes of opinion would be frequent in the course of the business & would fill the minutes with contradictions." Farrand, *Records*, vol. 1, p. 10.

51. The rules are printed in Farrand, *Records*, vol. 1, pp. 8–10, 17.

52. Madison, "Preface to Debates in the Convention of 1787," in Farrand, *Records*, vol. 3, p. 550.

53. Herbert J. Storing, "The Constitutional Convention: Toward a More Perfect Union," in Morton J. Frisch and Richard G. Stevens, eds., *American Political Thought: The Philosophical Dimension of American Statesmanship*, 2d ed. (Itasca, Ill.: F. E. Peacock, 1983), p. 68.

54. Farrand, *Records*, vol. 1, p. 21.

55. Ibid., p. 37.

56. Ibid., p. 193.

57. On the Monday following Paterson's Friday speech, Alexander Hamilton of New York presented the convention with still a third plan, a plan for a "high toned" government on the British model. Under it, both the executive and the senators would serve during good behavior, and the governors of the states would be appointed by the "General Government," which would have a negative over all laws enacted by the states. Farrand, *Records*, vol. 1, pp. 282–93. Hamilton's plan was given no consideration whatever, and by introducing it he succeeded in depriving himself of further influence in the convention's deliberations. But he also succeeded—and there is no way of knowing whether this was his intention—in making the New Jersey Plan appear to be extreme (the opposite of his own) and the Virginia Plan appear to be moderate.

58. Ibid., pp. 242–245.

59. Ibid., p. 492.

60. Storing, "The Constitutional Convention," p. 54.

61. Farrand, *Records*, vol. 1, p. 133.

62. Ibid., p. 134.

63. *Federalist* 10.

64. Farrand, *Records*, vol. 1, p. 166.

65. Madison "entreated the gentlemen representing the small states to renounce a principle wch. was confessedly unjust, which cd. never be admitted, & if admitted must infuse mortality into a Constitution which we wished to last forever." Farrand, *Records*, vol. 1, p. 464; see also pp. 49, 134, 446, 527.

66. Ibid., p. 253.

67. Ibid., p. 255.

68. Ibid., p. 324.

69. Ibid., p. 449.

70. Ibid., p. 461.

71. Storing, "The Constitutional Convention," pp. 65–66. The facts are taken from Luther Martin, "Genuine Information," Farrand, *Records*, vol. 3, pp. 187–188.

72. Farrand, *Records*, vol. 2, pp. 19–20.

73. The so-called supremacy clause (Article VI) reads, in part, that the Constitution, the laws made pursuant to it, and all treaties made or which shall be made "shall be the supreme Law of the Land; and the Judges in every State shall be bound thereby, any Thing in the Constitution or Laws of any State to the Contrary notwithstanding." It is not clear that the state sovereignty delegates appreciated that this would lead to judicial review by the Supreme Court of the United States.

74. On September 12, Elbridge Gerry of Massachusetts moved the appointment of a committee to prepare a bill of rights, a motion seconded by George Mason of Virginia, but the motion was defeated, zero to ten. Farrand, *Records*, vol. 2, pp. 587–588. Significantly, neither Gerry nor Mason signed the Constitution.

75. *Federalist* 84.

76. *Federalist* 10.

77. Farrand, *Records*, vol. 1, pp. 399, 401.

78. Ibid., p. 152.

79. Ibid., vol. 2, pp. 177–189.

80. Ibid., pp. 590–603.

81. Ibid., pp. 629–630. It is interesting in this connection to note that the amending provision embodies elements of both popular and state sovereignty. An amendment becomes part of the Constitution when ratified by a majority of the people of the United States (acting through either state legislatures or state conventions), but that

majority must be an extraordinary one, expressed as three-fourths of the states.

82. Ibid., p. 665.

83. Madison, "Preface to Debates in the Convention of 1787," Farrand, *Records,* vol. 3, p. 551.

84. Madison to George Washington, April 16, 1787, in William T. Hutchinson et al., eds., *The Papers of James Madison* (Chicago: University of Chicago Press, 1962–1977), vol. 9, p. 385.

85. Tansill, *Documents Illustrative of the Formation of the Union,* p. 1007.

86. Concord Town Meeting Resolutions, Oct. 21, 1776, in Handlin, *The Popular Sources of Political Authority,* pp. 152–153.

87. See Zera S. Fink, *The Classical Republicans: An Essay in the Recovery of a Pattern of Thought in Seventeenth Century England* (Evanston, Ill.: Northwestern University Press, 1945).

88. Tansill, *Documents Illustrative of the Formation of the Union,* p. 1062.

89. These constitutions are collected in (and kept up to date by) Albert P. Blaustein and Gisbert H. Flanz, eds., *Constitutions of the Countries of the World* (Dobbs Ferry, N.Y.: Oceana Publications, 1971–1986), 17 vols.

CHAPTER III

1. U.S. Congress, Senate, Committee on the Judiciary, Subcommittee on the Constitution, 96th Cong., 2d sess., July 1980.

2. Ibid., p. iii.

3. *Barron* v. *Baltimore,* 7 Pet. 243 (1833).

4. *Gitlow* v. *New York,* 268 U.S. 652 (1925).

5. *Dred Scott* v. *Sandford,* 19 How. 393 (1857); *Hepburn* v. *Griswold,* 8 Wall. 603 (1870), overruled by *Knox* v. *Lee,* 12 Wall. 457 (1871).

6. *Lamont* v. *Postmaster General,* 381 U.S. 301 (1965); *Tilton* v. *Richardson,* 403 U.S. 672 (1971).

7. *Boyd* v. *United States,* 116 U.S. 616 (1886).

8. The exceptions were *The Justices* v. *Murray,* 8 Wall. 274 (1870) (Seventh Amendment); and four Sixth Amendment cases: *Kirby* v. *United States,* 174 U.S. 47 (1899); *Wong Wing* v. *United States,* 163 U.S. 228 (1896); *Rassmussen* v. *United States,* 197 U.S. 516 (1905); and *United States* v. *Cohen Grocery Co.,* 255 U.S. 81 (1921).

9. James Madison to Thomas Jefferson, October 17, 1788, in Gaillard Hunt, ed., *The Writings of James Madison* (New York: Putnam, 1900–1910), vol. 5, pp. 271–275.

10. "The Congress shall have power . . . to promote the Progress of Science and useful Arts, by securing for limited Times to Authors and Inventors the exclusive *right* [*sic*!] to their respective Writings and Discoveries." Article I, section 8, #8. As far as I know, my colleague Robert A. Goldwin was the first person to remark this. See his "Rights Versus Duties," in Arthur L. Caplan and Daniel Callahan, eds., *Ethics in Hard Times* (New York: Plenum, 1981), p. 130.

11. *Federalist* 84.

12. "It is evident that [only the republican] form [of government] would be reconcilable with the genius of the people of America." *Federalist* 39.

13. Aristotle, *Politics*, book 8 (1337a10–19).

14. "Centinel" (Judge George Bryan?), the leading Anti-Federalist of Pennsylvania, complained of the "wealthy and ambitious [who] think they have a right to lord it over their fellow creatures"; John De Witt of Massachusetts, having observed that the "aristocratical hath ever been found to have the most influence, and the people in most countries have been particularly attentive in providing checks against it," objected to the Constitution precisely because, in his judgment, it failed to provide such checks; Patrick Henry of Virginia said the Constitution was deformed, that it had an "awful squinting; it squints toward monarchy"; and, for one more example, a farmer from western Massachusetts writing under the name of "A Watchman" warned that a perfect "democratical" constitution was being superseded by an "aristocratical one" devised by "designing men" intent on leading the people into "vassalage and slavery." Herbert J. Storing, *The Complete Anti-Federalist* (Chicago: University of Chicago Press, 1981), vol. 2, p. 137; vol. 4, p. 26; vol. 5, p. 224; vol. 4, p. 232.

15. *Federalists* 47, 48, 71; Thomas Jefferson, *Notes on the State of Virginia* (New York: Harper Torchbook, 1964), query XIII.

16. The best account of Montesquieu's teaching can be found in Thomas L. Pangle, *Montesquieu's Philosophy of Liberalism: A Commentary on the Spirit of the Laws* (Chicago: University of Chicago Press, 1973), esp. pp. 107–138.

17. *Federalist* 39.

18. Max Farrand, ed., *The Records of the Federal Convention of 1787* (New Haven: Yale University Press, 1937), vol. 1, pp. 150–153.

19. Ibid., p. 48.

20. *Federalist* 78.

21. *Federalist* 10.

22. *Federalist* 63.

23. See Walter Berns, *The First Amendment and the Future of American Democracy* (New York: Basic Books, 1976), pp. 119–128.

CHAPTER IV

1. Thomas Babington Macaulay, "Francis Bacon," in Macaulay, *Critical and Historical Essays*, Everyman's Library ed. (New York: Dutton, 1951), vol. 2, p. 373.

2. Herbert J. Storing, "American Statesmanship: Old and New," in Robert A. Goldwin, ed., *Bureaucrats, Policy Analysts, Statesmen: Who Leads?* (Washington, D.C.: American Enterprise Institute, 1980), p. 97.

3. Harry C. Mansfield, Jr., "Impartial Representation," in Robert A. Goldwin, ed., *Representation and Misrepresentation* (Chicago: Rand McNally, 1968), p. 104.

4. Philip B. Kurland and Ralph Lerner, eds., *The Founders' Constitution* (Chicago: University of Chicago Press, 1987), vol. 1, p. 383.

5. Mansfield, "Impartial Representation," p. 95.

6. Thomas Jefferson, *Notes on the State of Virginia* (New York: Harper Torchbook, 1964), query XVII.

7. Alexis de Tocqueville, *Democracy in America* (Garden City, N.Y.: Doubleday, 1969), p. 177 (vol. 1, pt. 2, ch. 2).

8. *The Three Charters of the Virginia Company of London*, Jamestown 350th Anniversary Historical Booklet, no. 4, 1957, p. 127.

9. William Penn, "A Preface to the Frame of Government," in Merrill Jensen, ed., *American Colonial Documents to 1776*, vol. 9, p. 175, of David C. Douglas, ed., *English Historical Documents* (New York: Oxford University Press, 1969). Kurland and Lerner, *The Founders' Constitution*, vol. 1, p. 608.

10. Thomas Jefferson to Roger C. Weightman, June 24, 1826, in Paul Leicester Ford, ed., *The Writings of Thomas Jefferson* (New York: 1899), vol. 10, p. 343.

11. Thomas Babington Macaulay, *History of England* (Leipzig: Tauchnitz, 1849), vol. 2, p. 135.

12. John Locke, *Two Treatises of Government*, II, sec. 1.

13. Locke, *Discourse of Miracles*, in *Works* (1812 ed.), vol. 9, p. 259; Hobbes, *Leviathan*, book 3, ch. 37; Spinoza, *Theologico-Political Treatise*, in *Works of Spinoza*, trans. R. H. M. Elwes (New York: Dover, 1951), vol. 1, ch. 6. For a fuller discussion of the issue, see Berns, *The First Amendment and the Future of American Democracy* (New York: Basic Books, 1976), ch. 1.

14. James Madison to Thomas Jefferson, October 24, 1787, in Gaillard Hunt, ed., *The Writings of James Madison* (New York: Putnam, 1900–1910), vol. 5, pp. 28–29.

15. See Appendix, pp. 242–251.

16. S. Gerald Sandler, "Lockean Ideas in Thomas Jefferson's *Bill for Establishing Religious Freedom*," *Journal of the History of Ideas* 21 (1960): 110–116. In three parallel columns, Sandler cites five ideas concerning toleration as they appear first in Locke's *Letter*, second in Jefferson's notes on the *Letter*, and third in the bill that, with amendments, became the statute. The similarity is remarkable.

17. Macaulay, *History of England*, vol. 2, pp. 115–116.

18. John Locke, *A Letter Concerning Toleration* (Indianapolis: Bobbs-Merrill/Library of Liberal Arts, 1955), p. 52. The passage cited is in paragraph 70 (of 86) in this edition of the *Letter*.

19. Thomas Jefferson, *Notes on the State of Virginia*, query XVIII, p. 152.

20. Locke, *A Letter Concerning Toleration*, p. 30 (paragraph 36).

21. Ibid., p. 52 (paragraph 70).

22. 1 William and Mary, ch. 18.

23. Macaulay, *History of England*, vol. 4, pp. 84 ff.

24. Washington to the Hebrew Congregation of Newport, R.I., August 17, 1790, in John C. Fitzpatrick, ed., *The Writings of George Washington from the Original Manuscript Sources, 1745–1799* (Washington, D.C.: Government Printing Office, 1931–1944), vol. 31, p. 93n.

25. Francis Newton Thorpe, ed., *The Federal and State Constitutions, Colonial Charters, and Other Organic Laws of the States, Territories and Colonies now or heretofore forming the United States of America* (Washington, D.C.: Government Printing Office, 1909), vol. 1, p. 566.

26. Ibid., vol. 6, p. 3743.

27. Petition of the Philadelphia Synagogue. . . . December 23, 1783, in Anson Phelps Stokes, ed., *Church and State in the United States* (New York: Harper, 1950), vol. 1, pp. 287–289.

28. *Annals of Congress*, vol. 1, p. 784 (August 17, 1789), p. 434 (June 8, 1789). Madison's proposed amendment reads as follows in its entirety: "No state shall violate the equal rights of conscience or the freedom of the press, or the trial by jury in criminal cases."

29. Adam Smith, *The Wealth of Nations* (New York: Modern Library, 1937), p. 745 (book 5, ch. 1, art. 3, "Of the Expence of the Institutions for the Instruction of People of all Ages").

30. Ibid., pp. 748, 755.

31. Thomas Hobbes, *Leviathan*, ch. 15.

32. Locke, *Treatises*, II, sec. 42.

33. Macaulay, "Francis Bacon," in *Critical and Historical Essays*, vol. 2, p. 373.

34. Locke, *Treatises*, II, secs. 123, 124.

35. *McCulloch* v. *Maryland*, 4 Wheat. 316, 408 (1819).

36. Locke, *Treatises*, II, sec. 34.

37. George Wilson Pierson, *Tocqueville and Beaumont in America* (New York: Oxford University Press, 1938), p. 115.

38. Locke, *Treatises*, II, secs. 26, 31, 34, 40, 42, 43.

39. Pierson, *Tocqueville and Beaumont in America*, p. 582.

40. Jean-Jacques Rousseau, *Discourse on the Sciences and Arts*, in Roger D. Masters, ed., *The First and Second Discourses* (New York: St. Martin's Press, 1964), p. 51.

41. Montesquieu, *Spirit of the Laws*, vol. 1, book 20, ch. 1. See Thomas L. Pangle, *Montesquieu's Philosophy of Liberalism: A Commentary on "The Spirit of the Laws"* (Chicago: University of Chicago Press, 1973), pp. 203–209.

42. James Madison, "Property," *National Gazette*, March 27, 1792, in *Letters and Other Writings of James Madison* (Philadelphia: Lippincott, 1884), vol. 4, p. 478.

CHAPTER V

1. *Federalist* 10.

2. Alexis de Tocqueville, *Democracy in America* (Garden City, N.Y.: Doubleday, 1969), pp. 698–699 (vol. 2, pt. 4, ch. 7).

3. Ibid., p. 606 (vol. 2, pt. 3, ch. 14).

4. Harvey C. Mansfield, Jr., "The Forms and Formalities of Liberty," *Public Interest*, no. 70 (Winter 1983): 128.

5. Tocqueville, *Democracy in America*, p. 238 (vol. 1, pt. 2, ch. 6).

6. John Locke, *Two Treatises of Government*, II, secs. 87, 128, 131, 142, 147.

7. Ibid., sec. 138.

8. *I.N.S.* v. *Chadha*, 462 U.S. 919, 944 (1983).

9. This is the clear conclusion to be drawn from the events reported in *Lucas* v. *Forty-Fourth General Assembly of Colorado*, 377 U.S. 713 (1964), a legislative reapportionment case. The people of Colorado approved an amendment to the state constitution apportioning the seats in the state house of representatives on the basis of population but retaining the existing apportionment in the state senate, which, to some extent, was based on factors other than population. To put it simply, the amendment recognized the right of counties to be represented as counties no matter how sparsely

populated they were. This plan was approved by a two-to-one statewide majority; not only that, it was approved by a majority of the voters in every county of the state, including the urban and heavily populated counties, which allegedly were discriminated against by the plan because it allowed sparsely populated counties representation beyond that to which their populations alone would have entitled them. Nevertheless, the Supreme Court declared the apportionment plan unconstitutional. Both houses of a bicameral legislature, the Court said, "must be apportioned on a population basis."

10. *West Virginia State Board of Education* v. *Barnette,* 319 U.S. 624, 670 (1943) (dissenting opinion).

11. *Federalist* 49.

CHAPTER VI

1. Max Farrand, ed., *The Records of the Federal Convention of 1787* (New Haven: Yale University Press, 1937), vol. 2, p. 221.

2. Alexis de Tocqueville, *Democracy in America* (Garden City, N.Y.: Doubleday, 1969), p. 238 (vol. 1, pt. 2, ch. 6).

3. *Annals of Congress,* vol. 1, p. 757 (August 15, 1789). For a complete account of the debates on the religious clauses of the First Amendment, see Walter Berns, *The First Amendment and the Future of American Democracy* (New York: Basic Books, 1976), ch. 1.

4. Farrand, *Records,* vol. 2, pp. 344, 606.

5. Herbert J. Storing, ed., *The Complete Anti-Federalist* (Chicago: University of Chicago Press, 1981), vol. 6, pp. 221, 233.

6. Tocqueville, *Democracy in America,* p. 99 (vol. 1, pt. 1, ch. 6).

7. Ibid., pp. 102–103.

8. Farrand, *Records,* vol. 1, p. 21; vol. 2, pp. 80, 298.

9. Ibid., vol. 2, pp. 79, 74.

10. Ibid., vol. 1, pp. 97–98; vol. 2, pp. 76–77, 298, 300.

11. In the event, of course, the British monarch has lost most of his or her prerogatives, whereas the president of the United States, despite the apprehensions expressed by Morris and Madison, and without the support of the judges serving on a council of revision, has (through 1976) vetoed a total of 2,342 bills, of which total only 86 (or 3.7 percent) have been overridden. *Congressional Quarterly's Guide to the Congress of the United States,* 2d ed. (Washington, D.C., 1976), p. 628. This record does not, however, prove Morris and Madison's fears to have been groundless. Presidents have not had the support of the judges, but they have had the support of the people. With the advent of political parties in the elec-

tion of 1800, the presidency became what it was not intended to be: a popular or democratic office.

12. *Marbury* v. *Madison*, 1 Cranch 137, 177–8 (1803).

13. *Griswold* v. *Connecticut*, 381 U.S. 479, 483–4 (1965).

14. *Roe* v. *Wade*, 410 U.S. 113, 153 (1973).

15. William J. Brennan, Jr., "The Constitution of the United States: Contemporary Ratification" (Paper presented at Georgetown University, October 12, 1985), p. 7.

16. *Home Building & Loan Assoc.* v. *Blaisdell*, 290 U.S. 398, 443 (1934). Brennan quoted Hughes in an address (August 8, 1986) before the American Bar Association.

17. *Marbury* v. *Madison*, at pp. 176, 177. The same idea was expressed even more emphatically by Justice William Paterson in 1795: "What is a Constitution? It is the form of government, delineated by the mighty hand of the people, in which certain first principles of fundamental laws are established. The Constitution is certain and fixed; it contains the permanent will of the people, and is the supreme law of the land; it is paramount to the power of the Legislature, and can be revoked or altered only by the authority that made it. The life-giving principle and the death-doing stroke must proceed from the same hand." *Van Horne's Lessee* v. *Dorrance*, 2 Dallas 304, 308 (1795).

18. *McCulloch* v. *Maryland*, 4 Wheat. 316, 407 (1819).

19. Ibid., p. 415.

20. John Marshall, "A Friend to the Constitution," in Gerald Gunther, ed., *John Marshall's Defense of McCulloch v. Maryland* (Stanford: Stanford University Press, 1969), p. 185.

21. *Federalist 57.*

22. An attempt to have the courts order imposition of the sanction against the state of Virginia was rebuffed in *Saunders* v. *Wilkens*, 152 F.2d 235 (C.A. 4, 1945), cert. denied, 328 U.S. 870 (1946).

23. *Slaughterhouse Cases*, 16 Wall. 36 (1873).

24. The case has been made by Professor Michael Zuckert of Carleton College in two as yet unpublished papers (one of them coauthored by Marshall McDonald) that, rather than being vaguely written, the three troublesome clauses of the Fourteenth Amendment are precisely drafted. Each one is addressed, as it were, to a different branch of the state governments: privileges or immunities to the legislative branch, due process to the judiciary, and equal protection to the executive. This literal reading of the amendment, while persuasive, gains little or no support from the legislative record; but, then, every reading derived from that record is refuted, or at least contested, by another reading. There is an enormous literature on this subject that I have ignored altogether here.

25. *Allgeyer* v. *Louisiana*, 165 U.S. 578 (1897).

26. The first was held to be a reasonable regulation because the Court was willing to concede that Utah was justified in finding mine work unhealthy; the second was declared to be an unreasonable regulation (and, therefore, a deprivation of liberty "without due process of law") because the Court was *not* willing to concede that New York was justified in finding bakery work unhealthy. *Holden* v. *Hardy*, 169 U.S. 366 (1898); *Lochner* v. *New York*, 198 U.S. 45 (1905).

27. *United States* v. *Carolene Products Co.*, 304 U.S. 144, 152–3 n. 4 (1938).

28. *Shelley* v. *Kraemer*, 334 U.S. 1, 20 (1948).

29. *Marbury* v. *Madison*, at p. 163.

30. Herbert Wechsler, "Toward Neutral Principles of Constitutional Law," in Wechsler, *Principles, Politics, and Fundamental Law* (Cambridge: Harvard University Press, 1961); Louis H. Pollak, "Racial Discrimination and Judicial Integrity: A Reply to Professor Wechsler," *University of Pennsylvania L.R.* 108 (November 1959): 1–34. Wechsler's article was first published in the November 1959 issue of the *Harvard Law Review*.

31. *Brown* v. *Board of Education*, 347 U.S. 483, 495 (1954).

32. Virginia Commission on Constitutional Government, *The Reconstruction Amendments' Debates* (Richmond, 1967), preface (unpaginated).

33. Kenneth L. Karst, "Invidious Discrimination: Justice Douglas and the Return of the 'Natural-Law-Due-Process Formula,'" *U.C.L.A. Law Review* 16 (June 1969): 720.

34. Joseph L. Rauh, Jr., "The Supreme Court: A Body Politic," Washington *Post*, March 5, 1980, p. A23.

35. Don E. Fehrenbacher, *Slavery, Law, and Politics: The Dred Scott Case in Historical Perspective* (New York: Oxford University Press, 1981), p. 5. The edition cited here is in fact an abridgement of his Pulitzer Prize volume, *The Dred Scott Case: Its Significance in American Law and Politics*.

36. Abram Chayes, "The Role of the Judge in Public Law Litigation," *Harvard Law Review* 89, no. 7 (May 1976): 1308, 1307.

37. Chayes is contemptuous of Congress: "And to retreat to the notion that the legislature itself—Congress!—is in some mystical way adequately representative of all the interests at stake, is to impose democratic theory by brute force on observed institutional behavior." Ibid., p. 1311.

38. *Sexton* v. *Wheaton*, 8 Wheat. 229, 239 (1823).

39. *Levy* v. *Louisiana*, 391 U.S. 68, 70 (1968).

40. *Labine* v. *Vincent*, 401 U.S. 532, 541 (1971) (dissenting opinion).

41. Tocqueville, *Democracy in America*, pp. 590, 591–592, 593, and generally, vol. 2, pt. 3, chs. 8–11.

42. Walter Berns, *The First Amendment and the Future of American Democracy* (New York: Basic Books, 1976), ch. 5.

43. *A Book (Fanny Hill) etc.* v. *Attorney General of Massachusetts*, 383 U.S. 415, 431 and Appendix (1966).

44. Allan Bloom, "Introduction," in Jean-Jacques Rousseau, *Politics and the Arts: Letter to M. d'Alembert on the Theatre*, trans. Allan Bloom (Ithaca: Cornell University Press, 1961), p. xv.

45. Tocqueville, *Democracy in America*, p. 544 (vol. 2, pt. 2, ch. 15).

46. *Wallace* v. *Jaffree*, 105 S.Ct. 2479 (1985). Only (then) Justice William H. Rehnquist recognized the extent to which the Court's religious establishment holdings are departures from the original intent of the First Amendment.

47. *Cohen* v. *California*, 403 U.S. 15 (1971), courthouse corridors; *Rosenfeld* v. *New Jersey*, 408 U.S. 901 (1972), schoolboard meetings; *Papish* v. *Board of Curators*, 410 U.S. 667 (1973), student newspapers; *Spence* v. *Washington*, 418 U.S. 405 (1974), flag hanging; *Smith* v. *Goguen*, 415 U.S. 566 (1974), flag wearing; *Street* v. *New York*, 394 U.S. 576 (1969), flag burning.

48. Harvey C. Mansfield, Jr., "The American Election: Towards Constitutional Democracy?" *Government and Opposition* 16, no. 1 (Winter 1981): 6.

49. *Bowers* v. *Hardwick*, 106 S.Ct. 2841 (1986).

50. Walter Barnett, *Sexual Freedom and the Constitution: An Inquiry Into the Constitutionality of Repressive Sex Laws* (Albuquerque: University of New Mexico Press, 1973), p. 13, *passim*.

51. *Van Horne's Lessee* v. *Dorrance*, at pp. 304, 310.

52. *Bowers* v. *Hardwick*, at p. 2848.

53. Ronald Dworkin, *Taking Rights Seriously* (Cambridge: Harvard University Press, 1977), pp. 200–201.

54. *Frontiero* v. *Richardson*, 411 U.S. 677 (1973).

55. Bob Woodward and Scott Armstrong, *The Brethren: Inside the Supreme Court* (New York: Simon and Schuster, 1979), p. 254.

CHAPTER VII

1. Thomas Jefferson to Thomas Mann Randolph, May 30, 1790, in Adrienne Koch and William Peden, eds., *The Life and Selected Writings of Thomas Jefferson* (New York: Modern Library, 1944), pp. 496–497.

2. William J. Brennan, Jr., "The Constitution of the United

States: Contemporary Ratification" (Address at Georgetown University, October 12, 1986), p. 4.

3. *Straight* v. *Wainwright,* 106 S.Ct. 2004 (1986).

4. Brennan, "The Constitution of the United States," p. 7.

5. *Bowen* v. *Roy,* 106 S.Ct. 2147, 2149 (1986).

6. Ralph Lerner, "The Supreme Court as Republican Schoolmaster," in Philip B. Kurland, ed., *The Supreme Court Review, 1967* (Chicago: University of Chicago Press, 1967), pp. 127–180.

APPENDIX

1. Garry Wills, *Inventing America: Jefferson's Declaration of Independence* (Garden City, N.Y.: Doubleday, 1978), pp. 308–309.

2. Alexander H. Stephens, speech at Savannah, Georgia, March 21, 1861. The speech is reported in Henry Cleveland, *Alexander H. Stephens, in Public and Private, with Letters and Speeches. . . .* (Philadelphia: National Publishing Co., 1866), pp. 717–729.

3. Thomas Hobbes, *Leviathan,* chs. 13, 14; Edmund Burke, *Reflections on the Revolution in France,* in *Works* (London: Bohn, 1855), vol. 2, p. 350.

4. See S. Gerald Sandler, "Lockean Ideas in Thomas Jefferson's *Bill for Establishing Religious Freedom," Journal of the History of Ideas* 21 (1960): 110–116.

5. Wills, *Inventing America,* p. xvi. Italics in the original.

6. These instructions may be found in Peter Force, *American Archives,* 4th ser. (Washington, D.C., 1846): vol. 6, p. 1364 (Virginia), p. 868 (Connecticut), pp. 1628–1629 (New Jersey), p. 1669 (Rhode Island), p. 1491 (Maryland), p. 1030 (New Hampshire), pp. 1675–1676 (Georgia), pp. 862–863 (Pennsylvania), p. 884 (Delaware); vol. 5, p. 860 (North Carolina), pp. 1687–1688 (South Carolina); vol. 4, p. 1266 (Massachusetts). On July 2, 1776, the New York delegate wrote the New York Congress asking for instructions (see vol. 6, p. 1212), and on July 9 that Congress voted to endorse the Declaration; four of New York's delegates subsequently subscribed their names to it.

7. Thomas Jefferson to Henry Lee, May 8, 1825, in Adrienne Koch and William Peden, eds., *The Life and Selected Writings of Thomas Jefferson* (New York: Modern Library, 1944), p. 719.

Index

Anti-Federalists, 77, 82, 85, 127,
173, 199
ratification of the Constitution and, 117–19
republican government and,
133, 134, 136
separation of powers and, 134
Arendt, Hannah, 31
aristocracy, 61–62, 111, 135–36,
138, 151
Aristotle, 69–70, 83, 130, 150,
151
Articles of Confederation and
Perpetual Union, 65, 66,
109–10, 248
amendment of, 66, 81, 85–89,
92–93, 100
inadequacies of, 85–87, 98, 132
state sovereignty and, 81–84,
89
Virginia Plan compared with,
98

Bacon, Francis, 147, 149
Baha'i, persecution of, 28–29
Bailyn, Bernard, 158
balance of power, governmen-
tal, 135–36
Baldwin, Abraham, 108
Barbé-Marbois, François, 38
Barron v. *Baltimore*, 126
Barton, William, 20*n*
Baxter, Richard, 156
Bayh, Birch, 125, 126
Beaumont, Gustave de, 175
Becker, Carl, 37
Bedford, Gunning, 101–2, 107,
109
Belknap, Jeremy, 50
Benezet, Anthony, 49
Bentham, Jeremy, 122–23
"Bill Declaring Who Shall be
Deemed Citizens of this

[Virginia] Common-
wealth," 55
Bill of Rights, U.S., 110, 124–
129, 193–94
purpose of, 126
ratification of, 125
see also First Amendment
Bill of Rights of 1689, 31
Blackmun, Harry A., 226–27,
237–38
blacks, 22, 40–58, 62–63
as citizens, 40–41, 54–55, 209–
211
colonization by, 40–41, 49–50,
52
Constitution and, 42–43, 54,
55, 113
Fourteenth Amendment and,
35, 209–14
free, 40, 49, 54–56
political isolation of, 211
poverty of, 195
rights of, 40–41, 46, 49, 210,
211
voting of, 113, 194, 210, 215,
238
see also abolition; slaves,
slavery
Blackstone, William, 122, 150
Bloom, Allan, 222
Book of Common Prayer, 31,
155
Boucher, Jonathan, 33
Bowers v. *Hardwick*, 237
Branagan, Thomas, 49–50
Brennan, William J., Jr., 208,
221, 233–37, 239, 241
Frontiero v. *Richardson* and,
229–31
on living Constitution, 206–7
Brown v. *Board of Education*,
128, 216–17
budget, federal, 239
Burke, Edmund, 246
Butler, Pierce, 42

Constitution, U.S. (*continued*)
blacks and, 42–43, 54, 55, 113
Brennan's views on, 233–34
deconstruction of, 206
democratizing of, 193–94
draft of, 113–14
as formal document, 188–89
ignorance of, 13
Indians in, 34–35
living, 206–7
longevity of, 12–13, 192
preamble to, 28, 115
predecessors of, 65
ratification of, 77, 80, 82, 114–21, 136
religion and, 59
respect for, 13
significance of, 65–66
slavery and, 42–43
uniqueness of, 12–13, 110–11, 120–21
We, the People in, 66, 67
women and, 113
see also specific topics
Constitutional Convention
(Philadelphia Convention; 1787), 93–115, 192, 198–99
agenda of, 100–101
call for, 65, 66–67, 92–93
Committee of Detail of, 113, 115
Committee of Style of, 43, 113
Committee of the Whole of, 99, 113
compromise at, 97–109
delegate selection for, 93
distinction of delegates to, 93–94
education and, 112
formal rules of, 95
homogeneity of members of, 94
judiciary branch and, 201–4

Madison's notes on, 96–97, 109
New Jersey Plan and, 100, 104–5
officers elected for, 94
procedural rules of, 95–96
religion and, 111–12
rules committee appointed for, 94–95
secrecy of deliberations of, 96
Virginia Plan and, 98–106, 109, 201–2
voter qualifications and, 112, 113
constitutionalism:
democracy and, 122–46, 181
forms and formalities and, 182–89
Locke and, 69, 71, 73–75
religious problem and, 147–80
respect for, 13
wisdom and, 189–90
see also specific topics
Constitution of Athens (Aristotle), 69–70
constitutions, 117, 120–21
ancient vs. modern, 70, 140–41
in classical antiquity, 69–70, 140–41
as novelty, 64–65
state, 65
unwritten, 69–70, 77, 120
written, necessity of, 69–77
constitution writing, conference on (1983), 12
Continental Congress, 16, 19–20, 83–84
Galloway Union plan and, 90
Indian letter of (1775), 37–38
Quebec letter of (1774), 47
"contraband" slaves, 50–52
Council of Censors of Pennsylvania, 168

Leonard, Daniel, 33
Lerner, Ralph, 154, 241
Letter Concerning Toleration
(Locke), 158–64, 248
liberals, 240, 241
liberty, material wealth and,
148–49
limited government, 74–75, 153,
184–85
Lincoln, Abraham, 15–19, 25,
61, 175, 195–96
Declaration of Independence
and, 16–19, 242–43
Gettysburg Address of, 15,
22, 249
slavery and, 44, 53, 54, 80
Union preserved by, 80–81
Locke, John, 70, 175, 176, 233,
246–48
constitutionalism and, 69, 71,
73–75
Hobbes compared with, 26–
27, 172, 287–88
Jefferson influenced by, 39,
158–61, 247–48
law making as viewed by,
187–88
property rights as viewed by,
178, 247
on rationality, 29, 73
religion as viewed by, 157–64
on state of nature, 24, 26–27,
32, 73, 152
Louis XIV, King of France, 163
Louisiana:
"contraband" slaves in, 52
due process case in, 213
Louisiana Territory, 50, 53
Lowndes, Rawlins, 43
loyalists (Tories), 22, 25, 32–
34, 40, 62

Macaulay, Thomas Babington,
147–48, 159–60, 165–66, 172

McCulloch v. *Maryland,* 207–8,
237
McGovern, George, 196
Madison, James, 39, 77, 86, 88,
92, 138, 190, 194, 198
blacks and slavery as viewed
by, 46–47, 49, 50, 52–53
commerce as viewed by, 173–
174, 175
on compacts of government,
23–27, 67–69, 76
at Constitutional Conven-
tion, 94, 96–97, 98, 102,
103–4, 106, 107, 109, 110,
111, 114–15, 192, 202, 203
dangers to private rights as
viewed by, 127–28
democracy as viewed by,
181, 182
factions as viewed by, 103,
124
Federalist writings of, 103–4,
117, 131, 133, 136, 139–43,
145–46, 168–69, 174, 193,
205, 240
naturalization as viewed by,
57
property as viewed by, 178–
179
on public good vs. private
rights, 205–6
ratification as viewed by,
116, 117
religion as viewed by, 60, 158,
168–69
representation as viewed by,
139–43, 209
Magna Carta, 31
majority rule, 71–72, 123–24,
181
constitutional vs. simple, 143
persuasion and, 224
Malcolm X, 62–63
Manchester, William, 61
Mansfield, Harvey C., Jr., 185

281

Marbury v. *Madison,* 204–5
Marshall, John, 34–35, 118, 173, 220, 232, 236
  McCulloch statement of, 207–8, 237
  Marbury v. *Madison* and, 204–5
Marshall, Thurgood, 234
Martin, Luther, 43, 105–6, 107, 109, 203, 214
Mary II, Queen of England, 165
Maryland, 250
  Constitutional Convention and, 107
Mason, George, 87, 118, 198–99
Massachusetts, 92, 250
  Constitutional Convention and, 109
  ratification of Constitution and, 116–17
middle class, 195
  polity of, 150–51
military, 112–13
militia, law enforcement and, 132–33
minority rights, 123, 125
Missouri, as slave state, 52, 54–55
Missouri crisis (1820), 46, 51–52, 54
Monroe, James, 79
Montesquieu, Baron de La Brède et de, 83, 134–35, 139, 150, 177, 233
morality:
  education and, 222–23
  Hobbes's views on, 171–72
Morris, Gouverneur, 94, 113, 203
Morris, Robert, 88, 94
Moslems, 162–64

National Association of Evangelicals, 61

National Reform Association, 61
naturalization, 35–36, 54
  Congressional debate on, 56–60
natural rights, 26–27, 41, 46, 68, 73, 225
  equality of, 70–71
  representation and, 152
  of self-preservation, 26, 27, 29, 246
  surrendering of, 27, 30–31, 73–74, 187
nature, Lockean state of, 24, 26–27, 32, 73
New Brunswick, 33–34
New Hampshire, 93, 118, 250
New Jersey, 118, 250
  blacks in, 48, 49
New Jersey (small state) Plan, 100, 104–5
New York, 249
  abolition in, 48
  anti-Catholicism in, 59, 60
  Congress of the United States in, 65
  ratification of Constitution and, 116, 117, 118, 119
Nigerian constitution, 12
Nineteenth Amendment, 113
North:
  abolition in, 48–51
  see also specific states
North America Act (1867), 117
North Carolina, 60, 118, 249
Northwest Ordinance (1787), 23, 89
Notes on the State of Virginia (Jefferson), 38–39, 44–45, 112, 160, 173*n*
Nova Scotia, 33

obscenity, 221–22
officeholding, qualifications for, 59

About the Author

Walter Berns is John M. Olin University Professor at Georgetown University and an adjunct scholar at the American Enterprise Institute. He has taught at Louisiana State University, Yale University, Cornell University, Colgate University, the University of Toronto, the University of Chicago, and the Salzburg Seminar in American Studies. He has been a Rockefeller Fellow, a Fulbright Fellow, a Guggenheim Fellow, a Phi Beta Kappa Lecturer, a winner of the Clark Distinguished Teaching Award (Cornell University), and a member of the Council of Scholars in the Library of Congress. His previous books include *The First Amendment and the Future of American Democracy* and *For Capital Punishment: Crime and the Morality of the Death Penalty*. His articles regularly appear in *Commentary* and *The Wall Street Journal*, as well as in professional journals.